Constructing
Undergraduate
Psychology
Curricula

Constructing Undergraduate Psychology Curricula

Promoting Authentic Learning and Assessment in the Teaching of Psychology

Joseph A. Mayo

American Psychological Association

Washington, DC

Published by
American Psychological Association
750 First Street, NE
Washington, DC 20002
www.apa.org

To order
APA Order Department
P.O. Box 92984
Washington, DC 20090-2984
Tel: (800) 374-2721; Direct: (202) 336-5510
Fax: (202) 336-5502; TDD/TTY: (202) 336-6123
Online: www.apa.org/books/
E-mail: order@apa.org

In the U.K., Europe, Africa, and the Middle East, copies may be ordered from
American Psychological Association
3 Henrietta Street
Covent Garden, London
WC2E 8LU England

Typeset in Goudy by Circle Graphics, Inc., Columbia, MD

Printer: Sheridan Books, Ann Arbor, MI
Cover Designer: Minker Design, Sarasota, FL

The opinions and statements published are the responsibility of the authors, and such opinions and statements do not necessarily represent the policies of the American Psychological Association.

Library of Congress Cataloging-in-Publication Data

Mayo, Joseph A.
  Constructing undergraduate psychology curricula : promoting authentic learning and assessment in the teaching of psychology / Joseph A. Mayo. — 1st ed.
      p. cm.
  Includes bibliographical references and index.
  ISBN-13: 978-1-4338-0563-9
  ISBN-10: 1-4338-0563-4
  ISBN-13: 978-1-4338-0718-3 (e-book)
  ISBN-10: 1-4338-0718-1 (e-book)
1. Psychology—Study and teaching (Higher)—United States. 2. Psychology—Study and teaching (Higher) I. Title.

  BF80.7.U6M39 2010
  150.71'1—dc22

                                                            2009029707

British Library Cataloguing-in-Publication Data

A CIP record is available from the British Library.

Printed in the United States of America
First Edition

I dedicate this book to the memory of my father, who, in his lifetime
of caring and giving, illuminated a personal pathway for me and countless
others in whose hearts and minds he continues to shine.

CONTENTS

ACKNOWLEDGMENTS

I am grateful to my family and friends for their ongoing support and encouragement throughout the time-intensive process of writing this book. A special heartfelt thank you goes to my wife and fellow educator and author, Becki, for her patient and skillful review of the manuscript in various stages of development. I also extend a lifetime of appreciation to my mother, Claudia, who is 90 years young, for instilling in me a quest for continuous learning.

I also applaud the efforts of the various reviewers and editors who helped me in shaping and molding the final version of this volume. In particular, I acknowledge Gary Fisk of Georgia Southwestern State University, Tom Pusateri of Kennesaw State University, and Trevor Butt of the University of Huddersfield, United Kingdom, for generously lending their subject-matter expertise to selected portions of the book. I am equally indebted to Emily Leonard, Linda McCarter, Devon Bourexis, Jeremy White, and other members of the American Psychological Association (APA) editorial staff for their cordial cooperation and expert guidance. Moreover, I recognize the APA Board of Educational Affairs, in collaboration with the APA Committee of Psychology Teachers at Community Colleges, for allowing me the formative opportunity of serving on the jointly appointed Task Force on Strengthening the Teaching and Learning of Undergraduate Psychological Science. Finally, I thank my students for their hard work and openness to classroom innovation.

Constructing
Undergraduate
Psychology
Curricula

INTRODUCTION

Teaching undergraduate psychology offers varied challenges to new and experienced educators alike. Beyond the need to organize and present a diverse array of names, terms, theories, and methods in a readily comprehensible manner, instructors constantly seek ways to stimulate students' engagement in learning and generate excitement for the subject matter.

Although courses differ widely across undergraduate institutions, dedicated psychology educators at all academic levels share an interest in uncovering optimal teaching practices. To aid the process of pedagogical discovery, this book addresses three contemporary concerns of psychology teachers and links these ideas to the first five learning goals and outcomes discussed in the American Psychological Association's (APA's; 2007) *Guidelines for the Undergraduate Psychology Major:* (a) knowledge base of psychology, (b) research methods in psychology, (c) critical thinking skills in psychology, (d) application of psychology, and (e) values in psychology. Within the broad framework of a constructivist educational perspective that promotes active and enduring learning, this book affords undergraduate psychology teachers opportunities to (a) align course content with APA-endorsed student learning outcomes, (b) integrate class-tested instructional strategies with authentic or "real-world" learning and assessment tools designed to foster higher order thinking, and

(c) assess students' understandings of course content along a developmental continuum that gauges academic progress from the introductory psychology course through receipt of the baccalaureate degree.

The impetus for my writing this book derives from two complementary sources. The first involves my ongoing interest in applying the scholarship of teaching and learning throughout undergraduate psychology education. The second pertains to my involvement in an APA task-force initiative aimed at establishing a measure of continuity within and across undergraduate psychology curricula (APA, 2008b). In the paragraphs that follow, I describe each of these sources and their logical intersection as it relates to the book's content.

Beginning in the early 1980s, and intensifying after the late 1990s, I undertook an active research agenda examining the effectiveness of student-centered constructivist pedagogy that encourages learners to actively and interactively build relationships between new and preexisting knowledge. Using my own undergraduate psychology classes as an observational platform, I have systematically compared parallel classes (innovative constructivist pedagogy vs. more conventional educational practices, such as assigning traditional term papers) while working to establish appropriate controls and equivalency across instructional conditions. In this manner, I have gathered both quantitative and qualitative evidence of the extent to which a constructivist curriculum contributes favorably to student learning without appreciably sacrificing breadth for depth of content coverage or adding inordinately to an instructor's time spent on grading assignments. The quantitative data derive from the results of objective testing, including *t* tests, analyses of variance, and matched-group comparisons. The qualitative data stem from measures such as anecdotal classroom reports, open-ended analysis of the thematic content of students' completed assignments, and students' assessments of constructivist techniques. These findings, along with additional empirical support for the heuristic benefits of constructivist pedagogy, lie at the core of the classroom approaches and exercises that I discuss throughout this book.

On the basis of the nature and scope of my classroom scholarship and its natural connection to authentic or performance-based measures of learning, I was asked in spring 2005 to serve on an APA task force that reexamined undergraduate psychology curricula in light of a developmental progression of student learning outcomes. My primary work on the Task Force on Strengthening the Teaching and Learning of Undergraduate Psychological Science focused on associations between constructivist pedagogy and embedded authentic assessments in the context of a developmentally coherent model for undergraduate psychology curricula. Our group was charged with bridging the gap between the *APA National Standards for High School Psychology Curricula* (APA, 2005a) and the *Guidelines for the Undergraduate Psychology Major*

(APA, 2007), with prior iterations of these documents setting the tone during the early stages of our discussions. Although designed originally for teaching high school psychology, the information included in the *National Standards* clearly applies to the first psychology offering at any academic level. Moreover, the *APA Guidelines* delineate behavioral expectations for learning outcomes upon completion of an undergraduate program of study. After merging the contents of these two documents, we found that a set of developmentally appropriate intermediate outcomes that students should attain as they progress from the first psychology course through the conclusion of the baccalaureate degree was still missing. In completing our report, *Teaching, Learning, and Assessing in a Developmentally Coherent Curriculum* (APA, 2008b), our group attempted to fill this informational gulf. As cited in our report,

> A very useful document would be one that combines the *APA Guidelines for the Undergraduate Psychology Major* (APA, 2007), the developmental model proposed in the [aforementioned task force] report, and links to assessment strategies for each outcome [identified in the model]. . . . as well as empirical identification of recommended teaching strategies for facilitating student learning in each outcome area. (APA, 2008b, p. 11)

These multiple focal points converge in the content of this book, which is steeped in both classroom assessment and classroom research. Consistent with Cross and Steadman's (1996) distinction between these two terms, this book not only addresses the *what* questions of teaching and learning inherent in the assessment process (e.g., What exactly did students learn in class today?) but also offers insight into *why* and *how* students learn by encouraging educators to use their classrooms as laboratories for investigating the learning process.

Before I construct a road map to the content of the present volume, I wish to clarify my intentions as author. This book is not meant to be prescriptive. Rather, it is intended as an advisory instructional resource to provide a general framework from which to approach undergraduate psychology curricula—one that permits maximum flexibility in relation to faculty, student, and institutional differences. Consequently, the ultimate worth of the book's substance should be judged on the basis of how psychology educators lend their unique pedagogical expertise to applying the forthcoming information to teaching, learning, and assessment within their own classes and departmental programs. As such, the book should especially appeal to those teachers committed to instructional innovation and improvement through critical examination of undergraduate psychology education and its resultant impact on teaching, learning, and assessment. Because the *APA Guidelines* (APA, 2007) can be traced to the earlier *National Standards* (APA, 2005a) in terms of guiding principles for teaching the first course in psychology at any level, the book should also prove useful to high school teachers of general psychology with an interest in connecting constructivist pedagogy to authentic learning and assessment.

Part I (chap 1) chronicles the history of psychology curriculum reform from the early 1900s through the present. As part of this discussion, I consider psychology educators' responses to accountability concerns at both secondary and postsecondary levels in American education. Of particular significance to applied classroom techniques appearing later in the book, I conclude this part by presenting a developmentally appropriate model grounded in the most recent APA curriculum guidelines for undergraduate psychology majors (APA, 2008b).

Part II (chaps. 2 and 3) examines constructivism as both a philosophy and an educational perspective. After briefly defining constructivist learning parameters at the start of chapter 2, I trace the epistemological underpinnings of constructivism from antiquity to modern times. In chapter 3, I discuss implications that a constructivist educational philosophy possesses for classroom practice emphasizing authentic teaching, learning, and assessment. At the end of chapter 3, I offer a structural guide to constructivist learning assignments that comprise the next part of the book.

Although chapters 1 through 3 lay a solid foundation for a developmentally coherent curriculum model with ties to constructivist learning and authentic assessment, this background material is contextual to practical classroom applications that I introduce in Part III (chaps. 4–8) as the "heart and soul" of this volume. In this part, I frame the content of each chapter with a description of the empirical and theoretical foundations of one or more constructivist classroom innovations. Afterward, I present detailed instructional methodologies and illustrative examples of how to embed authentic assessments over a wide array of constructivist learning assignments. In the paragraphs that follow, I provide a brief chapter-by-chapter breakdown of Part III.

Chapter 4 describes case-based instruction as an active-learning pedagogy in relation to fictional and real-life case studies. Using novel classroom applications, I implement this approach in the context of teaching introductory psychology, psychology of adjustment, research methods, and history and systems of psychology.

Chapter 5 examines narrative psychology as a way to enhance the connections between learners' life experiences and the comprehension and application of course content. Relying on learning assignments that tap into autobiographical and biographical narration, I use the principles of narrative psychology in various undergraduate classroom environments, including introductory psychology, psychology of adjustment, applied psychology, and life-span developmental psychology.

Chapter 6 looks at graphic organizers as effective tools for prefacing new concepts, helping students link new and preexisting knowledge, and assessing learners' static and dynamically evolving conceptual systems. I begin the chapter by discussing *concept maps*, which are hierarchical diagrams that students construct as pictorial depictions of conceptual differentiation and integration. After introducing a concept-mapping student training module, I integrate learners' concept-map construction into the instructional framework of an introductory psychology class. Next, I turn my attention to the *repertory grid*, a matrix-based approach for eliciting and analyzing knowledge. Although originally intended for use in clinical psychology, I modify and adapt this technique for instructional purposes. As an innovative pedagogical strategy, I use the repertory grid in teaching both life-span developmental psychology and history and systems of psychology as a vehicle for organizing course content, improving student comprehension, and sparking enthusiasm for learning.

Chapter 7 investigates pedagogical uses for analogical reasoning. After explaining how analogical reasoning can facilitate teaching and learning, I draw from teacher-provided and student-generated analogies in designing and implementing learning assignments within life-span development classes. Borrowing from the results of my classroom research on the efficacy of analogy-enhanced instruction, I also offer analogy-based classroom activities that highlight the component stages of an instructional model I developed for teaching with analogies.

Chapter 8 begins with a review of the literature on cooperative learning as one of the most researched teaching strategies. As classroom illustrations of interactive constructivist learning experiences, I describe cooperative learning tasks designed for small groups (educational psychology), large groups (applied psychology), and the entire class (history and systems of psychology).

Part IV (chaps. 9 and 10) addresses the succinct but broadly encompassing question, "What's next?" In chapter 9, I uncover connections between constructivism and educational technologies. In chapter 10, I explore the future of undergraduate psychology education, including promoting liberal education, psychology's role in preparing students for careers in other fields, internationalizing curricula, linking 2- and 4-year curricula, and new directions for educational reform.

In the face of the current challenges or future directions of undergraduate psychology education, psychology educators at all levels should search for meaningful links between teaching, learning, and assessment. Discovering these connections permits the establishment of a fully integrated approach to undergraduate psychology curricula. Drawing from classroom research and practice in learner-centered constructivist pedagogy and a well-articulated developmental model for course and program evaluation, this book offers the tools needed to promote authentic learning and assessment in the teaching of psychology.

I

SYSTEMATIC EXAMINATION OF PSYCHOLOGY CURRICULA

1

PSYCHOLOGY CURRICULUM INITIATIVES

Because psychology was still organizationally indeterminate as an academic discipline through the late 1800s, separate psychology departments did not yet exist at many American colleges and universities (C. L. Brewer, 1997, 2006). In the early years surrounding the American Psychological Association's (APA) establishment in 1892, course work bordering on the psychological could be found in numerous other departments, such as philosophy, physiology, education, humanities, history, ethics, religion, and pedagogy (APA, 2002; C. L. Brewer, 2006; Fancher, 1996). Until the early 1950s, psychology educators dedicated minimal effort toward systematically examining their evolving curricula (C. L. Brewer, 2006)—excluding sparsely dispersed analyses of undergraduate course offerings (e.g., Henry, 1938; Sanford & Fleishman, 1950; Wolfle, 1947).

LAYING THE GROUNDWORK FOR CURRICULUM REFORM

The first national conference on undergraduate psychology education, convened at Cornell University in 1952, resulted in establishing one model curriculum that focused on psychology as a scientific discipline in the liberal arts tradition (C. L. Brewer, 1997) and rejected courses in "applied areas with a vocational emphasis" (C. L. Brewer, 2006, p. 67). A 1960 follow-up conference conducted at the University of Michigan yielded essentially the same recommendations prescribed earlier by the Cornell conferees, except that the Michigan group could not concur on a single curriculum for all psychology undergraduate majors (McKeachie & Milholland, 1961). Similarly, Kulik's (1973) report cited the "undesirability of specifying what the curriculum should be for any program, much less for all programs" (C. L. Brewer, 2006, p. 68).

The 1980s ushered in two APA-initiated efforts to bolster the quality of undergraduate psychology education (C. L. Brewer, 1997). In 1982, the APA Committee on Undergraduate Education (CUE) called on the APA to formulate a recommended content base for undergraduate curricula (APA, 2002). The ensuing CUE-sponsored curriculum resolution encouraged the APA to periodically monitor undergraduate psychology education, with an eye toward developing curriculum guidelines or models (M. A. Lloyd & Brewer, 1992). A subsequent APA curriculum resolution in 1985 was a driving force behind organizing the 1991 National Conference on Enhancing the Quality of Undergraduate Education in Psychology at St. Mary's College of Maryland (C. L. Brewer & Halonen, 2003). Predicated on 3 years of advanced planning, the St. Mary's Conference was a far-reaching reform effort. In lending further support to the view that the study of psychology should be approached as a science in the liberal arts tradition, conferees identified six learning goals (i.e., attention to human diversity, breadth and depth of knowledge, methodological competence, practical experience and application, communication skills, and sensitivity to ethical issues) and four sequential levels of knowledge and skills (i.e., the introductory course, methodology courses, substantive content courses, and integrative experiences, such as internships or capstone courses; C. L. Brewer, 2006; C. L. Brewer & Halonen, 2003; see also C. L. Brewer et al., 1993; McGovern & Brewer, 2003). A book chapter on curriculum (C. L. Brewer et al., 1993) occupies a segment of the overall conference report, *Handbook for Enhancing Undergraduate Education in Psychology* (McGovern, 1993), which is an edited collection of works examining all critical areas of interest to conference participants. This seminal handbook "has been used by faculty as a source of ideas to renew undergraduate programs, as a stimulus for faculty development, and as a guide for the periodic reviews and evaluations mandated on different campuses" (McGovern & Reich, 1996, p. 252). Serving another, yet equally important, function from the St. Mary's Conference is a second document contained in the *Handbook*. This document, "Principles for Quality Undergraduate Psychology Programs" (Baum et al., 1993), is neither prescriptive nor proscriptive in offering concise and specific direction for innovation and change in undergraduate psychology education (C. L. Brewer & Halonen, 2003; McGovern & Reich, 1996).

In 1999, the APA Education Directorate and its decision-making body, the Board of Educational Affairs, sponsored an invitational conference aimed at establishing collaborative partnerships for solving problems among teachers of psychology at all academic levels and between psychology teachers and professional psychologists, teachers in other disciplines, and business and community organizations (Mathie, 2002). The National Forum of the Psychology Partnerships Project (P3; see Mathie, 2002) was held at James Madison University under the leadership of psychology faculty from the host institution. The P3 work groups most germane to our current discussion involve those on curriculum and assessment. In general, these two groups examined the changes in psychology education over the prior decade in an attempt to foster best educational practices. In supporting the conclusions derived previously from the St. Mary's Conference, the curriculum group reasserted the scientific foundation of psychology curricula at all academic levels. The assessment group undertook two projects of particular significance (C. L. Brewer, 2006). The first project led to publication of a groundbreaking rubric to guide teaching, learning, and assessing scientific inquiry as an essential educational component at all levels of psychology (Halonen, Bosack, Clay, & McCarthy, 2003). The second project involved sponsorship of the first discipline-specific assessment conference, "Measuring Up: Best Practices in Assessment in Psychology Education," which took place in 2002. An important byproduct of this assessment conference was an edited book featuring selected conference presentations (Dunn, Mehrotra, & Halonen, 2004).

In 2001, the APA Education Directorate, through its Board of Educational Affairs, sponsored the inaugural Education Leadership Conference in Arlington, Virginia. Of critical importance to future APA outcomes initiatives for undergraduate psychology education, participants at this historic conference, "Re-thinking Education in Psychology and Psychology in Education," discussed the relative advantages and disadvantages of developing national standards for the undergraduate psychology major (Murray, 2002).

Before I discuss a trio of relatively recent APA outcomes initiatives that are especially central to the theoretical and practical concerns of the present volume, it may be useful to recap some of the key events described thus far and the years in which those events occurred. Refer to Table 1.1 for a timeline of these important developments regarding psychology curriculum reform.

TABLE 1.1
Timeline of Selected Key Events in Psychology Curriculum Reform

Year	Event
1952	First national conference on undergraduate psychology education convened at Cornell University
1960	University of Michigan follow-up conference
1973	Kulik's report
1982	Curriculum resolution sponsored by APA Committee on Undergraduate Education
1985	APA curriculum resolution prompting the National Conference on Enhancing the Quality of Undergraduate Education in Psychology at St. Mary's College of Maryland
1991	St. Mary's Conference
1993	Publication of *Handbook for Enhancing Undergraduate Education in Psychology* and "Principles for Quality Undergraduate Psychology Programs"
1999	National Forum of the Psychology Partnerships Project conducted at James Madison University
2001	Inaugural Education Leadership Conference, "Re-thinking Education in Psychology and Psychology in Education"
2002	First discipline-specific assessment conference in psychology, "Measuring Up: Best Practices in Assessment in Psychology Education"
2003	Publication of precedent-setting rubric to guide teaching, learning, and assessing scientific inquiry at all academic levels of psychology (Halonen, Bosack, Clay, & McCarthy, 2003)

Note. APA = American Psychological Association.

ACCOUNTABILITY AND AN INTERRELATED TRILOGY OF THE AMERICAN PSYCHOLOGICAL ASSOCIATION'S OUTCOMES INITIATIVES

Consistent with the No Child Left Behind Act of 2001 that requires kindergarten through 12th grade education in America to demonstrate evidence of learning as its commitment to standards, a similar demand prevails in contemporary higher education involving college graduates' capacities to communicate, solve problems, and think critically (Executive Office of the President, 1990; S. White & Dillow, 2005). The present accountability movement in American higher education can be traced to the 1980s, with the convergence of the following three developments: (a) growing employer dissatisfaction with a rising number of college graduates who possessed underdeveloped thinking skills, (b) mounting interest in authentic assessment as part of curriculum reform, and (c) increased reliance on a constructivist model of learning that encourages students to actively link new and preestablished conceptualizations in creating their own enduring ways of knowing (Khattri & Sweet, 1996). The current zeitgeist of accountability in U.S. colleges and universities also originates from escalating costs of higher education and concerns about U.S. competitiveness on international comparisons of student learning (Clay, 2008). Accordingly, the accountability movement in American higher education has directed attention to higher education trends in other regions of the world and the effects of an increasingly interdependent global environment on how we educate our next generation of college students (Schneider, 2008). This focus stems, in part, from the recent emergence of the Bologna Process—a sweeping attempt to establish comparable quality assurance and degree standards throughout Europe (Tritelli, 2008) by "dissolving educational borders in the same way that economic borders had been dissolved" (Adelman, 2008, p. 8).

As a platform for U.S. educational improvement prescribed in a jointly developed report, the Association of American Colleges and Universities and the Council for Higher Education Accreditation (2008) came together to urge that

> each college and university . . . should develop ambitious, specific, and clearly stated goals for student learning appropriate to its mission, resources, tradition, student body, and community setting . . . [and] should gather evidence about how well students in various programs are achieving learning goals across the curriculum and about the ability of its graduates to succeed in a challenging and rapidly changing world. (¶ 8 and 9)

This paradigm shift from production measures of educational success (e.g., standardized test scores, course grades, degree-granting rates) to student learning outcomes reflects a major change within the higher education community in the United States (Millet, Payne, Dwyer, Stickler, & Alexiou, 2008).

Psychology educators have also mobilized over the past decade in response to increasingly insistent demands for accountability at both secondary and postsecondary levels in American education (see Dunn, Mehrotra, & Halonen, 2004). Under the auspices of APA leadership, psychology teachers have undertaken several outcomes initiatives to develop formal curriculum expectations for their students and directly measure student learning. The resulting APA reports are inspirational in intent, offering recommendations for future action. Of specific interest are three interrelated APA initiatives that have taken place since the mid-1990s. These three initiatives provide a requisite conceptual springboard from which to introduce content pivotal to the present volume.

Prompted by the content standards boom that began in the 1990s, the rising popularity of high school psychology courses in America, and the increased interest in promoting excellence in high school psychology instruction (Ernst & Petrossian, 1996), the APA Education and Science Directorates commissioned the Task Force for the Development of National High School

Psychology Standards in 1994. The task force consisted of experienced psychologists as well as secondary and university psychology educators. The resultant report, *National Standards for the Teaching of High School Psychology* (APA, 1999), promotes active learning and a suitably rigorous approach to teaching the science of psychology at the high school level. The report offers content outlines, performance standards, and performance indicators that delineate learning expectations within high school psychology curricula. The standards described in this report are categorized into five domains, or clusters of related content areas: (a) methods, (b) biopsychological, (c) cognitive, (d) developmental, and (e) variations in individual and group behavior. The High School Psychology Standards Working Group was formed in anticipation of the need for periodic revision of these standards because of ongoing advancement of psychology as both a natural and a social science. The original standards of 1999 were therefore revised to the *National Standards for High School Psychology Curricula* (APA, 2005a) to reflect an evolving vision of what students are expected to learn upon completing the high school psychology course. The document is currently undergoing its second revision, which is expected to be completed between 2010 and 2012.

Bolstered by the success of curriculum standards for high school psychology, the APA targeted development of goals and learning objectives at the undergraduate level. Consequently, the APA Board of Educational Affairs appointed the Task Force on Undergraduate Psychology Major Competencies in 2001 to establish suggested learning goals and outcomes for the undergraduate psychology major. The final product of this group's efforts, *Undergraduate Psychology Major Learning Goals and Outcomes* (APA, 2002), articulates behavioral expectations for student performance at the conclusion of the baccalaureate degree. This document outlines 10 learning goals and related outcomes, divided into two broad categories: (a) knowledge, skills, and values consistent with the science and application of psychology (theory and content of psychology, research methods in psychology, critical thinking skills in psychology, application of psychology, and values in psychology); and (b) knowledge, skills, and values consistent with liberal arts education that are further developed in psychology (information and technological literacy, communication skills, sociocultural and international awareness, personal development, and career planning and development). Moreover, each of these goals includes proposed strategies for how they can be demonstrated. Adopted as association policy by the APA Council of Representatives in August 2006, this document—reiterated and renamed the *APA Guidelines for the Undergraduate Psychology Major* (APA, 2007)—is supplemented by a CyberGuide of assessment resources and a template of effective assessment strategies.

In April 2005, the APA Board of Educational Affairs, in collaboration with the APA Committee of Psychology Teachers at Community Colleges, appointed the Task Force on Strengthening the Teaching and Learning of Undergraduate Psychological Science to fill the informational void between the *National Standards* (APA, 2005a) and the *APA Guidelines* (APA, 2007). Consequently, this group's final report, *Teaching, Learning, and Assessing in a Developmentally Coherent Curriculum* (APA, 2008b), proposes a set of intermediate competencies that psychology students should know, do, and value en route from the general psychology course through completion of the baccalaureate degree. The resulting developmental model attempts to establish necessary coherence within and across undergraduate psychology curricula. As this group noted, if students "string together course combinations that are not guided by the goals and objectives of a coherent curriculum, there may be gaps in the educational preparation they receive as undergraduate psychology majors" (APA, 2008b, p. 1). This legitimate concern becomes magnified in increasingly commonplace instances where students transfer between institutions or attend two or more institutions (either concurrently or in an alternating fashion) while pursuing a bachelor's degree (McCormick, 2003).

AN ORGANIZATIONAL FRAMEWORK FOR DEVELOPMENTALLY COHERENT UNDERGRADUATE PSYCHOLOGY CURRICULA

As an organizational framework for its developmental model, the APA Task Force on Strengthening the Teaching and Learning of Undergraduate Psychological Science relied on Halonen et al.'s (2003) developmental rubric for guiding teaching, learning, and assessing scientific inquiry skills in psychology. In this rubric, Halonen et al. identified eight domains of scientific inquiry and matched developmental outcomes in these domains to five levels of student proficiency, ranging from no initial exposure to scientific principles through complex scientific reasoning skills accompanying graduate school training. The middle three levels of this rubric (i.e., basic, developing, and advanced)—pertaining to anticipated behavioral outcomes in undergraduate psychology curricula—were of greatest interest to the task force in constructing its developmental model. The task force incorporated these levels into its model, with modest revision associated at the basic level. Originally, Halonen and associates conceived of basic skills as those learned by students in the introductory psychology course. In slight contrast, the task force adopted a broader perspective that *basic skills* may be best viewed as encompassing information acquired in *introductory-level* psychology courses, leaving open the possibility of other lower division undergraduate courses, such as psychology of adjustment, life-span developmental psychology, and applied psychology. In defining the parameters surrounding the developing and advanced levels of student proficiency, however, the task force remained wholly consistent with Halonen et al.'s perspective. *Developing skills* become apparent as students progress through lower and upper division undergraduate psychology courses, whereas *advanced skills* emerge as students approach the conclusion of a psychology major while completing capstone educational experiences.

In addition, the task force aligned the three levels of its developmental model with the cognitive domain in Bloom's revised taxonomy of educational objectives (Krathwohl, 2002). Linking six ascending levels of thinking represented in Bloom's scheme to three progressive levels of student proficiency in the developmental model (two levels of thinking per each level of proficiency), *retention* and *comprehension* relate to the basic level, *application* and *analysis* correspond to the developing level, and *evaluation* and *creation* connect to the advanced level.

The task force also incorporated into its developmental model a portion of the curriculum competencies expressed in the earlier *APA Guidelines* (APA, 2007). Congruent with the scientific and applied underpinnings of undergraduate psychology curricula, the task force devoted exclusive attention to the learning goals and outcomes tied to the science and application of psychology.

Blending the developmental conceptualizations of Halonen et al. (2003) and Krathwohl (2002) with the curriculum structure for the undergraduate psychology major reported in the *APA Guidelines* (APA, 2007), the present developmental model traces a progression of learning outcomes for each of five goals fitted to each of three levels of student proficiency. In proposing this model, the task force was careful to avoid a course-anchored curriculum representation. Rather, the model relies on an item-specific framework of knowledge, skills, and values within undergraduate psychology education that allows for considerable flexibility across courses constituting psychology programs.

Appendix 1.1 contains Tables 1A.1 through 1A.5, which together depict the developmentally coherent curriculum model that the task force proposed (APA, 2008b). Collectively, these tables identify knowledge-, skill-, and values-based expectations associated with the following five learning goals:

Goal 1: Knowledge base of psychology
Goal 2: Research methods in psychology
Goal 3: Critical thinking skills in psychology
Goal 4: Application of psychology
Goal 5: Values in psychology

Goal statements in each table are followed by behaviorally stated learning outcomes in terms of basic, developing, and advanced levels of student proficiency.

In Part II, I turn my attention to constructivism as both a philosophical theory of knowledge and a learning paradigm. After defining the characteristics of constructivism and tracing its epistemological roots from antiquity through modern times (chap. 3), I examine classroom practices associated with a constructivist educational perspective (chap. 4).

APPENDIX 1.1: DEVELOPMENTALLY COHERENT MODEL FOR UNDERGRADUATE PSYCHOLOGY CURRICULA

The tables that follow (Tables 1A.1–1A.5) are from *Teaching, Learning, and Assessing in a Developmentally Coherent Curriculum* (pp. 17–23), by the American Psychological Association, 2008b, Washington, DC: Author. Copyright 2008 by the American Psychological Association.

TABLE 1A.1

Knowledge Base of Psychology

Goal 1: Knowledge Base of Psychology
Demonstrate familiarity with the major concepts, theoretical perspectives, empirical findings, and historical trends in psychology.

Outcome areas	BASIC *retention and comprehension*	DEVELOPING *analysis and application*	ADVANCED *evaluation and creation*
Nature of psychology	**Define** psychology as the science that studies behavior and mental processes and the profession that applies that science	**Distinguish** the similarities and differences between the professional and scientific communities in psychology	**Evaluate** the influence of context in the evolving definition of psychology
Relationship of psychology to science	**Explain** how psychology meets the criteria of science	**Analyze** how psychological research reflects scientific principles	**Evaluate** psychological science as a means of understanding behavior and mental processes
Role of behavior in psychology	**Describe** behavior and mental processes empirically, including operational definitions **Distinguish** behavior from inferences about behavior	**Identify** antecedents and consequences of behavior and mental processes **Predict** likely patterns of behavior from context	**Interpret** behavior and mental processes at an appropriate level of complexity
Structure of psychology	**List** and **explain** the major research and applied subfields of psychology	**Differentiate** appropriate subfields to address specific research areas and/or assist in addressing specific behavioral concerns	**Speculate** about psychology's continuing evolution and refinement of subfields
Relationship of psychology to other disciplines	**Identify** the connections between psychology and other disciplines	**Compare** and **contrast** the assumptions, methods, and choice of problems of psychology with those of other disciplines	**Integrate** knowledge derived from psychological science with that of other disciplines

(continues)

TABLE 1A.1
Knowledge Base of Psychology *(Continued)*

Goal 1: Knowledge Base of Psychology
Demonstrate familiarity with the major concepts, theoretical perspectives, empirical findings, and historical trends in psychology.

Outcome areas	BASIC *retention and comprehension*	DEVELOPING *analysis and application*	ADVANCED *evaluation and creation*
Objectives of psychology (Describing, understanding, predicting, and controlling behavior and mental processes)	**Identify** and **explain** the primary objectives of psychology	**Compare** and **contrast** the primary objectives of psychology	**Evaluate** the strengths and limitations of the primary objectives of psychology
Historical perspectives in psychology	**Describe** the key eras of the major schools of thought in the history of psychology (including their founders, assumptions, explanatory concepts, and methods)	**Compare** and **contrast** historical perspectives.	**Assess** the relative importance of the major schools of thought in the history of psychology **Defend** a historical perspective
Contemporary perspectives in psychology • Behavioral • Biological • Cognitive • Evolutionary • Humanistic • Psychodynamic • Sociocultural	**Identify** and **describe** the major contemporary perspectives of psychology	**Compare** and **contrast** the assumptions, methods, and other elements of major contemporary perspectives in psychology	**Evaluate** the utility and effectiveness of contemporary psychological perspectives **Describe** how each perspective applies its findings to promote human welfare
Overarching themes of psychology • Interaction of heredity and environment • Variability and continuity of behavior and mental processes within and across species	**Identify** the overarching themes of psychology	**Apply** the overarching themes of psychology to explain specific behaviors **Debate** the merits of each side of the overarching themes of psychology	**Evaluate** the appropriateness of scientific explanations of behavior and mental processes from the standpoint of psychology's overarching themes

• Free will versus determinism • Subjectivism versus objectivism • Interaction of mind and body • Applicability of theories and measures across societal and cultural groups			
General content domains of psychology • Learning and cognition • Individual and sociocultural differences • Biological bases of behavior and mental processes • Development across the life span	**Identify** and **explain** basic concepts, theories, and research represented in the general content domains	**Apply** and **analyze** concepts, theories, and research in the general content domains	**Evaluate** and **synthesize** concepts, theories, and research in the general content domains
Role of ethics	**Describe** relevant ethical issues, as addressed by the APA code of ethics	**Apply** relevant ethical principles, as addressed by the APA code of ethics	**Evaluate** policies and procedures related to behavior and mental processes using relevant ethical principles, as addressed by the APA code of ethics
Career opportunities	**Identify** broad career opportunities associated with psychology at the bachelor's, master's, and doctoral levels	**Compare** and **contrast** the credentials, skills, and experiences required for a career in psychology	**Create** an appropriate career plan related to a specialized goal

APA = American Psychological Association.

TABLE 1A.2
Research Methods in Psychology

Goal 2: Research Methods in Psychology
Understand and apply basic research methods in psychology, including research design, data analysis, and interpretation.

Outcome areas	BASIC *retention and comprehension*	DEVELOPING *analysis and application*	ADVANCED *evaluation and creation*
Scientific method	**Describe** the basic characteristics of the scientific method in psychology	**Analyze** how primary behavioral research adheres to scientific principles	**Design** research that adheres to the principles of the scientific method
General research methods • Descriptive • Correlational • Experimental	**Describe** various general research methods, including advantages and disadvantages of use	**Select** and **apply** general research methods to address appropriate kinds of research questions	**Evaluate** the effectiveness of a general research method in addressing a research question
	Distinguish the nature of designs that permit causal inferences from those that do not	**Categorize** research articles that employ methods permitting causal and noncausal inferences	
Correlation	**Define** correlation	**Interpret** the meaning of correlational findings	**Speculate** about and **evaluate** the significance of correlational findings
Correlation versus causation	**Explain** the difference between correlation and causation	**Match** research questions to appropriate method	**Evaluate** whether a specific research method warrants a cause–effect conclusion
Controlled comparison	**Describe** the role of controlled comparison in justifying a cause–effect claim	**Analyze** research claims to identify legitimacy of cause–effect claims	**Develop** research strategies that appropriately address controlled comparison
Research elements	**Define** hypotheses, variables, and operational definitions	**Formulate** hypotheses, variables, and operational definitions from research articles and scenarios	**Deduce** testable research hypotheses based on operational definitions of variables

Experimental design	**Describe** experimental design strategies to address research questions	**Compare** and **contrast** different research methods used by psychologists **Design** basic experiments	**Design** appropriate experiments to maximize internal and external validity and reduce the existence of alternative explanations **Design** appropriate controlled conditions to minimize their effects, including random assignment to conditions
Participant selection and assignment	**Describe** random sampling and assignment	**Analyze** the potential influence of participant variables	**Evaluate** the validity of conclusions derived from psychological research
Design quality (internal validity)	**Define** validity and **describe** conditions that enhance valid findings	**Analyze** conditions that will enhance or detract from the validity of conclusions	**Generalize** research conclusions appropriately based on the parameters of particular research methods
Generalization (external validity)	**Describe** the relationship of research design to generalizability of results	**Analyze** the generalizability of research findings based on strengths or weaknesses of research design	**Recognize** that individual differences and sociocultural contexts may influence the applicability of research findings
Reporting research findings	**Apply** basic APA standards and style in writing about research	**Explain** (in writing) the methods, results, and conclusions of a data collection project	**Write** all sections of a research report, applying APA writing standards
Research ethics	**Describe** the basic principles of the APA code of ethics for research with human and animal participants, including the role of an institutional review board (IRB)	**Adhere** to the APA code of ethics in the treatment of human and nonhuman participants in the design, data collection, interpretation, and reporting of psychological research	**Evaluate** the contributions and constraints entailed in adherence to the APA code of ethics and appropriately **adjust** the research design **Complete** an IRB application

(continues)

TABLE 1A.2
Research Methods in Psychology   (Continued)

Goal 2: Research Methods in Psychology
Understand and apply basic research methods in psychology, including research design, data analysis, and interpretation.

Outcome areas	BASIC retention and comprehension	DEVELOPING analysis and application	ADVANCED evaluation and creation
Body of evidence	**Articulate** how an individual research study addresses a behavioral question	**Analyze** differences across related research studies	**Integrate** findings from several studies to produce a coherent set of conclusions
Sociocultural context	**Identify** variations in behavior related to sociocultural differences	**Apply** sociocultural framework to research strategies and conclusions	**Incorporate** sociocultural factors in the development of research questions, design, data collection, analysis, and interpretation
Database skills	**Identify** and **locate** relevant journals and databases in psychology	**Develop** and **adjust** search strategies to represent adequate range of research	**Create** efficient and effective search strategies to address research questions
Statistical skills	**Describe** the differences between descriptive and inferential statistical analysis	**Conduct** and **interpret** simple statistics from research results and in journal articles	**Evaluate** statistical power in results by addressing effect size and confidence intervals
Statistical significance	**Define** statistical significance and its role in interpreting research findings	**Distinguish** between statistical and practical significance	**Speculate** about the implications of using the conventions of statistical significance in interpreting results
Limits of scientific reasoning and evidence	**State** how evidence is contextual and tentative	**Discuss** the reasons why empirical findings and conclusions may change or require adjustment	**Justify** the evolving nature of scientific findings

APA = American Psychological Association.

TABLE 1A.3
Critical Thinking Skills in Psychology

Goal 3: Critical Thinking Skills in Psychology
Respect and use critical and creative thinking, skeptical inquiry, and, when possible, the scientific approach to solve problems related to behavior and mental processes.

Outcome areas	BASIC *retention and comprehension*	DEVELOPING *analysis and application*	ADVANCED *evaluation and creation*
Use of evidence in psychology	**Discern** difference between personal views and scientific evidence in understanding behavior	**Collect** and **use** scientific evidence in drawing conclusions and in practice	**Evaluate** the quality, objectivity, and credibility of scientific evidence in drawing conclusions and in practice
Association skills	**State** connections between diverse facts and theories	**Relate** connections between diverse facts and theories **Apply** diverse facts and theories over a wide range of contexts	**Assess** the quality of connections between diverse facts and theories
Argumentation skills	**Identify** arguments based largely on anecdotal evidence and personal experience	**Deduce** contradictory and oversimplified arguments based on a growing knowledge of the available facts and theories	**Develop** sound, integrated arguments based on scientific reasoning and empirical evidence
Detection of errors in psychological reasoning	**Identify** claims arising from myths, stereotypes, common fallacies, and poorly supported assertions regarding behavior	**Detect** and **reject** claims arising from myths, stereotypes, common fallacies, and poorly supported assertions regarding behavior	**Evaluate** the errors involved in claims arising from myths, stereotypes, common fallacies, and poorly supported assertions regarding behavior
Questioning skills	**Explain** the appropriateness and relevance of questions with direction and guidance	**Differentiate** independently between ill-defined and well-defined questions	**Evaluate** and **modify** questions to eliminate ambiguity throughout the process of scientific inquiry
Creativity	**Describe** elements of creativity	**Apply** alternative strategies to known protocols	**Generate** novel insights about the psychology of humans and nonhumans
Problem solving	**Define** the stages of problem solving	**Apply** problem-solving strategies to develop solutions to problems in diverse contexts	**Appraise** the quality of solutions **Select** an optimal strategy from multiple alternatives

TABLE 1A.4
Application of Psychology

Goal 4: Application of Psychology
Understand and apply psychological principles to personal, social, and organizational issues.

Outcome areas	BASIC *retention and comprehension*	DEVELOPING *analysis and application*	ADVANCED *evaluation and creation*
Healthy lifestyle	**Describe** elements of healthy lifestyle	**Analyze** personal lifestyle reflecting, among other factors, awareness of alternative cultural perspectives	**Evaluate** courses of action that can produce more beneficial outcomes
Abnormal behavior	**Summarize** general criteria of abnormality	**Define** criteria for abnormality relative to a given set of symptoms or characteristics	**Evaluate** the significance of symptoms in the sociocultural context
Psychological tests	**Explain** the elements and importance of effective testing	**Differentiate** between effective and less effective methods of testing and **ensure** that these methods show respect for alternative cultures and gender	**Design** and **evaluate** strategies to assess psychological phenomena
Potential for psychology as a change agent	**List** ways that psychological principles can facilitate personal, social, and organizational change	**Apply** a psychological principle to facilitate positive change in personal, social, or organizational behavior	**Evaluate** the power of psychological strategies to promote change
Major applied areas in psychology (e.g., clinical, counseling, school, industrial/ organizational)	**Identify** major and emerging applied areas in psychology	**Link** major and emerging applied areas to an appropriate psychological career	**Determine** whether an applied specialty can produce a solution for a given psychological problem
Emerging applied areas in psychology (e.g., health, forensic, media, military)			

TABLE 1A.5
Values in Psychology

Goal 5: Values in Psychology
Value empirical evidence, tolerate ambiguity, act ethically, and reflect other values that are the underpinnings of psychology as a science.

Outcome areas	BASIC *retention and comprehension*	DEVELOPING *analysis and application*	ADVANCED *evaluation and creation*
Curiosity	**Describe** how curiosity assists the scientific process	**Apply** curiosity to psychological phenomena of personal interest	**Sustain** curiosity for investigating complex behavioral questions
Skepticism	**Define** skepticism and its role in psychological thinking	**Distinguish** between scientific and pseudoscientific explanations of human behavior and **compare** their relative value	**Maintain** rigorous standards related to the quality of scientific evidence in support of a behavioral claim
Tolerance of ambiguity	**Define** tolerance of ambiguity and **explain** its role in psychological science	**Analyze** behavioral explanations with the intent of finding an alternative explanation	**Evaluate** psychological explanations with an expectation of complexity, tentativeness, and variance
Ethical orientation	**Describe** some elements of the ethical code	**Apply** an ethical orientation to hypothetical ethical dilemmas	**Implement** ethical orientation in novel psychological contexts
Protection of human dignity	**Describe** issues pertaining to psychological aspects of human dignity	**Predict** potential outcomes of scenarios in which protection of human dignity does not occur	**Design** psychology projects that protect human dignity and respect alternative cultural and gender perspectives
Human diversity	**Recognize** and **respect** human diversity	**Anticipate** that psychological explanations may vary across populations and contexts	**Exhibit** sensitivity to issues of power, privilege, and discrimination
Academic integrity	**Describe** academic integrity and **explain** its role in the discipline, profession, and society as a whole	**Predict** appropriate outcomes for actions that reflect academic integrity or violations thereof	**Integrate** academic integrity with personal code of honor
Personal responsibility/ service learning	**Describe** how psychology can foster positive civic, social, and global outcomes	**Identify** personal opportunities to apply psychological knowledge for enhancing positive outcomes	**Evaluate** a personal plan for engagement with respect to civic, social, and global responsibilities

II

WHAT IS CONSTRUCTIVISM?

2

THE EPISTEMOLOGICAL ROOTS
OF CONSTRUCTIVISM

Derived from the Latin *con struere*, the verb *to construct* means to organize, arrange, or give structure (Mahoney, 1999). Although contemporary educational literature is replete with a wide range of definitions for *constructivism* (Null, 2004), at the core level this term proposes that "knowledge is individually constructed and socially co-constructed by learners based on their interpretations of experiences in the world" (Jonassen, 1999, p. 217). As both a school of thought and a springboard for instructional practice, constructivism has a long and diverse history rooted in philosophy, psychology, and education (Null, 2004; von Glasersfeld, 1989b; Warrick, 2001).

According to Hein (1991), constructivism is "a position which has been frequently adopted ever since people began to ponder epistemology" (¶ 3) in investigating how people acquire, transmit, and apply knowledge (Bunge, 1983; Ozmon & Craver, 1999). Constructivism stresses the importance of self-discovery and life experiences in examining the genesis of knowledge. Rather than focusing on knowledge acquisition as something that exists outside of the individual, constructivism sees it as a uniquely inner experience. In believing that knowledge must be created in the mind of the knower, constructivism contrasts with *objectivism*, which posits that knowledge exists independently of the knower (Biggs, 1996) and thus people must learn passively about objective reality rather than actively construct working models of it (T. M. Butt, personal communication, November 10, 2008).

HISTORICAL OVERVIEW: CLASSICAL ANTIQUITY THROUGH THE MID-1900S

The link between epistemology and learning is several thousand years old, dating back to the considered ideas of ancient Greek philosophers. In general, pre-Socratic philosophy focused on the source of knowledge. As it pertains to the advent of constructivism in Western culture, however, the intellectual genealogy of links between epistemology and learning can be traced to Socrates' work. Socrates devised a method of teaching that explores knowledge seeking through a continual flow of probing questions, as opposed to ready-formed answers (Hintikka, 2007). As a means of fostering critical thinking, *Socratic questioning* is a disciplined process that allows learners to follow up all answers with facilitating questions that aid in self-derived knowledge acquisition (R. Paul, as cited in California Portable Assisted Study Sequence, 2006). Although Socrates is not directly associated with constructivism, his methodology speaks to the conceptual heart of a constructivist learning philosophy (Murphy, 1997). Contemporary constructivist educators still rely on variations of the Socratic method in evaluating students' learning and launching new learning experiences.

Despite the contributions of Socrates to a constructivist view of knowledge, 18th-century Italian philosopher Giambattista Vico proposed the "first explicit formulation of a constructivist theory of knowledge" (von Glasersfeld, 1989b, p. 162). As a precursor to constructivist thinking, Vico espoused the *verum factum* principle that locates the act of individual invention at the heart of verifying truth (Miner, 1998). Vico invoked a construction metaphor in his frequent reference to words such as *creates*, *builds*, and *shapes* (Sexton & Griffin, 1997). In the Latin treatise *De Antiquissima Italorum Sapientia ex Linguae Originibus Eruenda Librir Tres*, Vico (1710/1988) argued that knowledge is constructed by the knower. In von Glasersfeld's (1989a) words, "the human mind can know only what the human mind has made" (p. 3).

In the wake of Vico's revolutionary constructivist exposition, 18th-century German philosopher Immanuel Kant delineated the conditions for mathematical, scientific, and metaphysical knowledge. In *The Critique of Pure Reason*, Kant (1781/2003) "elaborated a monumental scaffolding to map the constructive activity of reason" (von Glasersfeld, 1999, ¶ 6). In assigning a leading epistemological role to inherent cognitive principles (*categories*) as conduits for organizing experience (Heylighen, 1997), Kant suggested that human beings construct their own bases for knowledge. Kant's description of categories is a predecessor of what are presently referred to as *constructs* and *schemata* in the popular vernacular of contemporary constructivists (Mahoney, 1999).

Jean-Jacques Rousseau, another influential 18th-century philosopher, can also be viewed as a major contributor to the intellectual history of constructivism. In *Emile*, Rousseau (1762/1993) laid the groundwork for a learning environment in which students construct their own knowledge through freedom to cultivate exploration and self-realization. In doing so, Rousseau advocated for a method of education that nurtures students' natural tendencies toward discovery. Instead of relying on the teacher's authority, students should develop ideas for themselves in arriving at conclusions from their own experiences. Rousseau's conception of education is akin to the modern-day constructivist emphasis on *discovery learning* (Doyle & Smith, 2007).

Influenced by the writings of Rousseau, 18th-century Swiss educator Johann Heinrich Pestalozzi offered a prescription for educational reform that holds powerful implications for current supporters of constructivism. In *How Gertrude Teaches Her Children*, Pestalozzi (1801/1894) discussed the principles underlying his famous *object teaching* method. In contrast to rote memorization and passive recitation of information read in books, he advocated for active engagement of students in using their senses to explore the environment. Pestalozzi guided his students in examining the size, shape, weight, and other quantifiable dimensions of objects found in their environment (e.g., rocks, plants, human-made artifacts). Moreover, he followed a developmental progression in his object teaching that proceeded from unknown to known, simple to complex, and concrete to abstract (Kilpatrick, 1951). Pestalozzi's active, hands-on approach to instruction—stressing spontaneity and self-activity as hallmarks of the learning process—bears marked similarity to defining characteristics of classroom practice among contemporary constructivist educators.

Although Socrates, Vico, Kant, Rousseau, and Pestalozzi have all left indelible marks on the development of constructivism, subsequent others had to further refine the constructivist learning model as a leading paradigm in modern educational psychology. Beginning with William James's contributions at the end of the 19th century, "the praxis of conceptual construction became an area of serious study" (von Glasersfeld, 1999, ¶ 6). A pioneering American philosopher, psychologist, and educational reformer, W. James presented ideas that would later become vital components of constructivism. W. James (1907) borrowed from the pragmatist principles of American philosopher and scientist Charles Peirce (1878/1992) in asserting that human beings are practical creatures who use their cognitive capacities to adapt to their environment. In a series of lectures presented to preservice teachers, W. James (1892/1958) spoke of *native reactions* that naturally drive people's cognitive processes. For example, the *reaction of curiosity* empowers us with a self-initiated drive to learn, and the *reaction of ownership* drives us to personalize the association between ideas. Both of these notions are crucial elements of a contemporary constructivist philosophy of education, which favors the interrelated processes of self-discovery and personalized meaning-making. Also relevant to a constructivist perspective is W. James's (1892/1958) discussion of the process of *apperception*, which results when people pay attention to matters of personal interest. As an organizational capacity of the human brain, the concept of apperception supports the constructivist position that human understanding is based on the ability to associate new experiences and ideas with cognitive frameworks already learned.

Like W. James, another leading American intellectual, John Dewey, spent decades in the late 19th and early 20th centuries both popularizing pragmatism and elaborating a constructivist theory of knowledge. In his famous article, "The Reflex Arc Concept in Psychology," Dewey (1896) criticized the standard psychology of his era for deemphasizing the ongoing relationship between organism and environment on the level of action. To Dewey (1896), human knowledge is composed of actions, and every act creates new meaning. Central to meaning construction is the role played by language in sharing ideas between people. This reliance on language within the context of a socially construed nature of mental activities remains an important element of contemporary constructivism. In objecting to the rote memorization that dominated American education in the early 1900s, Dewey (1916) also stated that "education is not an affair of 'telling' and being told, but an active and constructive process" (p. 43). Therefore, all knowledge must be subjected to continuous inquiry and revision because of its vulnerability to error. This *inquiry method* of teaching and learning is yet another tool of present-age constructivist educators.

The philosophy and psychology of John Dewey is found between the lines of 20th-century psychologist George Kelly's (1955) *personal construct theory*, which I consider in the next chapter. The importance of Kelly's work to the modern-day evolution of constructivism cannot be overstated, because it is "probably responsible for introducing more contemporary psychologists to constructivism than any other source" (T. W. Butt, personal communication, November 10, 2008).

CONTEMPORARY CONSTRUCTIVIST LEARNING PARADIGMS

Because constructivism is first and foremost a philosophy of knowledge acquisition, considerable current interest in constructivism pertains to its diverse applications to teaching and learning (Warrick, 2001). As a theoretical orientation with direct implications for classroom research and practice, contemporary constructivism falls into two broad schools of thought: (a) *cognitive constructivism* that focuses on how individuals make sense of the world and (b) *social constructivism* that stresses the social context of learning (Cobb, 1996). Cognitive constructivism traces its intellectual lineage to the cognitive developmental theory of Swiss psychologist Jean Piaget, whereas the roots of social constructivism can be found in the sociocultural developmental theory of Russian psychologist Lev Vygotsky (Pass, 2004). Although I focus on Piaget's and Vygotsky's pioneering developmental theories throughout the remaining discussion in this chapter, it is important to recognize that constructivist learning is not the result of development but rather is development, because it demands invention and self-organization on the part of the learner (Fosnot, 1996).

In his genetic epistemology, Piaget (1970) combined elements of philosophy, psychology, and biology in characterizing intelligence as a form of adaptation in which increasingly complex intellectual processes are built on earlier foundations of cognitive development. Piaget was the first modern theorist to synthesize into a comprehensive perspective the varied ideas about constructivism that came before him (S. D. Simon, 2001). Over a period spanning 6 decades, Jean Piaget revolutionized the field of cognition and opened the door to a cognitive constructivist educational philosophy. To Piaget, the purpose of human knowledge is to allow individuals the opportunity to intellectually adapt to and organize the world of experience (Fosnot, 1996). In Piaget's cognitive developmental psychology, intellectual development is an ongoing process of construction and reconstruction of knowledge through individual experience, discovery, and rediscovery (Piaget, 1973; Wadsworth, 1996).

In *Equilibration of Cognitive Structures,* Piaget (1977) explained that people organize their experiences into groups of interrelated ideas (cognitive structures referred to as *schemata*). When people encounter novel experiences, they must either *assimilate* the information into preexisting schemata or create entirely new ones to *accommodate* for this new knowledge. In this way, individuals maintain cognitive balance (*equilibration*) through a dynamic process of intrinsic, self-regulated behavior. For Piaget, neither internal maturation nor external teaching account for intellectual development. Instead, it is an "active construction process in which people, through their own activities, build increasingly differentiated and comprehensive cognitive structures" (S. D. Simon, 2001, p. 17). At various junctures in this spiraling equilibration, learners construct contradictions to their actions and ideas that provide the internal motivation for continued intellectual growth and change (Fosnot, 1996). Therefore, assimilation and accommodation serve as harmonizing components of transformative learning that results from a feeling of cognitive discomfort (*disequilibrium*) with what people currently think or know about the world (Piaget, 1987a, 1987b). From this viewpoint, learners acquire new conceptual frameworks through continuously developing (assimilation) or discontinuously restructuring (accommodation) preexisting schemata (Piaget,

1926/1959). For example, an 18-month-old girl with a pet Italian greyhound (a sleek, short-haired, small-dog breed) will assimilate information regarding larger and furrier dogs (e.g., collies) into her preexisting schema for "dog." To accommodate learning disparately new information, however, this child must construct a new schematic category for "horse" as a notably larger animal that is different from her Italian greyhound in numerous ways, though also four legged with a sleek appearance.

Despite their shared affinity for a constructivist stance, Piaget and Vygotsky differed in their views of cognitive development on the basis of their predominant unit of analysis: intrapersonal (Piaget) versus interpersonal (Vygotsky). Piaget emphasized knowledge construction within individuals—but not excluding the impact of social processes on learning (Fosnot, 1996)—whereas Vygotsky (1978) stressed social interaction between individuals as paramount to active construction of negotiated meaning—yet not precluding the eventual importance of an internalized knowledge base for each individual. In essence, Vygotsky posited that what learners can accomplish solely on their own is less indicative of their intellectual development than what they can do with the assistance of others in a social context (S. D. Simon, 2001). It was Vygotsky's decidedly social perspective on developmental psychology that paved the way for the rise of social constructivism as a prevailing educational model.

Vygotsky (1962/1986) differentiated between spontaneous and scientific concepts in his developmental theory. To Vygotsky, *spontaneous concepts* are similar to the immature conceptualizations that Piaget said develop naturally as individuals construct intuitive knowledge based on their personal reflections on everyday experience—apart from formal schooling in more systematized tracks of knowledge. In contrast, *scientific concepts* are "formulated by the culture rather than the individual . . . through instruction in a process of cultural transmission" (Au, 1990, p. 272). Vygotsky (1978) used the term *zone of proximal development* to refer to the process through which students move gradually from spontaneous knowledge (concept formation in the absence of assistance from a teacher or more experienced peer) to scientific knowledge (concept formation achieved in cooperation with a more knowledgeable guide)—what he called *guided participation*. In describing the developmental progression of conceptual thinking across these zones of proximal development, Vygotsky (1978) pointed to "the distance between the actual developmental level as determined by independent problem solving and the level of potential development as determined through problem solving under adult guidance, or in collaboration with more capable peers" (p. 86). Over time, a learner develops the ability to comprehend the systematic reasoning associated with scientific knowledge, without assistance from more accomplished others. Thus, in describing the chronology of events involved in intellectual development, Vygotsky (1962/1986) contended that conceptual formation initiates through social relationships; through the learner's actions, these concepts then become internalized on an intrapersonal level.

Central to his social constructivist view, Vygotsky (1962/1986) cited language as a mediator of cognition. As a psychological tool that stimulates new relations with the social world, language encourages jointly constructed knowledge. In stressing the dialogic nature of knowledge acquisition throughout each learner's zones of proximal development, Vygotsky discussed the pivotal role both teachers and learner's peers play in conversing, questioning, explaining, and otherwise arriving at socially negotiated meaning (Fosnot, 1996).

Although social constructivism and cognitive constructivism are often discussed as distinct psychoeducational paradigms, they are dynamically intertwined in practice. In characterizing the continuous interplay between these two models, socially shared knowledge is a whole that is greater than the sum of the individually structured cognitions it comprises (Fosnot, 1996). To continue, socially shared knowledge possesses its own structure that interacts with the individuals who are constructing it. As encapsulated by Lewontin, Rose, and Kamin (1984), "It is not just that wholes are more than the sum of their parts; it is that parts become qualitatively new by being parts of the whole" (p. 287). Keeping with this gestalt metaphorical framework, it all comes down to "whether the social or the cognitive is viewed as figure or ground" (M. Simon, 1993, p. 4) in determining whether social or cognitive constructivism occupies relatively greater weight in constructivist learning environments.

3

CONSTRUCTIVIST
EDUCATIONAL PRACTICE

In the preceding chapter, I examined the underpinnings of constructivism as a theory of knowledge and learning. However, constructivism is not a description of teaching in which a "'cookbook teaching style' or pat set of instructional techniques can be abstracted from the theory and proposed as a constructivist approach to teaching" (Fosnot, 1996, p. 29). Instead, various learning principles and experiences can be gleaned from constructivism and applied to educational practice.

Drawing from my own class-tested constructivist stance, learners (acting individually and/or collaboratively) are "architects of knowledge" influenced by preexisting knowledge, personal experience, and a propensity for reflection and discovery (Mayo, 2006c). This viewpoint takes into account the constituent elements of Kolb's (1984) model of the dynamic and cyclical processes involved in constructivist learning: concrete experience, reflection on that experience, abstract conceptualization resulting in the construction of underlying learning principles, and active experimentation in which learners construct ways to potentially modify the next occurrence of the experience. Figure 3.1 shows a hybrid model of constructivist learning that synthesizes the complementary components of each of these two perspectives.

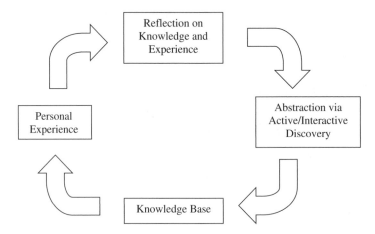

Figure 3.1. Constructivist learning model.

Constructivism blends the aims of effective learning and teaching in affording students opportunities to pursue their personal knowledge-building goals while still supporting clearly stated instructional objectives (Ng & Bereiter, 1991). Moreover, at the crossroads of cognitive and social constructivism, constructivist educators cast learners in one or more of the following three roles: active, creative, and social (Perkins, 1999; Phillips, 1995). *Active learners* acquire knowledge by continually hypothesizing and testing ideas, *creative learners* rediscover knowledge by alternatively constructing and reconstructing ideas, and *social learners* coconstruct knowledge in collaboration with others' ideas. Throughout the rest of the discussion in this chapter, it will quickly become apparent that matching constructivist learning principles to attendant instructional practices allows teachers considerable classroom flexibility while simultaneously adhering to the basic tenets of constructivism.

In recognition of the multiplicity of constructivist learning principles and the challenges for educators in aligning these principles with the practice of teaching (Fosnot, 1996), a comprehensive instructional model for constructivism would prove useful in categorizing and summarizing the relationship between learning principles and teaching practices. Although no such generally agreed-on model exists in higher education (either in or out of the psychology discipline), the Biological Science Curriculum Study—commissioned by the Miami Museum of Science (2001)—resulted in a promising instructional framework for constructivism designed specifically for elementary- and secondary-level teachers. However, this instructional model—called the *Five E's* (engage, explore, explain, elaborate, and evaluate)—has direct applications across all academic levels, including higher education. The model is intended to facilitate constructivist learning through a loosely defined stage-like process.

I rely on this instructional model as an overall organizational framework in considering a diverse array of constructivist implications for educational practice. As an alternative to viewing the component elements of the model as sequential stages in constructivist learning, it is also possible to regard these elements as characteristic themes observed throughout the constructivist educational literature.

ENGAGEMENT

To constructivists, learning is an active process in which learners engage with the world and extract meaning from their experiences. This view runs contrary to conceptions of learning as the passive reception of information through rote memorization and deference to authoritative proclamations of knowledge. In short, constructivism opposes memorization and recitation in favor of conceptual change and advancement of metacognitive and critical thinking skills (Tynjala, 1998).

During the process of engagement, students initially encounter and identify the learning task (Miami Museum of Science, 2001). How can constructivist educators stimulate student engagement? One answer lies within the practice of Socratic teaching, a system of learning based on inquiry and questioning in pursuit of independent thinkers (Hintikka, 2007). As introduced briefly in chapter 2, Socratic teaching continually probes into topics by asking students to respond to a series of open-ended questions that promote critical thinking and development of self-realized knowledge (Hintikka, 2007). Broadly construed, the term *Socratic teaching* refers to any interactive-engagement process of ongoing inquiry in the context of a dialogue, in which the teacher varies question difficulty in relation to audience background and subject-matter complexity. According to R. Paul (as cited in California Portable Assisted Study Sequence, 2006), the ultimate aim of Socratic teaching is for students to internalize a method of questioning that will prepare them to develop increasingly more sophisticated levels of reflective understanding. Therefore, both the underlying process and the long-range goal of Socratic teaching are consistent with the social constructivist learning perspective. Among the dimensions from which a teacher can draw in questioning students are the nature, implications, applications, and consequences of the issue or problem at hand; the existence of relevant supporting data for a given position; the potential for alternative interpretations of these data; and the appropriate generalized conclusions to be drawn from the available evidence (Seiferth, 1997).

There are tangible pedagogical advantages associated with the Socratic approach. As one of the most efficient ways to involve students in the learning process, Socratic teaching pushes students to uncover answers to questions on the basis of their own knowledge and experiences (Cheng, 2003). As such, Socratic teaching stimulates curiosity, imagination, creativity, and independent analytical thinking (Hativa, 2001). Through constant feedback, Socratic teaching also allows educators to evaluate students' understandings by dealing with misconceptions early in the inquiry process (Garlikov, 2000).

While reaping the benefits of Socratic teaching in their classroom environments, there are qualifying factors for constructivist educators to consider when using this instructional method. It is not only important for teachers to recognize errors in students' reasoning as they unfold during dialogue but also imperative that teachers formulate questions that require suitable logic to be answered correctly (Garrett, 1998). In the role of Socratic questioners throughout the course of dialogue, teachers should also periodically paraphrase what has been covered and summarize what has been missed (Seiferth, 1997). Moreover, the Socratic method of teaching appears to be best suited to smaller class sizes or small-group work within larger classes (Hake, 1998). In addition, the manner in which teachers pose questions will structure the success of student inquiry. Because reflective thought requires time to unfold and should produce more than merely "yes" or "no" answers, teachers should ask open-ended questions and permit appropriate wait-time for responses. Open-ended questions typically start with words such as *why* and *how*, which invoke a certain degree of elaboration on the part of respondents (Dillon, 1997). Drawing from research in higher education on wait-time in questioning (e.g., Khuwaileh, 1999; Kiewra, 1987), educators should allow at least 5 seconds when requesting students to answer a question—especially one that demands greater cognitive analysis.

Intellectual standards and derivative questions apply to using Socratic teaching (see R. Paul, as cited in California Portable Assisted Study Sequence, 2006). The following is a list of these standards, including corresponding examples of questions that teachers may pose to students:

- Significance: What is the central theme implied by the question?
- Clarity: Can you provide an illustrative example?
- Relevance: How do your statements relate to the question being addressed?
- Depth: What underlying variables need to be taken into account?
- Breadth: From what other perspective(s) can you examine this issue?
- Precision: Can you offer more details in response to the question?
- Accuracy: How can you confirm the veracity of your statements?
- Logic: Does your argument follow logically from available evidence?

From a constructivist stance, another important way for teachers to engage learners is to personalize learning by helping students build defensible connections between their past and present learning experiences (Miami Museum of Science, 2001). In introducing new concepts, a primary goal of teachers is to emphasize associations among ideas such that students are able to engage in meaningful learning. As a pedagogical tool that stresses relationships among ideas, *advance organizers* assist students in organizing and interpreting new incoming information on the basis of its relationship to preexisting cognitive structures (Ausubel, 1960). According to Mayer (2003), advance organizers can highlight relationships among newly presented ideas (*expository organizers*) and bridge the gap between old and new information (*comparative organizers*).

In developing and systematically investigating the instructional efficacy of advance organizers, David Ausubel (1963) revisited the Piagetian cognitive constructivist principle of assimilation—absorbing new information within the framework of preexisting superordinate concepts. To Ausubel, learners reorganize their established cognitive structures when they acquire novel conceptual understandings by means of verbal and visual cues in school settings. In this way, advance organizers act in tangibly different ways than content summaries that simply rehash key ideas. More specifically, advance organizers "are introduced in advance of learning itself, and are also presented at a higher level of abstraction, generality, and inclusiveness" (Ausubel, 1963, p. 81).

Ausubel (1963) discussed two guiding principles in organizing curriculum and instruction: progressive differentiation and integrative reconciliation. With *progressive differentiation*, teachers should begin by presenting the most general ideas first, followed by gradually increasing the detail and specificity of these ideas. In *integrative reconciliation,* the goal of instruction should be to integrate novel and previously presented information by means of comparing and cross-referencing new and old ideas. With regard to integrative reconciliation, the instructional utility of advance organizers becomes optimized in situations where a learner possesses limited background knowledge (Mayer, 2003). Under these circumstances, the advance organizers actually serve as the learner's prior knowledge before acquiring new information.

Joyce, Weil, and Calhoun (2000) developed a three-phase procedure for instructors to follow in correctly using advance organizers. In the first phase, teachers should clarify the aims of the instructional material and then present the advance organizer in a verbal (e.g., short anecdote) and/or visual (e.g., hyperlinked image) format. In this initial phase, it is useful to provide supplementary illustrations and prompt awareness of the learner's relevant knowledge base or experiences. In the second phase, instructors should present the learning task. During this intermediate phase, it is imperative to link material to the advance organizer in a logically and explicitly structured fashion. In the third phase, teachers should take steps to strengthen the learner's cognitive organization. Within this final phase, teachers should ask the learner to actively test or apply ideas and to compare and contrast new and old conceptualizations.

Advance organizers are effective pedagogical devices across a wide variety of instructional tasks. As an illustration, advance organizers can be useful heuristic tools before lectures, class discussions, question-and-answer periods, in-class videos, hands-on activities or demonstrations, homework or laboratory assignments, and student oral reports (Hassard, 2006).

In extending Ausubel's (1963) work, Charles Reigeluth (1987) proposed that instruction should be organized in an elaborative sequence of increasing complexity. As a result, the first lesson appropriately introduces the ideas and skills that follow. Applying Reigeluth's *elaboration theory of instruction* to classroom use of advance organizers, instruction is more effective if the teacher relies on epitomes (e.g., analogies) as advance organizers in sensitizing learners to forthcoming instructional content.

EXPLORATION

Regardless of each instructor's paradigmatic preference for cognitive or social constructivism, exploration demands that the emphasis be placed on learner rather than teacher (Thanasoulas, 2001). Instead of assuming the demonstrative role of "sage on the stage," the constructivist educator acts more as a facilitating "guide on the side" in providing food for thought, gently steering students' focuses, and otherwise encouraging students to discover and test their own current understandings. For those educators who are concerned that this teacher-as-guide approach will somehow usurp either their classroom hegemony or their place as reliable sources of expert knowledge, consider that promoting learner-centered instruction "does not suggest that all [student-generated] explanations are of equal value, nor does it eliminate the teacher's role as a knowledgeable authority" (Wong, 1993a, p. 378).

By casting exploration in light of the Socratic method of instruction, the process of student inquiry serves as the impetus behind instructional practice (Miami Museum of Science, 2001). According to Brooks and Brooks (1993), constructivist educators place in students' hands dynamic opportunities to follow trails of interest in exploring the world of available information. In nurturing learners' natural curiosities, constructivist teachers provide students with learning experiences designed to tap into learners' initiatives to discover information (exploring both what they know and what they aspire to know) that permit them to gain ownership of what they learn (Warrick, 2001).

Students' exploratory processes can be viewed from the vantage points of both cognitive and social constructivism. Active learners participate in independent discovery from Piaget's (1973) view on cognitive constructivism and assisted discovery from Vygotsky's (1978) perspective on social constructivism. In both cases, students in the role of active problem solvers attain their own intellectual identity as they analyze ideas, test hypotheses, and explore the answers to questions that relate to their abilities to learn effectively.

Regarding students' exploratory processes, the principal premises of Gestalt psychology are useful to constructivist educators. The focus of gestalt theory is higher order cognition in the context of perception and problem solving. According to Max Wertheimer (1923/1938), the intellectual founder of the gestalt movement, learners should be encouraged to discover the underlying nature of a problem. In doing so, learners should be challenged to uncover the overall structure of the problem and relationships among its elements. As important prompts for learning, the teacher should steer learners toward any gaps or incongruities in the whole–part relationship as a means to discover a "new, deeper structural view of the situation . . . [by] getting a whole consistent picture, and seeing what the structure of the whole requires for the parts" (Wertheimer, 1959, p. 212).

Shifting attention to George Kelly's (1955) *personal construct theory*, the "personal scientist" metaphor has monumental bearing on the exploratory aspects of a constructivist educational approach. Whether the unit of analysis is idiosyncratic or shared meaning-making, learners are incipient scientists who organize and revise their conceptual frameworks as they encounter events that challenge their assumptions. Like scientists, learners continuously explore their conceptual systems by generating and testing hypotheses about how the world operates. Because "anticipation is both the push and pull of the psychology of personal constructs" (Kelly, 1955, p. 49), the following connection exists between past, present, and future: Our present exploration is influenced by our past experiences, which, in turn, guide our prediction of future events. By permitting learners to explore course content on the basis of their past experiences, constructivist educators allow students the opportunity to organize and anticipate recurring phenomena.

The basic tenets of Carl Rogers's (1969) *experiential learning* are also relevant to the exploratory nature of constructivist knowledge acquisition. In experiential learning, the goal of education is facilitation of change and learning as embodied in the following quote:

> The only man who is educated is the man who has learned how to adapt and change; the man who has realized that no knowledge is secure, that only the process of seeking knowledge gives a basis for security. Changingness, a reliance on process rather than on static knowledge, is the only thing that makes any sense as a goal for education in the modern world. (Rogers & Freiberg, 1994, p. 152)

Rogers (1969) discussed the benefits associated with experiential learning when both learner-centered and properly facilitated by teachers. As learning mentors, teachers should provide an "interpersonal relationship in the facilitation of learning" (Rogers & Freiberg, 1994, p. 151). Consequently, teachers should balance intellectual and emotional components of learning as a means of guiding students to explore the depth and breadth of knowledge (Rogers, 1969).

Rogerian experiential learning is a learner-initiated process that addresses students' needs and wants (Rogers, 1969). During this process, students seek out educational materials and opportunities that are tied to applied knowledge and, at the same time, relevant to their personal interests. Thus, student exploration should be directed to practical, social, personal, or research problems. Throughout the process, teachers should create a classroom climate conducive to learning and organize a variety of available learning resources for students to investigate as they choose.

Another key contributor to the exploratory method in education is Jerome Bruner, who proposed a constructivist theory as a general framework for instruction grounded in the investigation of cognition. In *The Process of Education*, Bruner (1960) argued that learners are active problem solvers who are ready to explore the challenges of learning environments. In emphasizing intuition and subject-matter interest as internal stimuli crucial to learning, Bruner (1967) introduced *discovery learning* as an inquiry-based instructional approach. With discovery learning, students construct new ideas contingent on current or past experiential knowledge. Initially, students are encouraged to discover facts and relationships. Next, they are challenged to continually build on what they already know. This latter idea undergirds the development of a *spiral curriculum* that "should revisit basic ideas repeatedly, building upon them until the student has grasped the full formal apparatus that goes with them" (Bruner, 1960, p. 13).

Early on, Bruner's (1960, 1966) work was influenced by the intrapersonal concentration of Piaget's cognitive constructivism but subsequently—and to a greater extent—by the interpersonal emphasis of Vygotsky's social constructivism (Bruner, 1986, 1990, 1996). The changes in Bruner's thinking since the 1960s are reflected in the following excerpt from *The Culture of Education* (Bruner, 1996, p. xi): "Mental activity is neither solo nor conducted unassisted, even when it goes on 'inside the head'." As evidence of his increased focus on social interaction and collaboration as integral components of the learning process, Bruner (1975) developed the concept of *scaffolding*, borrowing from Vygotsky's (1962/1986) earlier work. To Vygotsky, through assistance from more capable or experienced mentors, learners are better prepared to accomplish tasks that they are unable to perform independently. As an instructional principle consistent with Vygotsky's view, Bruner described scaffolding as a systematic process wherein students are assisted by teachers while accomplishing new or difficult tasks. Once students begin to demonstrate task proficiency, the level of instructional assistance is decreased incrementally until responsibility for learning shifts from teacher to learners. Thus, scaffolded instruction uses a sequence of prompted content (e.g., compelling tasks, key questions, learning guides) and teacher or peer support aimed at optimizing learning skills and knowledge (Dickson, Chard, & Simmons, 1993). To be successful, however, scaffolded instruction must allow students to extrapolate beyond the information given (Bruner, 1973).

What are the most effective ways for constructivist educators to use scaffolded instruction to facilitate learning? From an overview of available literature on the topic (see Hogan & Pressley, 1997), the following elements of scaffolded instruction serve as general guidelines for optimal classroom practices:

1. Select tasks on the basis of curriculum goals and students' instructional needs.
2. Assess students' background knowledge in advance of curriculum design to gauge academic progress.
3. Plan instructional goals in tandem with students as a way to stimulate their personal motivation and vested interest in the learning process.
4. Create a learning environment that encourages students to explore alternatives and take appropriate risks in learning.
5. Help students remain task-focused by asking questions, soliciting clarification, and offering encouragement in the face of mounting learning successes.
6. Modify and adjust the teacher assistance offered (e.g., prompting, demonstrating, questioning) in correspondence with students' changing instructional needs.
7. Encourage students' conceptual internalization and independence from teacher assistance by providing sufficient opportunities to generalize learning to diverse contexts.
8. Summarize students' progress in an ongoing manner so that they can better learn to monitor their own progress.

EXPLANATION

Effective communication is crucial in explaining the elements of exploration undertaken by learners. Although learners can certainly engage in reflective analysis of direct experiences and make personal observations, explanatory communication involves interaction among classmates and between students and teachers (Miami Museum of Science, 2001). Social discourse encourages students to reinforce or alter their ideas. This perspective echoes Vygotsky's (1978, 1981) contention that cognition cannot be understood in isolation from the surrounding society because human beings are capable of using language skills to alter both their inner worlds as well as the world around them. Therefore, learning invites transformation of socially shared knowledge into individually constructed knowledge with cooperative learning groups as the underlying force in this process (Cobb, 1996). Working in collaboration, learners articulate their ideas and both support and critique each other's mental constructs. At the same time, teachers facilitate and guide learning by introducing explanatory cues and determining students' levels of understanding and possible misconceptions.

In emphasizing the central role of social learning, Albert Bandura's work relates to the complementary views of Vygotsky (1962/1986, 1978) and Bruner (1986, 1990, 1996) that learning requires social interaction. In Bandura's (1976) *social learning theory*, learning is a socially interactive process that occurs through exposure to respected social models that include teachers and highly accomplished peers. Learners emulate the behavior of these models in constructing mental frameworks and advancing cognitive understandings.

Consistent with Bandura's work, Reuven Feuerstein proposed that intellectual development proceeds within a mediated learning environment as a precursor to independent and self-regulated learning. In his *theory of mediated learning experience*, Feuerstein defined a *mediator* as a person who works in conjunction with learners in developing cognitive functions that clarify thinking and improve learning (Feuerstein & Feuerstein, 1991). Applying this theoretical model to classroom practice, both teachers and classmates can act as mediators by encouraging student learners to engage in shared problem solving as they internalize evolving knowledge bases.

Besides shared verbal communication between learners, what other types of communication can constructivist educators count on as evidence of a student's conceptual growth and development? Created works, such as writings, drawings, videos, or tape recordings, offer verifiable evidence of a learner's continual intellectual advancement that can also be shared to other learners' benefit (Miami Museum of Science, 2001).

ELABORATION

During elaboration, learners build on the concepts they have acquired, draw connections to related concepts, and apply their ideas to the world at large (Miami Museum of Science, 2001). Further inquiry and new cognitive understandings often unfold as learners interconnect concepts and extend and apply their knowledge bases.

In terms of elaboration on learning, a useful way to view conceptual change is to plot it along a continuum of gradations from modest to extreme (Dagher, 2006). Susan Carey (1985) discussed knowledge restructuring in a manner relevant to the respective poles of this continuum. To Carey, *weak restructuring* involves restricting or extending connections between already existing concepts and the contexts to which they apply, whereas *strong restructuring* leads to actual changes in core concepts themselves.

Vital to elaboration on learning is the context in which subsequent learning occurs. In his *situated learning theory*, Jean Lave (1988) offered that learning is a function of the activity and context in which it takes place. In sharp contrast with classroom learning that stresses knowledge "unsituated," or removed from natural contexts, knowledge should be presented within authentic settings and applications that reflect the ways in which that knowledge will be used. Consistent with Lave's view of situated cognition is the notion of a "cognitive apprenticeship" that enables students to learn in authentic domain activities, both inside and outside of the classroom (J. S. Brown, Collins, & Duguid, 1989). This *cognitive apprenticeship model* of learning resembles Vygotsky's (1978) concept of zones of proximal development. In both instances, learning is nestled in authentic tasks just beyond what a student can handle alone but can be accomplished with the support of teachers and/or mentoring peers.

In emphasizing the dual importance of context and authentic domain activities during learning, Thomas Sticht's (1975) *functional context approach* emphasizes the necessity of making learning germane to students' experiences. This approach enhances transfer of learning from classroom to real-life scenarios. In light of learners' prior experiences, it becomes possible for them to relate new information to preexisting knowledge and to transform old into new knowledge. Journaling (e.g., Mayo, 2003b) and reflective autobiographical narration (e.g., Mayo, 2004e) are viable learning strategies in terms of increasing the personal relevance of course content. These constructivist techniques also aid in effective transfer of learning by more closely linking learning framework to actual context of application.

In traditional classroom environments, students are often asked to solve well-defined problems in which reasoning derives almost exclusively from preformulated systems and rules. In these situations, learning results in fixed meaning that fails to transfer comfortably to new learning contexts (J. S. Brown et al., 1989). Using situated learning, however, conceptual understanding "continually evolve[s] with each new occasion of use, because new situations, negotiations, and activities inevitably recast it in a new, more densely textured form" (J. S. Brown et al., 1989, p. 33).

Because not all learning involves simple and well-structured problems, *cognitive flexibility theory* (Spiro, Feltovich, Jacobson, & Coulson, 1991) is a constructivist perspective that deals with the nature of learning in complex and ill-defined knowledge domains. Cognitive flexibility implies the

> ability to spontaneously restructure one's knowledge, in many ways, in adaptive response to radically changing situational demands . . . [as] a function of both the way knowledge is represented (e.g., along multiple rather than single conceptual dimensions) and the processes that operate on those mental representations (e.g., processes of schema assembly rather than intact schema retrieval). (Spiro & Jehng, 1990, p. 165)

Of particular concern to cognitive flexibility theory is the transfer of knowledge beyond initial learning environments to novel and unique situations (Spiro et al., 1991). In being flexible enough to apply important concepts to new situations, learners must be able to understand how to "crisscross," or interconnect, domain knowledge by comparing and contrasting information acquired from different thematic perspectives (Godshalk, Harvey, & Moller, 2004). Constructivist educators may draw from the following principles in applying cognitive flexibility theory to instructional design (see Jonassen, Ambruso, & Olesen, 1992):

1. Avoid content oversimplification by emphasizing knowledge construction over knowledge transmission.
2. Design instruction to be context dependent, as in the use of case-based teaching methods.
3. Allow learners to sample multiple representations of content.
4. Stress knowledge sources that allow learners to interrelate rather than compartmentalize knowledge.

EVALUATION

Evaluation, or assessment of learning, is an ongoing diagnostic process that can occur at all junctures throughout instruction. As tangible documentation of the need for modification in instructional design and delivery, demonstrations of learning attainment and academic progress can actually enhance students' educational experiences (Miami Museum of Science, 2001).

The first step in effective assessment is establishing student learning outcomes, or measurable descriptions of what instructors "intend for students to know (cognitive), think (attitudinal), or do (behavioral)" (Nichols & Nichols, 2000, p. 17), in connection with the learning task. According to the U.S. Department of Education's National Center for Education Statistics (1997), learning outcomes may be academic (e.g., content knowledge, critical thinking skills), occupational (e.g., work-readiness skills), or developmental (e.g., ethical decision making, respect for diversity).

Robert Gagne combined both behaviorism and a cognitive perspective in his theoretical stance and its implications for instructional design and assessment (Gagne, 1962, 1965, 1985; Gagne, Briggs, & Wager, 1992; Gagne & Driscoll, 1988). By assigning comparable significance to targeted behavioral changes and mental processes—including thinking and remembering—Gagne is recognized as a key "bridge theorist" (Lever-Duffy, McDonald, & Mizell, 2005, ¶ 2) within the constructivist educational tradition.

In *The Conditions of Learning and the Theory of Instruction*, Gagne (1965) described the relationship of learning goals and outcomes in appropriate instructional design. In Gagne's application of Skinnerian operant conditioning (Skinner, 1954) to the principles of learning, learning results in observable and measurable outcomes that are behaviorally stipulated descriptions of educational goals or performance objectives students are expected to accomplish through prescribed learning activities.

Gagne (1977, 1985) emphasized the cognitive conditions of learning that result from an individual's efforts to construct personal knowledge. In his work, Gagne extrapolated from *information-processing theory* (Atkinson & Shiffrin, 1968), which portrays the human learner as a processor of information analogous to a computer. Gagne was also influenced by Ausubel's (1980) *assimilation theory*, which stresses the processes by which learners integrate new information into their overall cognitive structures. Of special concern to Gagne was how best to plan instruction in predetermined chunks to avoid memory overload throughout knowledge construction.

Gagne (1985) classified various types of learning outcomes (intellectual skills, verbal information, cognitive strategies, motor skills, and attitudes) that stem from internal learning processes. These outcomes are distinguishable from one another on the basis of how learning can be demonstrated. Regarding intellectual skills, for example, concepts are demonstrated through labeling and classifying, rules are demonstrated through application, and problem-solving skills are demonstrated through generating solutions or procedures.

More recent constructivist influences on instructional design and assessment build on the earlier works of Gagne and others (e.g., Wittrock, 1974) that emphasize the importance of learner-generated ideas and the incorporation of these ideas within authentic learning contexts. In delineating prescriptive principles for constructivist learning, Driscoll (2000) called for educators to "embed learning in complex, realistic, and relevant environments" (p. 382). Similarly, Merrill (2002) recommended that instruction include demonstration, application, and integration of students' knowledge and skills in real-world learning activities.

Ideally, assessment strategies should both advance student competence (Wlodkowski & Ginsberg, 1995) and bolster teaching effectiveness (Austin, 1993). However, not all types of assessment are equally successful in satisfying these complementary educational aims. In contrast to traditional assessment instruments that invoke recall or recognition of knowledge on selected-response test items, such as multiple-choice, matching, or true–false questions (Wiggins, 1990), *authentic assessment* eschews rote learning and passive test taking in favor of real-world situations that encourage students to construct and apply knowledge in more meaningful, task-specific ways (Mueller, 2003). With authentic assessment, students demonstrate learning by actually doing something in situations that replicate a diverse range of real-life experiences and challenges.

According to Mueller (2003), teaching and learning converge in the practice of authentic assessment. As a vehicle for evaluating higher order cognitive competencies, the instructional designs used in authentic teaching applications sample contexts that are realistically connected to students' experiences. In these instructional designs, students learn to solve real-life problems, and teachers facilitate this learning process. Moreover, the solutions offered serve as measures of students' abilities to transfer learning from the classroom to the world at large.

Authentic assessment is an excellent means to accomplish embedded assessment as a normal consequence of the ongoing process of teaching and learning (American Psychological Association [APA], 2008b). Contrasted with *summative assessment* (e.g., A. H. Miller, Imrie, & Cox, 1998), which takes place at the completion of a course when student mastery of course-specific goals is being evaluated, *embedded assessment* (e.g., Gerretson & Golson, 2005) considers expected outcomes and evaluation criteria occurring as a routine component of assigned work while the course is being taught. Consequently, with embedded authentic assessment, students play a more prominent role in judging their own academic progress.

By its nature, authentic assessment should be created to evaluate the knowledge and skill development of all learners. Therefore, instructors should make efforts to design measures that canvas multiple pedagogical strategies in reaching desired learning outcomes while simultaneously maximizing the unique strengths of a diverse undergraduate student audience (APA, 2008b). To this end, rubrics can quantify and prioritize outcome expectations in a way that offers formative feedback to students about the strengths and weaknesses of their work (Allen, 2004).

Throughout Part III (chaps. 4–8), I embed authentic assessments in the context of constructivist learning assignments that I have used in teaching a variety of undergraduate psychology courses. In doing so, I cast these authentic assessments in the light of the developmentally coherent curriculum model presented at the end of chapter 1. Throughout this process, I emphasize item-specific knowledge, skills, and values over a course-specific curriculum orientation, which permits instructional flexibility and measurement of generalized learning throughout the entire range of undergraduate courses within a single psychology program or across different psychology programs. Therefore, the aforementioned developmental model "provides objective criteria that can also be used to evaluate [undergraduate psychology] course work that may differ with respect to course title, number of credit hours, or level of institution" (APA, 2008b, p. 10). This model is particularly useful in instructional designs with well-specified learning goals and performance-based assignments that contribute to progress toward meeting those goals. By matching behavioral descriptors within the model to performance expectations embedded within learning assignments, individual faculty members or departmental programs can link student proficiency levels and learning goals and outcomes with corresponding course work (APA, 2008b). With the present developmental model, I undertake a process comparable to the prior work of Bosack, McCarthy, Halonen, and Clay (2004), who provided illustrative examples of how to translate the general language of a developmental rubric for scientific inquiry skills into behavioral expectations of authentic assessments fitted to varying levels of sophistication. For the constructivist learning assignments that appear in chapters 4 through 8, illustrative examples include the following structural elements:

- levels of student proficiency associated with the assignments,
- undergraduate psychology courses associated with the assignments,
- instructional context of the assignments,
- purpose of the assignments,
- instructional methodology for completing the assignments,
- learning goals consistent with the science and application of psychology,
- constituent learning outcomes within each goal,
- student behaviors that demonstrate each outcome at each proficiency level, and
- evaluative criteria and grading rubrics for measuring the extent of student mastery of the learning goals and outcomes.

In considering these examples of embedded authentic assessments, it should prove helpful to reexamine the developmental model depicted in Tables 1A.1 through 1A.5 of Appendix 1.1 (see chap. 1), which correspond to each of five learning goals and outcomes for the undergraduate psychology major (i.e., knowledge base of psychology, research methods in psychology, critical thinking skills in psychology, application of psychology, and values in psychology) matched to each of three levels of student proficiency (i.e., basic, developing, and advanced). In applying this model to classroom practice, educators should recognize upfront that the model represents a flexible assessment instrument wherein "assignments may actually cover more than one level of student proficiency, despite the course designation in the undergraduate [psychology] curriculum (i.e., 1000, 2000, 3000, or 4000)" (APA, 2008b, p. 9).

In distinguishing between *course assessment* (undertaken to provide evidence of knowledge and skill mastery as a guide to improving learning performance in specific courses) and *program assessment* (aimed at securing "big picture" assessment data to improve teaching, modify programs, and document program strengths and weaknesses), it must be noted that both forms of assessment are addressed concurrently in aligning learning outcomes from the current developmental model with "determination of student progression toward meeting stated goals at preset points in [undergraduate psychology] courses or curricula" (APA, 2008b, p. 6).[1] This unified approach to assessment for learning is consistent with the principles of *formative assessment* (Nicol & Macfarlane-Dick, 2006). With the model as a starting point for a set of learning outcomes aligned to item-specific knowledge-, skill-, and values-based expectations within courses or curricula and embedded authentic assessments as guideposts to action, it then becomes possible to collect and review assessment data to determine what changes are needed for course- or program-level improvements and whether these changes have been successful in achieving desired outcomes. In promoting the scholarship of teaching and learning along with faculty innovations that can be shared with other teaching professionals (Gurung & Schwartz, 2008), faculty members may entertain how best to tailor assessments in their own courses to address learning outcomes at varying levels of student proficiency (T. P. Pusateri, personal communication, December 5, 2008). As a means to encourage assessment and "assurance of learning" at the programmatic level, faculty members within a psychology department may join forces to "identify core courses at different levels in which they will agree to embed assignments across sections of equivalent courses that address [student achievement at] appropriate levels of outcomes" (T. P. Pusateri, personal communication, December 5, 2008). In the words of the APA Task Force on Strengthening the Teaching and Learning of Undergraduate Psychological Science,

> This model of formative, embedded assessment clearly requires considerable front-loaded effort to yield a coherent curriculum. However, the reward is the integration of virtually all assessment efforts into the routine conduct of courses [or programs], and doing this saves the time and money associated with summative assessments. (APA, 2008b, p. 7)

---

[1] Dunn, McCarthy, Baker, Halonen, and Hill (2007) established a set of specific benchmarks for gauging the quality of a psychology program's assessment plan. These benchmarks allow for assessment of student learning outcomes (writing, speaking, research, collaborative, and technology skills) along a developmental continuum (underdeveloped, developing, effective, and distinguished).

III

AUTHENTIC ASSESSMENTS EMBEDDED IN CONSTRUCTIVIST LEARNING ASSIGNMENTS

4

CASE-BASED INSTRUCTION

Case-based instruction (CBI) has a long history of use in developing critical thinking and applied reasoning skills (McDade, 1995). This approach to learning, observed in law schools as early as the late 1800s, has also been popular in business schools since the early 1900s (Merseth, 1991). Today, college faculty continue to use case studies as instructional tools across a variety of disciplines, including medicine (S. M. Williams, 1992), nursing (DeMarco, Hayward, & Lynch, 2002), science (Yadav et al., 2007), and teacher education (Shulman, 1992). Particularly relevant to undergraduate psychology education, the case method has proven useful in teaching neuroanatomy (Sheldon, 2000), educational psychology (Gonzalez-DeHass & Willems, 2005), abnormal psychology (Lafosse & Zinser, 2002), developmental psychology (Cabe, Walker, & Williams, 1999), psychology of adjustment (Mayo, 2004d), and introductory psychology (Mayo, 2002a). In addition, computerized case simulations have served as heuristic instruments in teaching undergraduate counseling theories (Lambert & Lenthall, 1988).

The *case method* is an active learning pedagogy that stresses problem analysis and problem solving over a range of viewpoints and potential outcomes

(Cranston-Gingrass, Raines, Paul, Epanchin, & Roselli, 1996). In CBI, students apply their prior experiences to fictional or real-life cases (i.e., written narrative accounts of problem-centered environments) that they may encounter in applied settings. As a medium for teaching reasoning skills that connect in-class learning to out-of-class realities (R. A. Smith & Murphy, 1998), CBI presents authentic tasks that contextualize rather than abstract the learning process (Jonassen, 1994). Accordingly, effective cases for learning share several requisite characteristics (see Herreid, 1997; Lombardi, 2007; Schmidt, Waligora, & Vorobieva, 2008; Wasserman, 1994), including

- a short story that is believable and arouses reader interest;
- close alignment between case content and instructional objectives;
- concentration on an authentic situation that invokes real-world relevance;
- elements of ambiguity that necessitate problem solving or decision making;
- a broad level of generalizability that allows for transfer of learning across diverse contextual boundaries; and
- discussion that provides learners with opportunities to analyze, propose, and evaluate potential solutions to problems inherent in case content.

Consistent with Cobb's (1996) perspective, case-based teaching is a flexible model that highlights complementary aspects of cognitive and social constructivism. Although some instructors may assign cases as individual projects, others argue that group discussion frames CBI's success (Blackmon, Hong, & Choi, 2007). Classroom research has shown that "the use of discussion groups in case-based classes can be an effective and motivating method of instruction if students are prepared and time is available for both individual preparation and group discussion" (Flynn & Klein, 2001, p. 83). After reflecting individually on the predominant themes represented in a case, students are typically drawn into class discussion about its salient issues. Therefore, concerning CBI's capacity to foster higher order thinking and deeper understanding of targeted content, the primary distinction between a cognitive and social constructivist focus is the extent to which the instructor leads students directly or the instructor promotes learning activities (e.g., debating, role playing) through which students lead themselves (Blackmon et al., 2007).

APPLYING AUTHENTIC ASSESSMENT
TO A FICTIONAL CASE STUDY

As discussed earlier, CBI can apply to both fictional and actual case scenarios. Exhibit 4.1 describes an authentically assessed learning assignment that relates to a fictional case narrative used in teaching introductory psychology (Mayo, 2002a). This assignment encompasses a specific learning outcome from each of two learning goals for the undergraduate psychology major: (a) knowledge base of psychology and (b) critical thinking skills in psychology.

Exhibit 4.1 includes behavioral descriptors of student performance expectations grounded in the developmental model shown in Tables 1A.1 through 1A.5 of the appendix to chapter 1 of this volume. Also derived from this developmental model are the remaining exhibits throughout this book—except for the fictional case narrative appearing in Exhibit 4.2 and the concept-mapping student training module found in Exhibit 6.1—that are similarly designed to authentically assess other constructivist learning assignments.

APPLYING AUTHENTIC ASSESSMENT
TO REAL-LIFE CASE STUDIES

As a counterpart to applying CBI to a fictional case, this same instructional approach can also be used with real-world case scenarios (Mayo, 2004d). In the context of teaching psychology of adjustment, Exhibit 4.3 portrays an application of authentic assessment to a series of learning assignments involving real-life case narratives. These case assignments canvas learning outcomes from all five learning goals for the undergraduate psychology major: (a) knowledge base of psychology, (b) research methods in psychology, (c) critical thinking skills in psychology, (d) application of psychology, and (e) values in psychology.

APPLYING AUTHENTIC ASSESSMENT
TO THE LIFE-CHANGE LOG

As a logical extension of applying the case-study method to real-life case scenarios, CBI can also be used in the framework of a self-directed case analysis. Exhibit 4.4 presents an application of authentic assessment to a self-directed behavior change project known as the *life-change log* (Mayo, 2007). As reflected in teaching psychology of adjustment, this project samples learning outcomes from all five learning goals for the undergraduate psychology major: (a) knowledge base of psychology, (b) research methods in psychology,

(c) critical thinking skills in psychology, (d) application of psychology, and (e) values in psychology.

APPLYING AUTHENTIC ASSESSMENT TO "LIVE" RESEARCH CASE ANALYSIS

In contrast to the traditional instructional strategy of assigning one or more student-developed research projects in a research methods class, there is an alternative case-based approach to teaching students the components of psychological research. Exhibit 4.5 applies authentic assessment to this alternative instructional approach, called *"live" research case analysis* (Mayo, 2004b), which considers learning outcomes from all five learning goals for the undergraduate psychology major: (a) knowledge base of psychology, (b) research methods in psychology, (c) critical thinking skills in psychology, (d) application of psychology, and (e) values in psychology.

APPLYING AUTHENTIC ASSESSMENT TO THE DIALOGUE METHOD

In the framework of teaching history and systems of psychology, Exhibit 4.6 introduces a series of learning assignments that require students to apply case-based analysis to content-laden position statements espoused by preeminent contributors throughout psychology's history. These assignments, collectively referred to as the *dialogue method* (Mayo, 2002b), involve outcomes from three learning goals for the undergraduate psychology major: (a) knowledge base of psychology, (b) critical thinking skills in psychology, and (c) values in psychology.

EXHIBIT 4.1
Applying Authentic Assessment to a Fictional Case Study

Levels of student proficiency: Basic and developing

Course: Introductory psychology

Assignment: Fictional case study

Instructional context: The effectiveness of case-based instruction (CBI) is supported by *situated cognition theory* that emphasizes "the notion of learning knowledge and skills in contexts that reflect the way they will be used in real life" (Collins, 1988, p. 2). Adapted from my earlier work (Mayo, 2002a), this method exposes students to an instructor-generated, fictional case narrative in teaching conceptual applications of contemporary theoretical stances in introductory psychology.

Purpose of the assignment: As a teaching tool, CBI has been shown to successfully bridge the gap between theory and practice (Ertmer & Russell, 1995). In CBI, students are pushed in the direction of conceptual analysis and reflective decision making by using problem-centered narratives that provide authentic learning opportunities (Blackmon, Hong, & Choi, 2007). Relying on the content of the case-study narrative that follows, students learn to apply modern-day psychological theories over a number of contextual variables.

Instructional methodology: Over the initial week of the term, I introduce students to six psychological theories: biological, psychodynamic, learning, humanistic, cognitive, and cross-cultural. After preliminary lectures on the conceptual foundations of these perspectives, I provide students with an instructor-created, hypothetical case narrative (Mayo, 2002a). I design this narrative to reflect central components of each theory. Refer to Exhibit 4.2 for the content of a sample fictional case, including intended applications (in bold type) of the theories embodied within the case's content.

As a 50-minute in-class exercise, I divide students into six groups of four to six individuals. Each group discusses the case narrative's connection to a single psychological theory, with a different theoretical position assigned to each group. Each group designates one member to serve in the dual role of recorder–reporter, organizing and summarizing that group's responses and later reporting this information to the class. Following small-group discourse that lasts approximately 15 to 20 minutes, each reporter presents that group's conclusions to the entire class as a prelude to whole-class discussion that incorporates peer critique.

Graded assignment: Students receive a graded assignment, worth 10% of the final course average, which solicits conceptual application of the six psychological theories. Administered over a 50-minute class period, the assignment is a short-answer essay task that consists of 10 to 15 instructor-generated, fictional, problem-centered scenarios (2 or 3 per psychological theory). I ask students to correctly match theory to situation and offer a succinct explanation for each theoretical selection. A sample scenario, including (in bold type) the corresponding theory to which the situation pertains, is as follows:

> Professor Swisher investigates the relationship between long-term memory
> and ways in which college students categorize information while studying.
> What theoretical perspective does Professor Swisher's research illustrate?
> **(Cognitive perspective)** Briefly explain why.

Learning goals and outcomes:

1. Knowledge base of psychology: Contemporary perspectives in psychology
    _____ Identify, compare, and contrast contemporary psychological perspectives.
2. Critical thinking skills in psychology: Association skills
    _____ Apply contemporary theories in psychology across a diverse range of
    contexts.

Learning task and grading rubric: Applying contemporary psychological theories within a fictional case study.

A = Applies all psychological theories in a consistently accurate manner.
B = Demonstrates minor application errors with regard to psychological theories.
C = Displays a moderate level of inaccuracy in applying psychological theories.
D = Reveals marginal ability to apply psychological theories.
F = Applies psychological theories incorrectly in most or all instances.

EXHIBIT 4.2
Contemporary Psychological Theories Applied in a Fictional Case Narrative

Directions: Comment on how each of the following psychological perspectives can be applied in this hypothetical case narrative of a 15-year-old, American-born male named "William": biological, psychodynamic, behavioral, humanistic, cognitive, and cross-cultural. (*Note.* To elucidate my intended theoretical applications, I have inserted the names of the applicable theoretical perspective[s] in bold type after corresponding passages that sample aspects of one or more theories. For obvious reasons, I do not make this information available in advance to students who participate in this narrative exercise.)

William has been experiencing long-standing emotional and behavioral problems, including feelings of despair and fits of uncontrolled rage. These same psychological difficulties are evident in members of William's family. His father is chronically depressed and his older brother is frequently antisocial and aggressive in his interactions with others. **(Biological [hereditary] and learning perspectives)**

On his own, William has not shown the capacity for personal insight into his thoughts and feelings as possible causes of his psychological problems. In fact, when asked why he feels the way that he does about life, he offers little insight into the nature of his own troubles. **(Cognitive theory)**

William has received psychological counseling from two different therapists over the past year, the last several months of which he has been taking prescribed psychoactive medications with mixed success. **(Biological perspective)** The first of his therapists had used various environmental manipulations (e.g., progressive relaxation and anger management techniques) to assist William with his behavioral problems. However, none of these approaches were particularly effective. **(Learning perspective: Classical and operant conditioning)** William's more recent therapist, a clinical psychiatrist, has determined that William possesses underlying feelings of hostility and abandonment toward his mother, who divorced his father when William was 3 years old. Nonetheless, William is either unwilling or unable to come to terms with his deep-rooted, negative feelings about his mother. **(Freudian psychodynamic theory)**

William's circle of peers has also been questionable, since most of them have been involved in delinquent activities. In fact, William himself has recently been brought before juvenile court for assaulting a classmate on a bus ride home from school. In addition to seeking his peers' social approval, William appears to have modeled some of the same delinquent behaviors that he has observed in his peers **(Learning perspective: Operant conditioning and cognitive social learning theory)**

Nearly 2 months ago, William met a 43-year-old local preacher, Reverend Belton, who has taken an active interest in William's welfare. Reverend Belton holds a favorable view of human nature, believing that people are born basically good and that even the habitually wayward can make positive, life-affirming changes. **(Humanistic perspective)** Although it is too early to say conclusively, William seems to be establishing a working rapport and fundamental trust in this developing interpersonal relationship, despite their age and generational differences.

Another important figure in William's life is Woo-Jin, a 20-year-old man of South Korean descent, who is attending an American university near William's home. Woo-Jin has befriended William over the past 5 months. Drawing from his own cultural background and experiences, Woo-Jin has had several productive conversations with William about appropriate self-control, responsible decision-making, and harmonious group relations. **(Cross-cultural perspective)** Only time will reveal the full impact that Woo-Jin will have on William; however, early indications suggest that he is a stabilizing role model in William's life. **(Learning perspective: Cognitive social learning theory)**

Note. From "Case-Based Instruction: A Technique for Increasing Conceptual Application in Introductory Psychology," by J. A. Mayo, 2002a, *Journal of Constructivist Psychology, 15*, pp. 73–74. Copyright 2002 by Taylor & Francis. Adapted with permission.

EXHIBIT 4.3
Applying Authentic Assessment to Real-Life Case Studies

Levels of student proficiency: Basic and developing

Course: Psychology of adjustment

Assignment: Real-life case studies

Instructional context: As a way to promote connections between theoretical and applied knowledge, case-based instruction (CBI) that relies on real-life cases can be an effective teaching strategy in psychology classes (Hepler & Lloyd, 1999). According to Hepler and Lloyd (1999), tangible examples of psychological principles observed in the lives of real people can encourage students to think more reflectively about their own lives. As students apply psychological conceptions found in others' lives to their own life situations, they are afforded opportunities to link course content to personally relevant events (Cabe, Walker, & Williams, 1999).

Purpose of the assignment: There are learning benefits associated with CBI across multiple teaching contexts in psychology, including enhanced comprehension, analysis, synthesis, and evaluation of course content (Cabe et al., 1999). Although CBI can easily conform to many classroom environments, it is especially fitted to teaching psychology of adjustment, in which opportunities abound for instructors to use actual cases to convey how course content reflects the lives of real people (Hepler & Lloyd, 1999). Building on my preliminary success in teaching contemporary psychological theories to introductory psychology students by means of a single fictional case narrative (Mayo, 2002a), in the present assignment, I incorporate a series of real-life case narratives for students to analyze and discuss in a psychology of adjustment course (Mayo, 2004d).

Instructional methodology: Students complete a different experiential learning exercise for each chapter selected for coverage in the required text. These exercises are predicated on case narratives that feature material presented in each chapter. Each case narrative consists of a brief biographical account that stresses important events in the lives of actual characters. For example, a case narrative on postprison life of former South African President Nelson Mandela—who ushered in multiracial democracy in his country through a policy of reconciliation and negotiation—sets the stage for instructional coverage of leadership and intergroup relations in a chapter on psychology of group behavior.

In designing the case narratives, I draw from a variety of sources in print and electronic media. In preparing for a whole-class discussion on adjustment-oriented implications of each case narrative, students read each case before a designated class date. Following class discussion, students complete a short paper regarding the underlying psychological theme(s) evident in that case, what they have learned from reading the case and discussing its contents, and how to apply the principles derived from that case to life-adjustment issues of personal significance. Although I inform students that the content of their papers remains in strict confidence, they are encouraged to use appropriate discretion as part of their self-disclosure.

In completing each paper in line with current APA Style, students cite a minimum of one reference in support of adjustment concepts discussed. The required length of each paper varies somewhat based on the assigned topic. However, the typical length equals two pages, excluding the reference section.

Each paper is due two class periods from the date that the class discussion on the corresponding case narrative has been completed. Grade penalties are linked

(continues)

to late submissions. The numerical average of the case-narrative papers represents 25% of the final course grade.

Learning goals and outcomes:

1. Knowledge base of psychology: Overarching themes of psychology
    _____ Identify and apply overarching psychological themes (e.g., variability and continuity of behavior and mental processes) in relation to life-adjustment issues of relevance to self and others.
2. Knowledge base of psychology: General content domains of psychology
    _____ Explain and analyze concepts and theories in the general content domains of psychology most applicable to life-adjustment issues concerning self and others (e.g., learning and cognition, individual and sociocultural differences, development).
3. Research methods in psychology: Database skills
    _____ Identify, locate, and appropriately cite relevant reference sources in support of personal adjustment concepts discussed.
4. Critical thinking skills in psychology: Association skills
    _____ Apply diverse life-adjustment principles over a broad range of contexts in the lives of self and others.
5. Application of psychology: Healthy lifestyle
    _____ Describe elements of healthy lifestyle in the lives of self and others.
    _____ Analyze personal lifestyle in self and others that reflects an awareness of fundamental principles of psychology of adjustment.
6. Application of psychology: Potential for psychology as a change agent
    _____ Describe ways that psychological principles can facilitate positive adjustment in the lives of self and others.
7. Values in psychology: Human diversity
    _____ Anticipate that psychological explanations of life-adjustment concerns in the lives of self and others may vary across populations and contexts.

Learning task and grading rubric: Using real-life case studies to understand and apply psychological principles to life-adjustment issues in self and others.

A = Understands and accurately applies a wide variety of adjustment principles.
B = Demonstrates minor errors in understanding and applying adjustment principles.
C = Exhibits moderate difficulty in understanding and applying adjustment principles.
D = Displays restricted ability to understand and apply adjustment principles.
F = Shows insufficient evidence of understanding and applying adjustment principles.

EXHIBIT 4.4
Applying Authentic Assessment to the Life-Change Log

Levels of student proficiency: Basic and developing

Course: Psychology of adjustment

Assignment: Life-change log

Instructional context: Within higher education, interest in self-directed learning and its assessment dates back several decades. Kolb, Winter, and Berlew (1968) investigated the effectiveness of self-directed behavior change and the effects of variations in the change technique. Similarly, McGaghie and Menges (1975) described the use of goal-attainment scaling as a means of assessing self-directed learning. More recently, Harding, Vanasupa, Savage, and Stolk (2007) examined self-directed learning readiness in a project-based learning environment. Of particular appeal to teaching psychology of adjustment are self-directed behavior change projects derived from college textbooks that offer scientifically grounded precepts and practices of self-applied psychology.

Purpose of the assignment: To make material more personally relevant in a psychology of adjustment course, I ask students to complete a self-directed case analysis, called the *life-change log* (Mayo, 2007), which is aimed at instituting and assessing behavior change. Students begin by setting goals for behavior change in their own lives (e.g., losing weight, smoking cessation, studying more effectively, managing test anxiety, dealing more assertively with others) that translate into target behaviors. Then, using strategies for personal adjustment discussed throughout the course, they analyze the factors affecting or controlling each target behavior, develop and implement a systematic program for behavior change, measure the success of this program, and write a self-directed case analysis of the results.

Instructional methodology: The life-change log contains four sections, each marked as a distinct subheading in the body of the report. The procedures involved in completing each section (outlined next) borrow from guidelines for behavioral self-analysis and self-direction contained in both D. L. Watson and Tharp's (1997) and Weiten and Lloyd's (2000) adjustment texts.

1. *Target behavior:* Pinpoint a target behavior (e.g., cigarette smoking) and set a goal for behavioral change (i.e., reduce smoking behavior by how much? by when?).
2. *Baseline data:* Analyze the factors controlling the target behavior by gathering accurate baseline data. Begin by recording initial response level within a short time period (e.g., how often the target behavior occurs over a week), using physical or performance measurement (objective statistics), self-report (subjective narrative of attitudes, thoughts, and feelings), and/or visual presentation (e.g., charts, graphs). Next, identify events that normally precede the behavior (e.g., a big dinner) and typical consequences that are either sustaining the undesirable behavior (e.g., reward of "feeling relaxed" after smoking a cigarette) or preventing desirable behavior from occurring (e.g., threat of punishment in the form of anticipated weight gain upon smoking cessation).
3. *Program design:* Develop a program to modify the target behavior (e.g., decrease the frequency of smoking), spelling out the strategies (e.g., self-reinforcement) that will be used to accomplish the goals articulated in the program.
4. *Program implementation and evaluation:* Execute the program for a specified length of time, from several weeks to the remainder of the term, which indicates

(continues)

the need to get an early start on the assignment. Evaluate the ongoing success of the self-modification program by continuing to keep accurate records of progress. Moreover, address ways to handle backsliding to old, undesirable behavior patterns (if this does occur) and the conditions under which the intervention program will end (e.g., after reducing smoking behavior to less than five cigarettes a day? after completely eliminating smoking?).

Before proceeding with their assignments, I require that students seek my advance approval in terms of the targeted behavior and the accompanying behavior-change program. I automatically assign a grade of zero to any self-directed change project that is conducted and submitted without such prior approval.

Regarding the content of the life-change log, I take appropriate measures to guarantee student privacy and confidentiality. Additionally, I advise students to use reasonable discretion in their self-disclosure.

Students write the life-change log in accordance with current APA Style. There is no maximum page limit for this assignment. However, the completed assignment must contain a minimum of 12 pages, including the title page, abstract, reference section—if others' work is cited—and any tables or figures. I inform students that illustrations are meant to supplement, not replace, narrative presentation. Therefore, although I tell students that illustrations are useful in recording baseline data and in tracking the progress of a self-modification program, I also warn against overusing this mode of presentation.

The life-change log counts as 20% of the final course grade. The completed assignment is due in the final week of the term.

Learning goals and outcomes:

1. Knowledge base of psychology: Role of behavior in psychology
   _____ Identify antecedents and consequences of a selected target behavior.
   _____ Predict likely patterns of a target behavior based on contextual variables.
2. Research methods in psychology: Experimental design
   _____ Design a program to modify a target behavior that includes appropriate investigative strategies to accomplish this goal.
3. Research methods in psychology: Reporting research findings
   _____ Explain the goals, personal adjustment strategies, results, and conclusions derived from implementing a self-modification program, applying current APA Style throughout the process.
4. Research methods in psychology: Database skills
   _____ Identify, locate, and appropriately cite relevant reference sources (if others' work is cited).
5. Research methods in psychology: Limits of scientific reasoning and evidence
   _____ Discuss reasons why the findings and conclusions reached in a self-modification program may change or require adjustment.
6. Critical thinking skills in psychology: Use of evidence in psychology
   _____ Collect and use quantitative and/or qualitative evidence in drawing appropriate conclusions about a target behavior.
7. Critical thinking skills in psychology: Argumentation skills
   _____ Deduce contradictory and oversimplified arguments about a target behavior by relying on a growing body of available evidence.
8. Critical thinking skills in psychology: Detection of errors in psychological reasoning
   _____ Detect and reject conclusions about a target behavior arising from poorly supported assertions.

EXHIBIT 4.4
Applying Authentic Assessment to the Life-Change Log   *(Continued)*

9. Application of psychology: Healthy lifestyle
   _____ Use life-adjustment principles to analyze personal lifestyle in selecting a target behavior to change.
10. Application of psychology: Potential for psychology as a change agent
   _____ Apply one or more psychological principles to facilitate positive self-change in a target behavior.
11. Values in psychology: Tolerance of ambiguity
   _____ Analyze evidence-based conclusions about a target behavior with the intent of finding possible alternative explanations.

Learning task and grading rubric: Applying psychological principles of personal adjustment to evidence-based analysis, design, implementation, and evaluation of a self-directed behavior change program.

   A = Demonstrates clear and consistent understanding of how to apply principles of personal adjustment.
   B = Shows minor inaccuracies in applying principles of personal adjustment.
   C = Displays a moderate level of accuracy in applying principles of personal adjustment.
   D = Exhibits limited understanding of how to apply principles of personal adjustment.
   F = Reveals serious deficiencies in applying principles of personal adjustment.

EXHIBIT 4.5
Applying Authentic Assessment to "Live" Research Case Analysis

Levels of student proficiency: Basic, developing, and advanced

Course: Research methods

Assignment: "Live" research case analysis

Instructional context: Successful completion of an introductory course in research methods is vital to future psychology graduates who plan to conduct their own original research (Ball & Pelco, 2006) and/or need to make informed decisions about research findings as a consequence of their professional responsibilities and development (Zablotsky, 2001). However, the challenging nature of this course's technically complex content often renders it difficult to sustain high levels of student interest and motivation (Ball & Pelco, 2006) and to provide meaningful authentic learning experiences (Mayo, 2004b).

Purpose of the assignment: In teaching research methods, "some instructors supplement traditional lecture–text classes with active learning experiences such as a student-developed research project" (Ball & Pelco, 2006, p. 147). Short of the potentially time-intensive task of students developing and conducting one large or multiple smaller research projects throughout the term, is there any other way to authentically engage students in the content of this course? One such procedure involves the use of *"live" research case analysis* (Mayo, 2004b). Using this approach, students identify and evaluate the elements, methods, and stages of psychological research, as depicted in a carefully chosen empirical publication that serves as a reference case.

(continues)

EXHIBIT 4.5
Applying Authentic Assessment to "Live" Research
Case Analysis   *(Continued)*

Instructional methodology: A week before the assignment's due date, I provide students with a copy of an instructor-selected, peer-reviewed, research-anchored journal article that they are asked to read thoroughly. Students then bring the article to class on a designated date (or dates, if necessary) in anticipation of an in-class written exercise that they complete individually. Using the article as an in vivo case study in research methodology, I ask students a series of predesigned questions regarding the article's content. Organized into corresponding subheadings, students discuss and critique the article in terms of predetermined topics (as illustrated next). Within the overall framework of the assignment's intended purpose, the specific parameters of the assignment remain flexible. Therefore, individual instructors can customize the nature, breadth, and depth of topics to be addressed on the basis of each course's instructional concentration.

1. Hypotheses
    a. Experimental hypothesis
    b. Null hypothesis
2. Variables and operational definitions
    a. Independent variable(s)
    b. Dependent variable(s)
    c. Extraneous variable(s)
3. Participant selection and assignment
    a. Participant sampling
    b. Sample size
    c. Demographic characteristics
    d. Absence of bias
    e. Participant assignment to conditions
    f. Adherence to the American Psychological Association's code of ethics in treatment of participants
4. Instrumentation
    a. Assessment instruments used
    b. Rationale for instrument selection
    c. Absence of bias
5. General research methods
    a. Descriptive
    b. Correlational
    c. Experimental
6. Experimental validity
    a. Internal validity (design quality)
    b. External validity (generalization)
7. Statistical measures and data analysis
    a. Descriptive statistical measures
    b. Inferential statistical tests
    c. Qualitative measures
8. Conclusions and recommendations
    a. Conclusions reached by author(s)
    b. Recommendations for future research

The assignment, which counts as 10% to 20% of the final course grade (depending on the assignment's length and level of complexity), occurs near the end of the term. Once I have returned the scored assignments to respective students, I undertake a whole-class discussion of each component element of the assignment. This class discussion is designed to optimize the instructional utility of "live" research case analysis as a practical review tool in preparation for a comprehensive final examination.

Learning goals and outcomes:

1. Knowledge base of psychology: Relationship of psychology to science
   _____ Analyze how the research investigation reflects scientific principles.
2. Knowledge base of psychology: General content domains of psychology
   _____ Analyze and evaluate the psychological research in one or more of the general content domains (e.g., learning and cognition, biological bases of behavior, development) represented in the research.
3. Knowledge base of psychology: Role of ethics
   _____ Evaluate research practices (e.g., treatment of participants) by means of relevant ethical principles addressed in the APA code of ethics.
4. Research methods in psychology: Scientific method
   _____ Analyze the extent to which the research methodology adheres to scientific principles.
5. Research methods in psychology: General research methods
   _____ Evaluate the effectiveness of research methodology in addressing the question(s) inherent in the research.
6. Research methods in psychology: Correlation versus causation
   _____ Evaluate whether research methodology warrants a cause–effect conclusion.
7. Research methods in psychology: Controlled comparison
   _____ Analyze purported research claims.
   _____ Evaluate the legitimacy of cause–effect assertions.
8. Research methods in psychology: Research elements
   _____ Identify and describe hypotheses, variables, and operational definitions.
9. Research methods in psychology: Experimental design
   _____ Describe experimental design strategies used to address the research question(s).
10. Research methods in psychology: Participant selection and assignment
    _____ Describe the participant sampling and assignment procedures used.
    _____ Analyze the potential influence of participant variables.
11. Research methods in psychology: Design quality (internal validity)
    _____ Analyze conditions that enhance or detract from the validity of conclusions drawn.
    _____ Evaluate the validity of conclusions derived from the research investigation.
12. Research methods in psychology: Generalization (external validity)
    _____ Analyze the generalizability of research findings based on strengths or weaknesses of the research design.
    _____ Recognize that individual differences and sociocultural contexts may impact the generalizability of research findings.
13. Research methods in psychology: Reporting research findings
    _____ Critique the results and conclusions derived through data collection, analysis, and interpretation.
14. Research methods in psychology: Body of evidence
    _____ Articulate how the research investigation addresses one or more behavioral questions.

(continues)

15. Research methods in psychology: Sociocultural context
_____ Apply sociocultural context to the research methods and conclusions.
16. Research methods in psychology: Database skills
_____ Analyze whether the literature review and discussion represent an adequate range of research in addressing the research questions(s).
17. Research methods in psychology: Statistical skills
_____ Evaluate statistical power in the reported results by examining effect size and confidence intervals.
18. Research methods in psychology: Statistical significance
_____ Distinguish between statistical and practical significance in interpreting the reported results.
19. Research methods in psychology: Limits of scientific evidence and reasoning
_____ Discuss reasons why the research findings and conclusions are subject to change.
20. Critical thinking skills in psychology: Use of evidence in psychology
_____ Evaluate the quality, objectivity, and credibility of the research findings in drawing appropriate conclusions and recommending a direction for future research.
21. Critical thinking skills in psychology: Association skills
_____ Assess the quality of connection between the research findings and conclusions and supporting theoretical frameworks.
22. Critical thinking skills in psychology: Argumentation skills and detection of errors in psychological reasoning
_____ Detect, deduce, and/or evaluate contradictory, oversimplified, or poorly supported arguments based on the reported body of research evidence.
23. Critical thinking skills in psychology: Questioning skills
_____ Evaluate the research question(s) in relation to the potential for ambiguity throughout the process of scientific inquiry.
24. Application of psychology: Psychological tests
_____ Evaluate instrumentation used (if applicable) to determine whether it reflects respect for alternative cultures and gender.
25. Values in psychology: Skepticism
_____ Assess whether the research investigation maintains rigorous standards relative to the quality of research evidence in support of valid inferences and claims.
26. Values in psychology: Tolerance of ambiguity and consideration of human diversity
_____ Evaluate the research conclusions based on tentativeness, complexity, and variability across populations and contexts.

Learning task and grading rubric: Identifying and evaluating the elements, methods, and stages of psychological research by means of a "live" research case analysis.

A = Displays thorough proficiency in identifying and evaluating the components of psychological research.
B = Exhibits minor difficulties in identifying and evaluating the components of psychological research.
C = Demonstrates moderate proficiency in identifying and evaluating the components of psychological research.
D = Shows limited proficiency in identifying and evaluating the components of psychological research.
F = Fails to identify and evaluate the components of psychological research in most or all instances.

EXHIBIT 4.6
Applying Authentic Assessment to the Dialogue Method

Levels of student proficiency: Developing and advanced

Course: History and systems of psychology

Assignment: Dialogue method

Instructional context: According to Sanzenbacher (1997), the meaning of language is predicated on the social context and ideological influences of the time and place in which it is offered. The contextual relevance of language is especially important to teaching history and systems of psychology. In this capstone course, recorded intellectual contributions of significant figures from antiquity through the present are cast against the times in which these individuals lived. Extending the logic underlying this argument, discourse from each major contributor to psychology constitutes a content-laden position statement, or "mini-case study," which offers a snapshot of a signature ideological stance and the sociohistorical milieu in which it is articulated.

Purpose of the assignment: In the *dialogue method,* students reflect on the shaping powers of language as a way of knowing (Sanzenbacher, 1997). By using content-laden position statements as mini-case studies to establish active dialogue between reader and writer, the classroom focus shifts from passive knowledge transmission by the instructor to self-constructed explanations on the part of students (Yager & Tweed, 1991). In the present pedagogical application of the dialogue method, I ask students to identify contributors to psychology associated with diverse position statements that represent these individuals' intellectual, philosophical, or theoretical views.

Instructional methodology: Consistent with the organizational layout of Hunt's (1993, 2007) text, the course traces the history of psychology within the backdrop of short biographies of leading contributors. This structural format lends itself particularly well to student consideration of the mini-case studies inherent in content-laden position statements put forth by intellectual giants who have helped to shape psychology's historical evolution. Course coverage includes three units: (a) the development of philosophical/prescientific psychology from antiquity through the 19th century, (b) the early decades of scientific psychology at the start of the 20th century, and (c) the growth of psychology's principal subfields over the past century.

Adapted from my prior classroom research and practice (Mayo, 2002b), the dialogue assignments consist of written position statements (a minimum of 10 per unit) in the form of direct or translated quotations from original sources and paraphrased excerpts from secondary sources, including history of psychology texts. I select these statements to capture the perspectives of noteworthy contributors throughout psychology's historical development—as shown here in quotes from ancient Greek naturalist Aristotle, 17th-century rationalist René Descartes, and 20th-century behaviorist John B. Watson, respectively.

> If ever [the facts have been sufficiently established], then credit must be given rather to observation than to theories, and to theories only if what they affirm agrees with the observed facts. (Aristotle, 2007 version, Part II, Book III, § 10, ¶ 8)
>
> Finally, it is known that all these motions of the muscles, as also all the senses, depend on the sinews, which are as little strings, or like small tunnels coming all from the brain, and containing as that does a certain air, or exceeding[ly] subtle wind, which is termed the animal spirits. (Descartes, 1649/2008, Part I, Article 7, lines 25–27)
>
> Give me a dozen healthy infants, well-formed, and my own specified world to bring them up in and I'll guarantee to take any one at random and train him to

(continues)

become any type of specialist I might select—doctor, lawyer, artist, merchant-chief and, yes, even beggar-man and thief, regardless of his talents, penchants, tendencies, abilities, vocations, and race of his ancestors. (J. B. Watson, 1924, p. 104)

Without my advance notification of contributors' identities in relation to their respective position statements, students name the contributor to psychology most directly linked to each statement. Students also offer supporting rationale for their responses, discussing each perspective on the basis of sociohistorical overtones in both current times and the times in which each contributor lived. Concerning paraphrased materials from secondary courses, I permit students to attribute position statements to more than one contributor—provided that the accompanying rationale reflects the shared philosophical or theoretical stance.

I administer the written dialogue assignments as in-class exercises for each of the three units in the course. These assignments are worth a total of 15% of the final course grade (5% per unit). Students work individually in completing each assignment in one class period. Once returned to students, each scored assignment serves as a catalyst for whole-class discussion that focuses on evaluating the expressed views of key figures throughout psychology's history. In some instances, follow-up discussion moves in the direction of role-play exercises (e.g., B. F. Skinner vs. Carl Rogers) that invite open-ended inquiry in comparing and contrasting differing perspectives (see Robertson & Rane-Szostak, 1996).

Learning goals and outcomes:

1. Knowledge base of psychology: Nature of psychology
   _____ Evaluate the influence of sociohistorical context in an evolving definition of psychology.
2. Knowledge base of psychology: Historical perspectives in psychology
   _____ Compare and contrast historical perspectives in psychology.
   _____ Assess the relative importance of historical perspectives in psychology.
   _____ Defend one or more historical perspectives in psychology.
3. Knowledge base of psychology: Contemporary perspectives in psychology
   _____ Compare and contrast the assumptions, explanatory concepts, methods, and other elements of contemporary psychological perspectives, including the behavioral, biological, cognitive, evolutionary, humanistic, psychodynamic, and sociocultural views.
   _____ Evaluate the utility and efficacy of contemporary perspectives in psychology.
4. Knowledge base of psychology: Overarching themes of psychology
   _____ Debate the relative merits of each side of overarching themes expressed over psychology's history, including nature versus nurture, mind versus body, free will versus determinism, subjectivity versus objectivity, and variability versus continuity of behavior and mental processes.
   _____ Evaluate the appropriateness of competing explanations of behavior throughout psychology's history from the vantage point of overarching themes of psychology.
5. Knowledge base of psychology: General content domains of psychology
   _____ Analyze and evaluate historical and contemporary psychological perspectives in the general content domains of psychology: learning and cognition, individual and sociocultural differences, biological bases of behavior and mental processes, and development.

6. Critical thinking skills in psychology: Argumentation skills
     _____ Deduce contradictory and oversimplified intellectual, philosophical, and theoretical perspectives over psychology's history based on burgeoning and expanding knowledge bases in the field.
7. Critical thinking skills in psychology: Detection of errors in psychological reasoning
     _____ Detect, reject, and evaluate erroneous claims throughout the history of psychology that stem from myths, stereotypes, common fallacies, and poorly supported assertions.
8. Values in psychology: Skepticism
     _____ Distinguish between scientific and pseudoscientific explanations of human behavior over psychology's history.
     _____ Compare the relative value of competing scientific and pseudoscientific explanations of human behavior throughout the history of psychology.
9. Values in psychology: Tolerance of ambiguity and consideration of human diversity
     _____ Evaluate competing explanations of human behavior over psychology's history, with anticipation of complexity, tentativeness, and variability across populations and sociohistorical contexts.

Learning task and grading rubric: Identifying and discussing perspectives captured in dialogic position statements that reflect views from leading contributors throughout psychology's history.

   A = Demonstrates consistent ability to accurately identify and discuss contributors' perspectives.
   B = Exhibits minor difficulties in identifying and discussing contributors' perspectives.
   C = Displays modest proficiency in identifying and discussing contributors' perspectives.
   D = Evidences restricted proficiency in identifying and discussing contributors' perspectives.
   F = Fails to identify and discuss contributors' perspectives in most or all cases.

5

NARRATIVE PSYCHOLOGY

In a groundbreaking investigation, Bower and Clark (1969) demonstrated the effectiveness of narrative stories as an aid to information recall. Since that time, the psychological and pedagogical literature has witnessed a growing interest in narrative psychology as it pertains to comprehension, recall, and organization of events (e.g., Graesser & Ottati, 1995; Stein & Trabasso, 1982). As a resounding endorsement of the educational benefits of narrative psychology, Schank and Abelson (1995) contended that narrative stories are the foundation for nearly all knowledge, memory, and comprehension. In practical terms, people acquire conceptual understandings by associating their narrative stories with others' narrative perspectives. Even if this emphatic claim is open to dispute (W. F. Brewer, 1995), the educational utility of narrative psychology appears to be undeniable. Consistent with the *self-referral effect* (Millis, 2002), students are better able to retain and retrieve content knowledge in narrative learning situations where they can cast that knowledge in a personal context. Consequently, educators should allow students to place new learning in their own words and discover connections between course content and their life experiences (Jensen, 2000).

Although the educational value of narrative psychology is often overlooked, narratives are vital components in the process by which a person derives meaning about inner self in relation to surrounding culture (Bruner, 1996). Congruent with this sociocultural conception, narrative accounts of life experiences are helpful in describing and interpreting the meaning of these events within their social contexts (Bertaux & Kohli, 1984). As everyday cognition involves a combination of generalizations abstracted from experiences encoded in memory (B. J. Reiser, Black, & Abelson, 1985), narrative psychology occupies a prominent position in the retrieval of autobiographical memories relevant in analyzing and explaining human behavior.

Research has emerged that examines autobiographical memories within the overall structure of experiential learning and development (Pillemer, Picariello, Law, & Reichman, 1996; Rothenberg, 1994; Walls, Sperling, & Weber, 2001). With particular emphasis on an undergraduate psychology audience, the study of autobiographical memories has also spilled over into classroom research and practice. For instance, in teaching developmental principles from a constructivist perspective, educators have successfully used narrative accounts of individual development as an undergraduate learning tool. As part of an instructional technique called *connected teaching* (Belenky, Clinchy, Goldberger, & Tarule, 1986), students have used narratives of personal experiences as a vehicle for constructing meaningful knowledge about developmental psychology (Clinchy, 1995). According to Singer (1996), narrative reflections on developmental stages of the life cycle are crucial to an individual's understanding of these time periods.

In addition to life-story narration from autobiographies that provide students with opportunities to "validate classroom learning in their own interpersonal experiences" (Grasha, 1998, p. 85), narrative psychology exists within narrative storytelling involving biographical sketches (Neysmith-Roy & Kleisinger, 1997), case studies (McManus, 1986), and stories from classic literature (Boyatzis, 1992) that afford students a contextual background for examining human behavior (Fernald, 1996). Journaling has also been shown to be an effective narrative learning strategy in various undergraduate psychology courses, from introductory psychology (Finke & Davis, 1988) to experimental psychology (Hettich, 1980). As a learning assignment, journal writing holds the potential to integrate elements of both autobiographical and biographical narration. Students can use journals to analyze everyday circumstances in psychological terms, permitting opportunities to apply psychological principles not only to personal illustrations from their own lives but also to examples arising from others' lives, current events, and the mass media. Connecting journal writing to case-based methodology (Silverman & Welty, 1990), journal entries may be written as brief case descriptions that depict real-life experiences through which students can extract applied psychological principles.

APPLYING AUTHENTIC ASSESSMENT TO THE LIFE ANALYSIS AND THE LIFE-NARRATIVE JOURNAL

Exhibit 5.1 applies authentic assessment to two related autobiographical narrative assignments used in teaching life-span developmental psychology. Both assignments are rooted in a self-reflective developmental framework, with the *life analysis* (Mayo, 2001a) taking the form of a term-length narrative report and the *life-narrative journal* (Mayo, 2006b) being a term-length journal. Each of these assignments encompasses outcomes from all five learning goals for the undergraduate psychology major: (a) knowledge base of psychology, (b) research methods in psychology, (c) critical thinking skills in psychology, (d) application of psychology, and (e) values in psychology.

APPLYING AUTHENTIC ASSESSMENT TO THE LIFE-ADJUSTMENT NARRATIVE

Exhibit 5.2 discusses a term-length autobiographical learning assignment intended to teach students how to apply life-adjustment principles to their personal experiences. Relative to teaching psychology of adjustment, the *life-adjustment narrative* (Mayo, 2003a) assignment addresses outcomes from all five learning goals for the undergraduate psychology major: (a) knowledge base of psychology, (b) research methods in psychology, (c) critical thinking skills in psychology, (d) application of psychology, and (e) values in psychology.

APPLYING AUTHENTIC ASSESSMENT TO MINI-AUTOBIOGRAPHICAL NARRATIVES

Applied psychology classes—with a natural focus on applications of the science of psychology to real-world contexts—afford ideal opportunities to integrate autobiographical learning exercises into the flow of instruction. Exhibit 5.3 offers a term-long series of short autobiographical learning assignments that capitalize on these opportunities (Mayo, 2004e). These assignments speak to outcomes from all five learning goals for the undergraduate psychology major: (a) knowledge base of psychology, (b) research methods in psychology, (c) critical thinking skills in psychology, (d) application of psychology, and (e) values in psychology.

APPLYING AUTHENTIC ASSESSMENT TO THE OBSERVATIONAL DIARY

Exhibit 5.4 ties authentic assessment to a term-length journaling assignment in introductory psychology that involves features of both autobiographical and biographical narration. This assignment, referred to as the *observational diary* (Mayo, 2003b), relates to outcomes from all five learning goals for the undergraduate psychology major: (a) knowledge base of psychology, (b) research methods in psychology, (c) critical thinking skills in psychology, (d) application of psychology, and (e) values in psychology.

EXHIBIT 5.1
Applying Authentic Assessment to the Life Analysis and the Life-Narrative Journal

Levels of student proficiency: Basic and developing

Course: Life-span developmental psychology

Assignments: Life analysis, life-narrative journal

Instructional context: Successful college educators act as "midwife teachers" who assist learners in "giving birth to new ideas, in making tacit knowledge explicit and elaborating on it" (Belenky, Clinchy, Goldberger, & Tarule, 1986, p. 217). In these ways, instructors lend credence to students' sources of internal knowledge while also facilitating the process by which learners reflect on this knowledge. In the context of teaching life-span developmental psychology, narrative-based instruction promotes an active inner dialogue between students and course content that pushes learners to search inside for answers that become, at once, both intellectually and personally meaningful (Mayo, 2001a). As a result, students move progressively in the direction of viewing course conceptions not as arbitrary collections of facts, but rather as verifiable constructions of the human psyche (Clinchy, 1995). Even though traditional-minded academics may conclude that narratives of personal experiences are limited and biased sources of evidence, teachers of human development should consider blending this personalized information base into the fabric of learning and instruction (Clinchy, 1995).

Purpose of the assignments: The life analysis and related life-narrative journal are both term-length assignments that can be used to assess students' knowledge of the principles inherent in life-span developmental psychology classes. Each of these autobiographical learning assignments integrates students' comprehension of these principles with realistic self-assessment of their own physical, cognitive, and socioemotional development across the life cycle.

Instructional methodology for the life analysis: In the *life analysis* (Mayo, 2001a), each student theoretically examines his or her own life—past, present, and future. In the case of developmental periods that have already transpired, students offer an analysis of the events that have impacted their personal development. In doing so, I encourage students to talk with significant others (e.g., parents, siblings, former teachers, friends) in obtaining historical information about their own development. For future developmental periods, students discuss anticipated or potential life successes and disappointments. To earn maximum credit, students must weave

EXHIBIT 5.1
Applying Authentic Assessment to the Life Analysis
and the Life-Narrative Journal *(Continued)*

a variety of developmental principles into their respective life analyses. Although I inform students that I will keep the content of each life analysis in strict confidence, I encourage students to apply reasonable discretion in their self-disclosure.

The life analysis assignment, worth 20% of the final course average, consists of seven sections: (a) infancy (0–2 years), (b) early childhood (2–6 years), (c) middle and late childhood (6–12 years), (d) adolescence (13–19 years), (e) early adulthood (20–40 years), (f) middle adulthood (40–60 years), and (g) late adulthood (age 60 years onward). Students identify each section as a separate subheading in the body of the report. Students also separately discuss physical, cognitive, and socioemotional development as yet another level of subheading within each section. In citing a minimum of seven references, students include at least one reference in support of developmental principles that they discuss in each section. By establishing the project's due date for the final week of the term, I permit optimal in-class coverage of material pertaining to middle and late adulthood.

Written in current APA Style, each life analysis consists of a 12-page minimum, including the title and reference pages. Distinct from fulfilling the minimum page requirement, illustrations (e.g., photographs, diagrams, drawings) appear in a separate appendix.

Along with delineating project guidelines in the course syllabus, during the first class meeting I provide students with a brief, instructor-generated sample life analysis that chronicles the physical, cognitive, and socioemotional development of a fictitious person during a designated stage in the life cycle. As an example, the following narrative excerpt uses middle childhood as an illustrative developmental period and discusses a concept tied to Vygotsky's (1981) sociocultural theory.

> My parents often remind me that, as a grade school child, I seemed to ask the people closest to me a steady stream of probing questions. I agree with my parents when they tell me that I learned much about the world through my endless questioning and hunger for knowledge. This example fits well with Vygotsky's (1981) idea of *guided participation,* where social experiences and explorations lead to cognitive growth through the support and guidance of parents, older siblings, and teachers.

Instructional methodology for the life-narrative journal: A variation of the life analysis assignment is called the *life-narrative journal* (Mayo, 2006b). In the life-narrative journal, which covers infancy through late adulthood, each student adheres to a journaling format in describing significant events throughout his or her life that have shaped, are shaping, or may conceivably shape the course of personal development. Similar to the life analysis, each student analyzes his or her life over its historical and hypothetical span, relating developmental milestones to salient developmental principles. Once again, I guarantee confidentiality and privacy in terms of journal content but recommend reasonable discretion in students' self-disclosure.

The life-narrative journal consists of 28 sequentially numbered entries, including 4 entries for each of the same seven developmental periods covered in the life analysis assignment. Like the life analysis, this journaling project counts as 20% of the final course average and is due in the last week of the term. It also includes a library research component that requires students to cite—in current APA Style within the body of the journal—a minimum of seven references (at least one per developmental

(continues)

EXHIBIT 5.1
Applying Authentic Assessment to the Life Analysis
and the Life-Narrative Journal   *(Continued)*

period) in support of developmental principles presented. To ensure a focus on each of the three domains of development pertinent to studying the life span, each student offers one entry per domain (physical, cognitive, and socioemotional) for each developmental period.

At the beginning of the term, I provide students with several instructor-generated fictitious journal entries (in conjunction with detailed instructions in the course syllabus) to familiarize learners with the guidelines for project completion. As shown in this sample entry that relates to a Piagetian concept applicable to preschool cognitive development, each entry for the life-narrative journal consists of two headings: (a) description of life event and (b) supporting developmental principle:

Description of life event	Supporting developmental principle
When I was 3 years old, I thought that my "Mr. Potato Head" doll was a real person with whom I could speak before bedtime. I would not only talk to him, but also answer each of my questions on his behalf. I'd even get angry when I thought that he was ignoring me as I spoke.	Based on Piaget's (1929) cognitive developmental theory, this example describes *animism,* or the way in which preschoolers assign life-like qualities to inanimate objects.

Learning goals and outcomes for the life analysis and the life-narrative journal:

1. Knowledge base of psychology: Overarching themes of psychology
   _____ Identify and apply overarching themes of developmental psychology (e.g., interaction of heredity and environment, variability and continuity of behavior across the life span, applicability of theories across societal and cultural groups) in explaining behaviors affecting personal development.

2. Knowledge base of psychology: General content domains of psychology
   _____ Identify and apply concepts, theories, and research in the general content domain involving life-span development.

3. Research methods in psychology: Database skills
   _____ Identify, locate, and appropriately cite relevant reference sources in support of developmental principles discussed.

4. Critical thinking skills in psychology: Association skills
   _____ State and relate connections between diverse developmental principles.
   _____ Apply developmental theories, concepts, and research over a broad range of personal experiences.

5. Application of psychology: Healthy lifestyle
   _____ Analyze personal lifestyle on the basis of developmental theories, concepts, and research.

6. Values in psychology: Curiosity
   _____ Apply curiosity to examining patterns and milestones of personal development.

Evaluative criteria and grading rubric: Three equally weighted evaluative criteria serve as anchors in scoring both the life analysis and the life-narrative journal assignments: (a) completeness in following stated guidelines for finishing the

EXHIBIT 5.1
Applying Authentic Assessment to the Life Analysis
and the Life-Narrative Journal   *(Continued)*

assignment, (b) accuracy in connecting personal life events to supporting developmental principles, and (c) variety across life events and supporting developmental applications.

A = Displays exemplary completion of all evaluative criteria.
B = Exhibits minor difficulties with completeness, accuracy, and/or variety.
C = Demonstrates a moderate range of errors regarding completeness, accuracy, and/or variety.
D = Evidences missing entries, inaccurate connections between life events and supporting principles, and an overall absence of variety across applications.
F = Fails to meet evaluative criteria in most or all entries.

EXHIBIT 5.2
Applying Authentic Assessment to the Life-Adjustment Narrative

---

Levels of student proficiency: Basic and developing

Course: Psychology of adjustment

Assignment: Life-adjustment narrative

Instructional context: As a way to engage students in meaningful self-exploration that can concurrently lead to intellectual gains, Webb (1999) suggested a class activity in teaching psychology of adjustment that involves the use of daily journal narratives. Using Webb's recommendation as a point of departure, I designed the *life-adjustment narrative* (Mayo, 2003a) for classroom use.

Purpose of the assignment: The life-adjustment narrative is a term-length autobiographical learning assignment in which students record salient factors impacting their personal adjustment, including perspectives toward self and others, life events, and interpersonal relationships. The primary goal of this project is to increase the personal relevance of course content such that students can integrate sound theoretical knowledge of the adjustment process with a working understanding of the variables influencing their personal adjustment.

Instructional methodology: The life-adjustment narrative contains two sections that appear as distinct subheadings in the body of the report: understanding self and understanding others. Among the topics that relate to understanding self are self-concept, decision making, stress management, self-control in daily living, career selection, and self-discovery in adolescence and adulthood. Topics pertaining to understanding others include impression formation, group dynamics, interpersonal relationships, communication, living with families, and working on the job. In completing this assignment, students may engage in a topical analysis of issues influencing their current personal adjustment. Alternatively, students may adopt a developmental framework both in addressing issues relevant to their own past and present adjustment and in speculating about their future life adjustment. As an illustration of the latter stylistic approach to assignment completion, a former student of mine cited the following quote from Kubler-Ross (1969): "A well-rounded life should

(continues)

have a beginning, a middle, and an end" (p. vi). On the basis of this quote, this student argued that

> life is a continual process of adjustment that begins at the moment of birth. I have come to realize that every action I take, every thought I have, counts in the grand scheme of my existence. As a young adult, I can now reflect on the joys and frustrations of my earlier life. As I look toward the future, I hope to draw on the inner peace I've gained from life's joys, plus the inner strength I've developed from life's frustrations. In the twilight of my life, I hope to accept what was, is, and will be (Erikson, 1959).

As reflected in the student's citation of Kubler-Ross's (1969) quote and its connection to the final stage in Erikson's (1959) developmental theory (ego integrity vs. despair), the life-adjustment narrative incorporates a library research component. Students must write their narratives in adherence with current APA Style and must cite a minimum of eight references (at least four per section) that support adjustment concepts discussed. Appearing separately from the body of a 10-page minimum report (including the title and reference pages), ancillary materials, such as self-report rating scales, are reserved for an appendix that does not factor into the minimum page requirement for the assignment.

In the course syllabus, I explain the project guidelines for completing the life-adjustment narrative and review these guidelines during the first class meeting. Even though I take necessary steps to protect privacy and confidentiality, I urge students to exercise calculated discretion in their self-disclosure.

The life-adjustment narrative is due the last week of the term. The assignment counts as 20% of the final course average.

Learning goals and outcomes:

1. Knowledge base of psychology: Overarching themes of psychology
    _____ Identify and apply variability and continuity of behavior with respect to personal adjustment issues.

2. Knowledge base of psychology: General content domains of psychology
    _____ Identify and apply concepts and theories in the general content domains of psychology most applicable to personal adjustment issues, including learning, cognition, and development.

3. Research methods in psychology: Database skills
    _____ Identify, locate, and appropriately cite relevant references that support principles of personal adjustment discussed.

4. Critical thinking skills in psychology: Association skills
    _____ Relate and apply diverse psychological principles over a wide range of personal adjustment contexts.

5. Critical thinking skills in psychology: Problem solving
    _____ Apply psychologically sound problem-solving strategies in proposing solutions to personal adjustment concerns across diverse contexts.

6. Application of psychology: Healthy lifestyle
    _____ Analyze personal lifestyle in terms of psychological principles of life adjustment.

7. Application of psychology: Potential for psychology as a change agent
    _____ Describe ways in which psychological principles of life adjustment can facilitate favorable personal change.

EXHIBIT 5.2
Applying Authentic Assessment to the
Life-Adjustment Narrative   *(Continued)*

8. Values in psychology: Curiosity
   _____ Apply curiosity to examining psychological principles of personal adjustment.

9. Values in psychology: Skepticism
   _____ Distinguish between scientific and pseudoscientific psychological principles as applied to personal adjustment issues, comparing the relative value of these principles.

Learning task and grading rubric: Using term-length autobiographical narration to apply psychological principles across diverse personal adjustment contexts dealing with self and others.

A = Demonstrates clear understanding of how to consistently apply personal adjustment principles.
B = Displays minor difficulties in applying personal adjustment principles.
C = Evidences moderate success in applying personal adjustment principles.
D = Shows limited proficiency in applying personal adjustment principles.
F = Fails to apply personal adjustment principles in most or all instances.

EXHIBIT 5.3
Applying Authentic Assessment to Mini-Autobiographical Narratives

Levels of student proficiency: Basic and developing

Course: Applied psychology

Assignments: Mini-autobiographical narratives

Instructional context: In teaching undergraduate psychology, merely lecturing about content application may fall well short of the intended instructional mark (Grasha, 1998). By increasing course relevance and applicability to students' lives, autobiographical narration successfully links the depth and breadth of classroom learning to meaningful introspection and knowledge construction and application in real-world contexts (Klos, 1976). According to Hettich (1976), autobiographical narration connects psychological concepts to students' cognitive structures in ways that personalize teacher- and textbook-provided examples through the use of students' everyday experiences.

Purpose of the assignments: To emphasize the practical significance of psychology as an applied science, an important instructional objective within undergraduate psychology education should be to instruct students how to generalize and apply important principles to authentic contexts (Grasha, 1998). Instead of a single, term-length life-narrative project (Mayo, 2001a, 2003a, 2006b), I ask students to complete a term-long series of brief written autobiographical reports as graded assignments in the instructional framework of applied psychology (Mayo, 2004e). In completing each of these *mini-autobiographical narratives,* students describe and apply psychological principles to their lives across a diverse array of course content and past and present experiences.

(continues)

Instructional methodology: Each mini-autobiographical narrative corresponds to material from one chapter covered in the course. A separate narrative report pertains to each of the following general topics, although instructors can tailor the nature and number of topics to suit their individual needs:

- examining psychology's perspectives, methods, subfields, and career opportunities;
- sensation and perception;
- learning and changing behavior;
- improving memory;
- thinking and problem solving;
- motivation;
- emotions;
- communication;
- interpersonal attraction;
- attitude formation and change;
- group processes; and
- career planning and job satisfaction.

Students prepare each mini-autobiographical narrative in accordance with current APA Style. As a library research component, students include a minimum of one reference in support of psychological applications discussed in each narrative. Although the length of each narrative varies slightly in accordance with the assigned topic, the body of each report typically consists of two pages, excluding a reference page and an optional abstract not to exceed 100 words. Ancillary illustrations appear in a separate appendix that is also extraneous to the page requirement for the body of each report. Despite the fact that I ensure their privacy and anonymity, I encourage students to use appropriate discretion in their self-disclosure.

Within the course syllabus, I describe the guidelines for completing the mini-autobiographical narratives. I also take class time to review these guidelines during the initial class meeting.

Each chapter-specific assignment is due within two class periods after I have covered that respective chapter, with grade penalties attached to late submissions. The numerical average of these assignments represents 20% of the final course grade. For illustrative purposes, a narrative excerpt from a selected mini-autobiographical narrative appears in the following paragraph. The excerpt, written by a former student of mine, pertains to course content covered under learning and behavioral change. In this passage, the student presents an early life experience with stimulus associations that depicts processes involved in classical conditioning.

> Over the years, I have developed a habit of drinking two cups of coffee with breakfast. Although I know that I'm certainly not alone in my taste preference for coffee, I've often wondered about the physical and psychological mechanisms that have drawn me to this habit. Coffee contains caffeine, a stimulant that excites the central nervous system and can be mildly physically addictive when consumed in moderate doses (Fredholm, Battig, Holmen, Nehlig, & Zvartau, 1999). So, there are definitely physiological explanations for why I drink coffee every day. But research has also shown that liking the taste and aroma of coffee can be acquired through *classical conditioning.* People can learn to associate taste and smell with physiological arousal, a common side effect of caffeine consumption (Fredholm et al., 1999). On a psychological level, this explains why I often feel "alive and awake" right after drinking coffee each morning, even

though it can take caffeine up to 45 minutes to become absorbed in my body (Arnaud, 1993).

Learning goals and outcomes:

1. Knowledge base of psychology: Role of behavior in psychology
   _____ Identify antecedents and consequences of behavior stemming from personal experiences.

2. Knowledge base of psychology: Contemporary perspectives in psychology
   _____ Identify and describe contemporary psychological perspectives (e.g., behavioral, biological, cognitive, evolutionary, humanistic, psychodynamic, sociocultural) in light of personal experiences.

3. Knowledge base of psychology: Overarching themes of psychology
   _____ Identify and apply variability and continuity as it pertains to behavior originating in personal experiences.

4. Knowledge base of psychology: General content domains of psychology
   _____ Identify and apply principles in the general content domains of psychology concerning personal experiences, including learning, cognition, sociocultural framework, biological bases of behavior, and development.

5. Research methods in psychology: Database skills
   _____ Identify, locate, and appropriately cite relevant reference sources in support of the applied psychological principles.

6. Critical thinking skills in psychology: Association skills
   _____ Relate and apply diverse psychological principles to personal experiences.

7. Application of psychology: Healthy lifestyle
   _____ Analyze personal lifestyle practices by means of applicable psychological principles.

8. Application of psychology: Potential for psychology as a change agent
   _____ Describe ways in which psychological principles can promote positive personal change.

9. Application of psychology: Applied areas in psychology
   _____ Link major and/or emerging applied areas in psychology with appropriate career choices (if applicable).

10. Values in psychology: Curiosity
    _____ Apply curiosity to psychological phenomena in terms of questions surrounding personal experiences.

11. Values in psychology: Skepticism
    _____ Compare and contrast the relative worth of scientific and pseudoscientific psychological principles related to personal experiences.

Learning task and grading rubric: Using mini-autobiographical narration to describe and apply psychological principles over a broad assortment of personal experiences.

   A = Demonstrates consistent ability to accurately describe and apply psychological principles to personal experiences.
   B = Reveals minor difficulties in describing and applying psychological principles to personal experiences.

(continues)

C = Shows moderate difficulty in describing and applying psychological principles
to personal experiences.

D = Displays an incomplete range of ability to describe and apply psychological
principles to personal experiences.

F = Exhibits prominent and recurring difficulties in describing and applying
psychological principles to personal experiences.

EXHIBIT 5.4
Applying Authentic Assessment to the Observational Diary

Levels of student proficiency: Basic and developing

Course: Introductory psychology

Assignment: Observational diary

Instructional context: In matching course content to everyday experiences comprising or surrounding learners' lives, student journals have been shown to foster self-understanding and applied reasoning in numerous undergraduate psychology classes (e.g., Grasha, 1998; Hettich, 1976, 1980; Klos, 1976; McManus, 1986). In the context of teaching introductory psychology, the *observational diary* (Mayo, 2003b) is a term-length journaling assignment that combines elements of autobiographical and biographical narration. In creating an observational diary, students keep a running record of situations in which they observe psychological principles at work in their own and others' lives. Drawing from these personal observations, students discuss practical uses of basic psychology over diverse contexts.

Purpose of the assignment: It is important for psychology educators to stress pragmatic applications of psychological principles in consideration of psychology's vanguard position as an applied behavioral science (Grasha, 1998). Connecting the classroom environment to the real world is particularly important to students who are just beginning their studies in psychology. As a pedagogical tool, the observational diary links theory to practice in teaching introductory psychology.

Instructional methodology: The observational diary, due during the final week of the term, counts as 20% of the final course grade. Each observational diary consists of 40 to 50 entries across various topics covered in the course. In recording each diary entry, students include a date, source, description of event (five sentences or fewer), and psychological application (five sentences or fewer). In a minimum of 15 entries, students cite a different reference (appearing in current APA Style within the body of the diary) in support of each corresponding psychological application. During the first class meeting, I review the guidelines for assignment completion appearing in the course syllabus. At that same time, I also distribute and examine several instructor-generated fictitious diary entries, such as this sample entry:

EXHIBIT 5.4
Applying Authentic Assessment to the Observational Diary   *(Continued)*

Date	Source	Description of event	Psychological application
04-20-09	College classroom	During a meeting of my Physical Fitness for Life class, a female class-mate indicated how frustrated she was with unsuccessful dieting. When our professor asked her if she snacked regularly, she said, "Yes, but only on health food that I buy at the local nutrition center." As the professor probed deeper, the student revealed that this included whole-milk yogurt. The professor explained that whole-milk yogurt contained much saturated fat. Regard-less, the student argued that since she bought the yogurt at a nutrition center, it was somehow healthier for her to eat than the exact same product available at a supermarket.	The student's reaction to the professor's com-ments demonstrates the powerful impact that *framing* (Tversky & Kahneman, 1981) can have on thinking and decision making. With framing, a person is influenced by the way that something is pre-sented. In this case, the student believed that she was eating "health food" simply because she bought it at a nutri-tion center. I doubt that she would have felt exactly this way if she'd bought the same item at a supermarket and carefully read the ingre-dient label.

Learning goals and outcomes:

1. Knowledge base of psychology: Nature of psychology
   _____ Define psychology as the applied science that investigates behavior and mental processes.

2. Knowledge base of psychology: Relationship of psychology to science
   _____ Illustrate how psychology satisfies the criteria of science.

3. Knowledge base of psychology: Relationship of psychology to other disciplines
   _____ Identify connections between psychology and other disciplines.

4. Knowledge base of psychology: Contemporary perspectives in psychology
   _____ Identify and describe contemporary perspectives for understanding behavior.

5. Knowledge base of psychology: Overarching themes of psychology
   _____ Identify overarching themes of psychology, including free will versus determinism, subjectivism versus objectivism, applicability of psychologi-cal principles across societal and cultural groups, and interaction of heredity and environment and of mind and body.

(continues)

6. Knowledge base of psychology: General content domains of psychology
   _____ Identify and explain basic psychological principles from among the following general content domains: learning and cognition, individual and sociocultural differences, biological foundations of behavior and mental processes, and development.

7. Research methods in psychology: Scientific method
   _____ Describe basic features of scientific methodology in psychology.

8. Research methods in psychology: Correlation versus causation
   _____ Explain the difference between correlation and causation (where applicable).

9. Research methods in psychology: Sociocultural context
   _____ Identify variations in behavior that may be due to sociocultural differences.

10. Research methods in psychology: Database skills
    _____ Identify, locate, and appropriately cite relevant reference sources in support of psychological applications discussed.

11. Critical thinking skills in psychology: Use of evidence in psychology
    _____ Distinguish between personal views and scientific evidence in understanding behavior.

12. Critical thinking skills in psychology: Association skills
    _____ Apply diverse psychological theories over a broad range of contexts.

13. Critical thinking skills in psychology: Argumentation skills
    _____ Identify arguments based on anecdotal evidence and personal experience.

14. Critical thinking skills in psychology: Detection of errors in psychological reasoning
    _____ Identify myths, stereotypes, common fallacies, and poorly supported assertions in psychological reasoning.

15. Application of psychology: Healthy lifestyle and abnormal behavior
    _____ Identify appropriate applications of psychology in solving problems that may include the pursuit and effect of healthy lifestyle and/or origin and treatment of abnormal behavior.

16. Application of psychology: Potential for psychology as a change agent
    _____ Describe how psychological principles can be used to facilitate personal, social, and/or organizational change.

17. Application of psychology: Applied areas in psychology
    _____ Identify and illustrate major and/or emerging applied specialty areas in psychology.

18. Values in psychology: Curiosity
    _____ Apply curiosity to examining psychological phenomena.

19. Values in psychology: Skepticism
    _____ Differentiate between scientific and pseudoscientific explanations of human behavior.

20. Values in psychology: Ethical orientation
    _____ Identify relevant ethical principles applied in psychological contexts (where applicable).

21. Values in psychology: Human diversity
    _____ Recognize that psychological explanations may vary across populations and contexts.

22. Values in psychology: Personal responsibility/service learning
    _____ Describe how psychology can promote positive civic, social, and/or global awareness and outcomes.

Evaluative criteria and grading rubric: Three equally weighted variables constitute the evaluative criteria for this assignment: (a) completeness in adhering to the guidelines for finishing the assignment, (b) accuracy between descriptions of events and their respective psychological applications, and (c) variety across psychological applications.

A = Demonstrates superior performance in completing all evaluative criteria.
B = Displays minor problems with completeness, accuracy, and/or variety.
C = Exhibits modest success in satisfying the parameters of completeness, accuracy, and/or variety.
D = Shows missing entries, inaccurate psychological applications, and a general lack of variety across applications.
F = Fails to satisfy evaluative criteria in most or all entries.

Note. Adapted from *Teaching, Learning, and Assessing in a Developmentally Coherent Curriculum* (pp. 24–26), by the American Psychological Association, 2008b, Washington, DC: Author. Copyright 2008 by the American Psychological Association.

6

GRAPHIC ORGANIZERS AS LEARNING AND ASSESSMENT TOOLS

Graphic organization strategies, such as *concept mapping* and the *repertory grid technique* (RGT), can be used not only to introduce new material to students but also to provide learners with a visually elucidating conceptual framework from which to link new knowledge with preexisting knowledge (Mayo, 2009). A primary instructional benefit of using graphic organizers for optimal comprehension is that they encourage holistic understanding not always communicated as effectively by words alone (Plotnick, 1997). As a necessary condition for learning, students usually engage in their best thinking when they represent concepts graphically (Jonassen, 1996)—which they do, for example, in working with concept-mapping computer tools (Anderson-Inman & Zeitz, 1993). Similarly, the RGT encourages students to engage in reflective analysis and metacognition (Liu & Lee, 2005).

Graphic organizers can also prove useful in assessing conceptual learning. Accurately evaluating students' conceptual systems can be tenuous, labor intensive, and restricted in scope (Fetherstonhaugh & Treagust, 1992). Student drawings (Quiggin, 1977), sorting tasks (Gobbo & Chi, 1986), interviews (Pines, Novak, Posner, & Vankirk, 1978), open-ended and multiple-choice test questions (Bloom, Hastings, & Madaus, 1971), and other quantitative and qualitative assessment instruments have all been used with mixed success. As an alternative means to more effectively assess students' conceptual structures, graphic organizers can be used to detect incomplete and deficient conceptions that may impair learning. Classroom research and practice have shown that concept mapping (Jacobs-Lawson & Hershey, 2002; Liu, Don, & Tsai, 2005) and the RGT (Liu & Tsai, 2005) are useful instruments for monitoring students' conceptual systems and improving their conceptual awareness. As educational diagnostic tools with inherent versatility, concept mapping (Anderson-Inman & Ditson, 1999) and the RGT (Mayo, 2008; Winer & Vazquez-Abad, 1997) can be used to assess construct systems at a given moment in time or to evaluate dynamically evolving concept formations across time. In the latter instance of *concept-formation tracking* (Anderson-Inman & Ditson, 1999; Ditson, Kessler, Anderson-Inman, & Mafit, 2001), students may be asked to generate concept maps or repertory grids at various stages throughout the learning process—pretesting before instruction and posttesting after designated instructional activities.

CONCEPT MAPPING: BACKGROUND, EXEMPLAR, AND STUDENT TRAINING MODULE

In the early 1970s at Cornell University, Joseph D. Novak and his research team (see Novak, 1977; Novak & Musonda, 1991) developed concept mapping by borrowing from Ausubel's (1960, 1963, 1968) seminal work with advance organizers. As discussed in chapter 3 of this volume, Ausubel's cognitive theory of learning relies on the underlying belief that meaningful learning occurs through assimilation of new concepts into existing conceptual structures. From this perspective, concept mapping helps learners "organize their cognitive frameworks into more powerful integrated patterns . . . [while serving] as a metaknowledge and metalearning tool" (Jegede, Alaiyemola, & Okebukola, 1990, p. 952).

With concept mapping, the learner organizes networks of concepts in a diagram resembling a hierarchical flow chart that proceeds from the most inclusive general concept to more specific subordinate ones (Wandersee, 1990). In these visual depictions of conceptual differentiation and integration that facilitate a learner's hierarchical cognitive organization (Novak & Gowin, 1984), *nodes* are points or vertices representing concepts with keywords or short phrases; *links* are connecting lines indicating temporal or causal relationships between concepts; *propositions* are two or more concepts joined together with descriptive words to form meaningful statements; *hierarchies* are concepts appropriately situated in the top, middle, or bottom segments of the map; and *cross-links* are connections between initially discrete concepts in relatively distant parts of the map that illustrate recognition of broad associations within a domain of knowledge (Novak & Canas, 2006; Plotnick, 1997). A one- or two-way directional link between subordinate concepts, combined with descriptive connecting words, portrays comprehension of a semantic or ideational relationship between concepts in a learner's knowledge set (Novak, 1998).

Figure 6.1 shows a student-generated concept map of the human nervous system. This map was originally hand drawn in class by a student participant in a collaborative pilot investigation—examining concept mapping in both introductory psychology and biology classes—in which I had taken part (Mayo & Salata, 2002). For illustrative purposes, I have reconstructed the map through CmapTools (Institute for Human and Machine Cognition, 2009), a free, downloadable, user-friendly software toolkit that allows users to construct, share, and critique concept maps.

The instructional efficacy of concept mapping has been well documented in natural science courses (e.g., C. V. Lloyd, 1990; Wallace & Mintzes, 1990). However, far less documentation exists in courses within the behavioral and social sciences. Of special relevance to psychology education from a constructivist vantage point, though, two relatively recent empirical investigations have explored the use of concept mapping in undergraduate psychology classes. Jacobs-Lawson and Hershey (2002) reported the results of a study of concept mapping as an assessment instrument in the introductory psychology course. Their findings showed that students who have never constructed a concept map are best served by initially viewing a sample map before creating a map on their own. In another experiment, Anthis (2005) examined concept mapping within a personality theories course. Central to the purpose of this study, the researcher found that student-produced concept maps are influenced by the type of instructions that students receive prior to concept-map construction. Consistent with the related findings of these two studies, classroom success with concept mapping demands that students receive appropriate advance training on how to construct a good concept map.

Data gathered in the aforementioned interdisciplinary study of concept mapping point to a direct relationship between student training and the quality of concepts maps that students produce (Mayo & Salata, 2002). Since my involvement in this pilot investigation, I have used concept mapping more extensively throughout introductory psychology and other undergraduate psychology classes that I teach. Overall, my classroom observations indicate that learners require well-defined preliminary training as an essential ingredient in constructing accurate concept maps. As a result, I have codesigned (Mayo

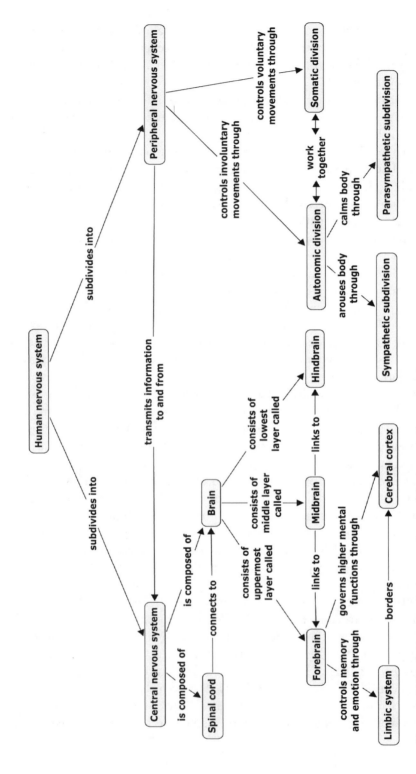

Figure 6.1. Student-generated concept map of the human nervous system.

& Salata, 2002) and subsequently refined (Mayo, 2005b) an in-class training module for concept mapping that takes approximately 30 minutes for students to complete on their own. I normally follow this module with a 15- to 20-minute period during which students ask questions and share and critique responses among the entire class. Refer to Exhibit 6.1 for this concept-mapping student training module.

EXHIBIT 6.1
Concept-Mapping Student Training Module

When learning, we often align new material with prior knowledge that is either directly or indirectly related. This activity involves processes that lead to new understandings and, perhaps, a cognitive transformation from old to new conceptual realities. With new learning experiences, we are frequently confronted with new terminology and concepts. As students, the task is to cognitively wrestle with these ideas and display an understanding of them. Concept mapping, pioneered by influential psychologist Joseph D. Novak, has been used across a wide variety of educational environments as a way for students to better organize their thoughts, retain information for longer time periods, and experience fewer misconceptions during the learning process.

Today's classroom exercise focuses on comparing and contrasting some diagrams and then formulating a proper concept map according to a series of basic steps. The first task is to examine a good and bad example of a concept map (see Figure 6.2) before answering these two questions: What is common between the two examples? and What is different between the two examples?

A concept map is a hierarchically arranged diagram that displays relationships between and among concepts under a category of knowledge. The key steps for creating a concept map are as follows.

1. Create or find a list of terms from a knowledge category.
2. Rank those terms on a continuum from abstract to specific. In doing so, assign numbers to the concepts (1 = most abstract and 2, 3, 4, etc. = increasingly specific).
3. Group the concepts into levels of abstraction.
4. Decide whether all concepts can be categorized under the most abstract item. If not, add a concept to the list under which all other concepts will fit.
5. Place the most abstract concept in a central location at the top of the paper.
6. Choose the next level of abstraction and place the corresponding concept(s) underneath the main one in a horizontal row, leaving sufficient space between them. Continue this step until the diagram is complete.
7. Draw lines to connect concepts on the basis of their relationships, writing connecting words to describe each relationship. Connecting lines with one- and two-way arrows should proceed from top to bottom.
8. Similarly, place special cross-connections between concepts in distant locations on the map. Again, include descriptive connecting words.

During the second task, use these terms in following the previously listed steps for concept-map construction: *written, computer, keyboard, paper, typewriter, pencil, eraser, mouse, word processor, notepad, "Post-It" note, essay, printout, communication, electronic,* and *media.* Brainstorm (e.g., define terms and write down possible relationships) and generate a first-draft concept map. Then use a separate page for a revised concept map. Last, write a final revision on yet another page. Be sure to label each concept map as "First Draft Map," "Revised Map," and "Final Revision," accordingly.

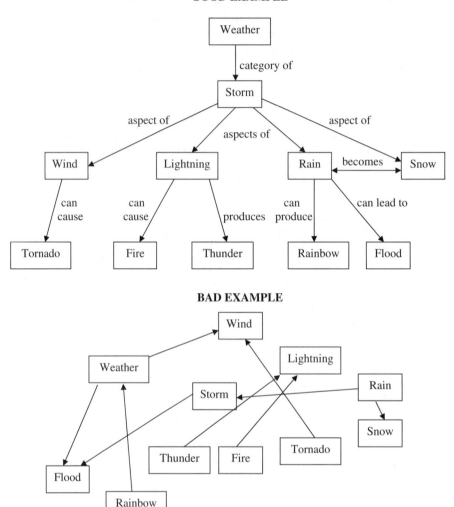

GOOD EXAMPLE

BAD EXAMPLE

Figure 6.2. Good and bad examples of a concept map for the following terms: *fire, thunder, storm, rainbow, rain, tornado, lightning, snow, weather, flood,* and *wind.*

APPLYING AUTHENTIC ASSESSMENT TO CONCEPT MAPPING

Exhibit 6.2 presents a term-long series of learning assignments in which introductory psychology students work alone in completing concept maps. The content of the maps, combined with the metacognitive processes involved in completing them, addresses outcomes from all five learning goals for the

EXHIBIT 6.2
Applying Authentic Assessment to Concept Mapping

Levels of student proficiency: Basic and developing

Course: Introductory psychology

Assignment: Concept mapping

Instructional context: In teaching introductory psychology, it is important to provide students with "a broad and deep knowledge base" (C. L. Brewer et al., 1993, p. 170). However, it is precisely for this reason that introductory psychology can be a challenging class for instructors to teach and students to complete. Because of the potentially voluminous information to be covered in as little time as a single term, the issue of balancing depth and breadth of coverage has been explored in both the psychological and teaching literature (e.g., C. L. Brewer et al., 1993). Although opinions vary from teachers feeling obligated to cover as much material as possible to the view that teaching less is teaching more (Wade, 1998), a reasonable compromise is available through the use of concept mapping as a heuristic tool. *Concept maps* are concise, two-dimensional, graphic representations of learners' conceptual knowledge sets (Passmore, 1995) that permit students to organize multiple conceptions (e.g., summarizing readings and lectures, reviewing for exams, brainstorming in the early stages of essay writing) and teachers to assess the gamut of students' conceptual knowledge bases (University of Victoria Counselling Services, 2003; Plotnick, 1997).

Purpose of the assignment: Enduring learning requires that students not only tie new information to what they already know but also connect new pieces of knowledge with one another (Ausubel, 1963; Fisher et al., 1990). Academic success relates to students' abilities to rise above rote memorization in conducting metacognitive activities that afford acquisition of knowledge links (Wandersee, Mintzes, & Novak, 1994). Unlike conventional tables, graphs, and other such abbreviated visual representational systems of knowledge, concept maps allow students to schematically represent a collection of concepts and their linking relationships (Fisher, 1990; Wallace, Mintzes, & Markham, 1992). Therefore, constructing concept maps—as required in the present assignment—enables students to seek and develop parsimonious and meaningful conceptual relationships (Novak, 1990).

Instructional methodology: After preliminary training at the beginning of the term on how to properly construct a concept map (Mayo, 2005b; see Exhibit 6.1), I ask students to generate maps that depict their comprehension of various concepts covered throughout an introductory psychology course. As part of this training, I introduce students to operational definitions of terms applied to concept maps (nodes, links, hierarchies, propositions, and cross-links) and to grading criteria as illustrated in preselected examples of scored maps.

In all cases, concept-mapping assignments take place after classroom instruction on respective concepts, considering the relatively basic entry level of student proficiency expected in a general psychology course prior to educational intervention. Although the number and conceptual focus of concept-mapping assignments are contingent on an instructor's preferences, available class time, and the types of other required assignments, I usually concentrate on the following 10 topics:

- contemporary psychological perspectives,
- research methods in psychology,
- biological bases of behavior and mental processes,
- learning,

(continues)

EXHIBIT 6.2
Applying Authentic Assessment to Concept Mapping   *(Continued)*

- memory,
- problem solving,
- personality theory and assessment,
- life-span development,
- psychological disorders, and
- psychological and biomedical therapies.

Each assignment, worth 2% of the final course grade, is completed in class and due at the conclusion of that given class period.

For each assignment, I give students an instructor-generated "Key Concepts Sheet" that contains terms associated with the topic. The number of terms ranges from 12 to 14, dependent on the level of conceptual depth and complexity inherent in the assigned topic. The procedure for concept-map construction mimics the steps invoked within the preliminary training module shown earlier in Exhibit 6.1. Using as many of the terms as possible, students create a first draft map by brainstorming about the definition and relationships between terms. This initial step is followed, in turn, by constructing a revised map and then a final revision. Students design their concept maps so as to demonstrate to an uninformed audience the mechanisms underlying the topic. Students label and write all of their work in bound blue books before submitting their materials to me for grading. This affords me an orderly opportunity to gauge changes in conceptual understandings from the brainstorming–draft stage through the construction of the final concept map.

In the present assignment, students work alone in completing their concept maps. However, it is also possible to assign concept mapping as a cooperative learning task (e.g., Novak & Canas, 2006; Okebukola, 1992). In the case of cooperative learning, students work collaboratively in small groups (e.g., 3–5) and select one student to record the name of each group participant and all work completed, including a summary of salient group discussion that may occur during this exercise.

In addition to scoring the concept-mapping assignments and factoring them into each student's course grade, educators may use these graded assignments as structural platforms for class discussion and review in preparation for unit tests and/or a comprehensive final examination.

Learning goals and outcomes:

1. Knowledge base of psychology: Contemporary perspectives in psychology
   _____ Describe, compare and contrast contemporary perspectives in psychology: behavioral, biological, cognitive, evolutionary, humanistic, psychodynamic, and sociocultural.
2. Knowledge base of psychology: General content domains of psychology
   _____ Explain and interrelate concepts in the general content domains of psychology, including learning and cognition, individual and sociocultural differences, biological bases of behavior and mental processes, and life-span development.
3. Research methods in psychology: General research methods
   _____ Describe and interrelate research methods in psychology, including descriptive, correlational, and experimental methods.
   _____ Distinguish the nature of research methods in psychology that permit causal inferences from those methods that do not.

EXHIBIT 6.2
Applying Authentic Assessment to Concept Mapping   *(Continued)*

4. Critical thinking skills in psychology: Association skills
    _____ State and relate connections between diverse facts and theoretical concepts in psychology.
5. Critical thinking skills in psychology: Problem solving
    _____ Define and interconnect the stages of problem solving.
    _____ Define and interrelate cognitive roadblocks to effective problem solving.
6. Application of psychology: Abnormal behavior
    _____ Summarize and interconnect general criteria of abnormality within and between given sets of symptoms or characteristics for various psychological disorders.
    _____ Summarize and interrelate the component elements of different types of psychological and biomedical therapies for treating abnormal behavior.
7. Values in psychology: Skepticism
    _____ Distinguish between scientific and pseudoscientific explanations of human behavior and compare and contrast their relative value.

Evaluative criteria and grading scheme: The evaluative criteria used in assessing the concept-mapping assignments represent a synthesized and adapted amalgam of available scoring systems (see McClure, Sonak, & Suen, 1999; Wallace & Mintzes, 1990; West, Park, Pomeroy, & Sandoval, 2002). Although the final revision of each concept map is the primary scoring focus, I also devote attention to conceptual refinement displayed from the first draft map through the revised map and, ultimately, the final revision.

- Nodes: 1/2 point for each concept (from the "Key Concepts Sheet") included as a node.
- Links: 1 point for each appropriate choice of connecting lines.
- Propositions: 2 points for each meaningful relationship between a pair of concepts.
- Hierarchies: 3 points for each appropriate level of hierarchy.
- Cross-links: 4 points for each valid cross-link.
- Conceptual change: up to 10 points for evidence of conceptual growth from first draft map to revised map to final revision.

Within stated parameters for calculating letter grades (A = 90–100%, B = 80–89%, C = 70–79%, D = 60–69%, and F = below 60%), I convert total points earned on each assignment into numerical grades by using the following scheme:

75+ points = 100%	48–50 points = 64%	21–23 points = 28%
72–74 points = 96%	45–47 points = 60%	18–20 points = 24%
69–71 points = 92%	42–44 points = 56%	15–17 points = 20%
66–68 points = 88%	39–41 points = 52%	12–14 points = 16%
63–65 points = 84%	36–38 points = 48%	9–11 points = 12%
60–62 points = 80%	33–35 points = 44%	6–8 points = 8%
57–59 points = 76%	30–32 points = 40%	3–5 points = 4%
54–56 points = 72%	27–29 points = 36%	1–2 points = 2%
51–53 points = 68%	24–26 points = 32%	0 points = 0%

undergraduate psychology major: (a) knowledge base of psychology, (b) research methods in psychology, (c) critical thinking skills in psychology, (d) application of psychology, and (e) values in psychology.

THE REPERTORY GRID TECHNIQUE: BACKGROUND AND EXEMPLARS

The RGT derives from the work of clinical psychologist and personality theorist George Kelly (1955), who designed this approach (originally known as the *role construct repertory test*) as a psychotherapeutic interview strategy to subtly guide a patient in exploring his or her own thoughts. For instance, using the RGT to tap into a patient's self-image, Kelly might have introduced school, work, and leisurely contexts as *elements* (i.e., persons, objects, events, or problems of personal interest or concern). In prompting the patient to pair two of these elements in contrast with the third (e.g., "I am self-confident at work and with my friends, but I struggle with self-doubts in my college classes"), Kelly would have then permitted the patient to elicit a *personal construct,* or bipolar meaning dimension (i.e., self-confidence/self-doubt), with minimal therapist intervention or bias.

Along with continued clinical use of the RGT, modified applications of this technique have also been observed in diverse educational environments (Bezzi, 1996; Olsson, 1997; Winer & Vazquez-Abad, 1997). For instance, in the instructor-provided construct form of the RGT (Tobacyk, 1987), the instructor furnishes students with elements (e.g., names of influential persons throughout psychology's history) that comprise the columns of the grid and bipolar constructs (e.g., reductionistic–nonreductionistic) that compose its rows (see Tobacyk, 1987). By placing an X in the applicable location on the grid, students evaluate each construct against each element in working, row by row, through the grid. In completing this task, students often use numerical ratings on a Likert-type scale (Likert, 1932), with anchors at 1 and 5, 7, 9, or 11. Refer to Figure 6.3 for an example of a repertory grid on the writings of 17th-century British empiricist John Locke, who helped to engender the eventual rise of scientific thinking in psychology. A former student of mine completed this grid as a required assignment in a history and systems of psychology class as part of evaluating the contributions of key figures throughout psychology's historical evolution. In this grid, the student rates Locke's intellectual position on a series of 1 to 11 scales relative to each of six bipolar constructs: mind–body, nature–nurture, subjectivism–objectivism, holism–elementalism, free will–determinism, and utility–purity.

Consistent with Kelly's (1955) definition of bipolar constructs as meaning dimensions that allow each person to organize and interpret information, such constructs have served as vital components of undergraduate psychology texts

	Construct ratings											
	1	2	3	4	5	6	7	8	9	10	11	
1. Mind	—	X	—	—	—	—	—	—	—	—	—	Body
2. Nature	—	—	—	—	—	—	—	—	—	—	X	Nurture
3. Subjectivism	—	—	—	—	—	—	—	X	—	—	—	Objectivism
4. Holism	—	—	—	—	—	X	—	—	—	—	—	Elementalism
5. Free will	—	—	—	—	—	—	—	—	—	—	X	Determinism
6. Utility	—	X	—	—	—	—	—	—	—	—	—	Purity

Figure 6.3. Student-generated repertory grid on John Locke's writings.

in personality theories (e.g., Hjelle & Ziegler, 1992), developmental psychology (e.g., Santrock, 2004), and history and systems of psychology (e.g., Lundin, 1996). Moreover, bipolar constructs are pedagogical tools that instructors can readily create for use in teaching abnormal psychology (e.g., functionality–dysfunctionality), social psychology (e.g., conformity–nonconformity), and other undergraduate classes. Therefore, drawing from thematically based textbook-provided and/or self-generated meaning dimensions, educators can use the RGT as a versatile instrument to facilitate student learning and explore personal constructs across a wide range of instructional contexts.

In the illustrative case of teaching life-span developmental psychology (Mayo, 2004c, 2008), I begin by selecting elements in the form of principal proponents of major developmental theories. Afterward, I match proponents to respective theoretical perspectives, such as ethological (John Bowlby), contextual (Urie Bronfenbrenner), psychodynamic (Sigmund Freud and Erik Erikson), learning (B. F. Skinner and Albert Bandura), humanistic (Abraham Maslow), cognitive (Jean Piaget and Lawrence Kohlberg), and sociocultural (Lev Vygotsky). Relying on both textbook- and self-derived sources of inspiration, I then formulate a list of bipolar constructs pertaining to salient developmental issues (e.g., nature–nurture). To sensitize students to the factors underlying these issues, I lecture succinctly on these constructs at the beginning of the term.

Applying the RGT, students evaluate the intellectual positions of each developmental proponent on the basis of each construct. Using a series of Likert-type rating scales, students print an X on the appropriate line within each bipolar continuum that typifies the corresponding person's stance. To exemplify this process, Figure 6.4 contains a student-completed repertory grid on the seminal cognitive developmental theory of Jean Piaget. A former student of mine created this grid in partial fulfillment of grading requirements in a life-

	Construct ratings							
	1	2	3	4	5	6	7	
1. Heredity	—	—	—	—	X	—	—	Environment
2. Continuity	—	—	—	—	—	—	X	Discontinuity
3. Stability	—	—	—	—	—	X	—	Change
4. Internality	—	—	X	—	—	—	—	Externality
5. Unidimensionality	—	—	—	X	—	—	—	Multidimensionality
6. Testability	—	—	—	X	—	—	—	Lack of testability

Figure 6.4. Student-completed repertory grid on Jean Piaget's theoretical work.

span developmental psychology class. In this example, the student uses 7-point rating scales to critique Piaget's work across six bipolar constructs: heredity–environment, continuity–discontinuity, stability–change, internality–external-ity, unidimensionality–multidimensionality, and testability–lack of testability.

Once students complete a repertory grid for each developmental propo-nent, they compile a comprehensive repertory grid matrix that properly cat-egorizes all perspectives. In this way, students tabulate the aggregate results of their repertory grid assignments throughout the term. Refer to Figure 6.5 for a comprehensive repertory grid matrix completed by the same student who composed the grid shown in Figure 6.4. In this matrix, the student rates the following 10 theorists on 7-point continua for the same six bipolar constructs appearing in Figure 6.4: Albert Bandura, John Bowlby, Urie Bronfenbrenner, Erik Erikson, Sigmund Freud, Lawrence Kohlberg, Abraham Maslow, Jean Piaget, B. F. Skinner, and Lev Vygotsky.

I assign students both the ratings of individual developmental propo-nents and the comprehensive repertory grid matrix as take-home paper-and-pencil projects to be completed independently and then submitted to me for grading immediately upon completion.[1] Because of their concise organiza-

---

[1] If class time permits (or as extra-credit assignments), I also train students to use WebGrid (Gaines & Shaw, 2009), which is a Web-based implementation of the RGT that allows for computer-generated grid elicitation and interpretation. See chapter 9 for further discussion of this topic.

	Construct ratings							
	1	2	3	4	5	6	7	
1. Heredity	Bo	F	M		K, P	E	Ba, Br, S, V	Environment
2. Continuity	Ba, S, V	Bo		Br, M			E, F, K, P	Discontinuity
3. Stability	F	Bo		M		K, P	Ba, Br, E, S, V	Change
4. Internality	Bo	F	K, P	Ba, M		E	Br, S, V	Externality
5. Unidimensionality	Bo, F, S	Br, E		K, P	M, V	Ba		Multidimensionality
6. Testability	Ba, S	Br, V	Bo	K, P	E		F, M	Lack of testability

Figure 6.5. Student-completed, repertory grid matrix based on the work of leading developmental proponents. Bo = Bowlby; F = Freud; M = Maslow; K = Kohlberg; P = Piaget; E = Erikson; Ba = Bandura; Br = Bronfenbrenner; S = Skinner; V = Vygotsky. From "Repertory Grid as a Means to Compare and Contrast Developmental Theories," by J. A. Mayo, 2004c, *Teaching of Psychology, 31,* p. 179. Copyright 2004 by Taylor & Francis. Adapted with permission.

tional structure, the instructor-scored comprehensive matrices serve as objects of whole-class discussion at the end of the term. The primary purpose of this discussion is to prepare students for a comprehensive final examination that accentuates important similarities and differences among developmental proponents' views. The individual-proponent rating assignments and the comprehensive matrix combine to determine 10% of each student's final course grade.

APPLYING AUTHENTIC ASSESSMENT TO THE REPERTORY GRID TECHNIQUE

The RGT is the hallmark of assessment in Kelly's (1955) *personal construct theory.* To Kelly, human beings continually push to explore their personal knowledge constructions and test their conceptual systems. Exhibit 6.3 discusses a classroom application of the RGT within history and systems of psychology (Mayo, 2004a). This application samples all five learning goals for the undergraduate psychology major, with selected outcomes covered under each goal: (a) knowledge base of psychology, (b) research methods in psychology, (c) critical thinking skills in psychology, (d) application of psychology, and (e) values in psychology.

EXHIBIT 6.3
Applying Authentic Assessment to the Repertory Grid Technique (RGT)

Levels of student proficiency: Developing and advanced

Course: History and systems of psychology

Assignment: The RGT

Instructional context: Although targeted originally for clinical use (Kelly, 1955), successful adaptations and applications of the RGT have also found their way into higher education settings (Davis, 1985; Mayo, 2004c; Thomas & Harri-Augstein, 1985). Tobacyk (1987) outlined the process by which learners may use the instructor-provided construct form of the RGT in the framework of a history and systems of psychology class. After exposure to the names of significant contributors to psychology's intellectual history (elements) and a teacher-generated list of dichotomous constructs similar to Robert Watson's (1967) contrasting prescriptions of psychology (e.g., conscious vs. unconscious, functionalism vs. structuralism), students rate each element based on each bipolar construct. Drawing from Tobacyk's prior instructional application of the RGT, I also applied and extended this technique in the context of teaching history and systems of psychology (Mayo, 2004a).

Purpose of the assignment: Teaching history and systems of psychology offers an exceptional medium for synthesizing the diverse content of other undergraduate psychology courses (Tobacyk, 1987) while at the same time affording a solid platform for teaching and practicing critical thinking (Keniston, 2005). Owing to these instructional opportunities and their accompanying classroom challenges, instructors often search for pedagogical strategies to enhance student comprehension and active involvement. As a teaching and learning instrument in history and systems of psychology, the RGT can be used to organize course content and bolster student understanding and enthusiasm for the subject matter (Mayo, 2004a; Tobacyk, 1987). In the present term-long series of assignments, I ask students to evaluate the positions of key contributors to philosophical/prescientific, early scientific, and contemporary psychology.

Instructional methodology: The course traces the intellectual history of psychology from antiquity through the present. I divide course content into three units (see Hunt, 1993, 2007): (a) the evolution of philosophical/prescientific psychology, (b) competing psychological systems during the infancy of scientific psychology, and (c) the chronological development of contemporary psychology's principal subfields.

    To begin, I present students with an instructor-generated list of bipolar constructs linked to 11-point rating scales (see Figure 6.6) on which they rate 24 preselected contributors (8 per unit) to psychology's historical development (see Table 6.1). The first six bipolar constructs (mind–body, nature–nurture, subjectivism–objectivism, holism–elementalism, free will–determinism, and utility–purity) represent ongoing debates throughout psychology's intellectual history. By means of preliminary lecture at the beginning of the term, I introduce students to factors underlying the two construct poles for each of these six meaning dimensions. On the final two constructs (verity–falsity and major contribution–minor contribution), which assess students' views on strictly subjective grounds, students' ratings are predicated on sociohistorical overtones relative to both contemporary times and the milieu in which each contributor lived.

    Working independently, students complete each of three take-home repertory grid assignments (one per unit) as a paper-and-pencil task. For each repertory grid assignment, students work through the construct scales, one contributor at a time, by printing an *X* on the appropriate line within the 1-to-11 rating continuum that best fits each contributor's perspective. Although not included in a more traditional administration of the RGT, students offer written justification for each of their construct ratings. Exhibit 6.4 shows an exceptionally well-articulated example of a student-completed repertory grid with both Likert-type numerical ratings and accompanying justifying rationales. Composed by a former student of mine, the grid represents a critique of Aristotle's writings.

Comprehensively, the repertory grid assignments count as 30% of the final course grade (10% per unit). The assignments permit enhanced depth and clarity in examining each student's work because they include numerical ratings in tandem with written justifications. Accordingly, I advise students that their ratings are unsubstantiated judgments unless supported by evidence-based, logical arguments.

Students submit their completed unit assignments to me at designated due dates in advance of respective unit exams. Once I return each graded assignment to students, I devote 30 to 45 minutes of class time to whole-class discussions centered on the scored grids. These teacher-facilitated discussions are intended to assist in preparing students for corresponding unit exams. Throughout these deliberations, I encourage students to actively share and debate their analyses and conclusions.

Learning goals and outcomes:

1. Knowledge base of psychology: Nature of psychology
   _____ Evaluate the impact of contextual variables in psychology's evolving definitions.
2. Knowledge base of psychology: Relationship of psychology to science
   _____ Evaluate competing perspectives of psychological science as a means of understanding behavior and mental processes.
3. Knowledge base of psychology: Structure of psychology
   _____ Speculate about psychology's continuing evolution and refinement of subfields.
4. Knowledge base of psychology: Relationship of psychology to other disciplines
   _____ Compare and contrast the assumptions, methods, and choices of problems in psychology with those of other disciplines that have served as predecessors to the development of psychological science, including philosophy and the natural and physical sciences.
5. Knowledge base of psychology: Objectives of psychology
   _____ Compare, contrast, and evaluate the descriptive, explanatory, and predictive value of different intellectual, philosophical, and theoretical perspectives throughout the history of psychology.
6. Knowledge base of psychology: Historical perspectives in psychology
   _____ Compare and contrast intellectual perspectives throughout psychology's history.
   _____ Assess the relative importance of intellectual perspectives over psychology's historical evolution.
   _____ Defend historical perspectives in psychology.
7. Knowledge base of psychology: Contemporary perspectives in psychology
   _____ Compare and contrast the assumptions, methods, and other features of contemporary psychological perspectives.
   _____ Evaluate the relative utility and efficacy of contemporary perspectives in psychology.

(continues)

8. Knowledge base of psychology: Overarching themes of psychology
_____ Debate the relative merits of each side of the following overarching themes throughout psychology's history: nature versus nurture, mind versus body, free will versus determinism, subjectivism versus objectivism, holism versus elementalism, and utility versus purity.
_____ Evaluate the appropriateness of competing intellectual, philosophical, and theoretical perspectives over the history of psychology using ongoing debates related to psychology's overarching themes.

9. Knowledge base of psychology: General content domains of psychology
_____ Analyze, evaluate, and synthesize the work of important contributors in the general content domains of psychology: learning and cognition, individual and sociocultural differences, biological bases of behavior and mental processes, and development.

10. Research methods in psychology: Sociocultural context
_____ Apply historical and sociocultural framework to prominent research discoveries across the historical evolution of psychology.

11. Research methods in psychology: Limits of scientific reasoning and evidence
_____ Discuss reasons why empirical findings and conclusions are subject to modification over the course of psychology's history.
_____ Justify the evolving nature of scientific findings throughout psychology's historical development.

12. Critical thinking skills in psychology: Use of evidence in psychology
_____ Analyze and evaluate the quality, objectivity, and credibility of evidence in diverse contexts as it relates to the formation of influential intellectual, philosophical, and theoretical perspectives across the historical development of psychology.

13. Critical thinking skills in psychology: Association skills
_____ Relate and assess the quality of connections between diverse facts and theories espoused during the course of psychology's historical development.

14. Critical thinking skills in psychology: Argumentation skills
_____ Develop sound, integrated supporting arguments that tie to diverse intellectual contributions throughout psychology's history.

15. Critical thinking skills in psychology: Detection of errors in psychological reasoning
_____ Detect, reject, and evaluate errors involved in poorly supported assertions by contributors to psychology's intellectual history, with an eye toward sociohistorical context as a basis of judgment.

16. Critical thinking skills in psychology: Problem solving
_____ Appraise the quality of solutions to problems offered by key contributors to the intellectual history of psychology.

17. Application of psychology: Psychological tests
_____ Distinguish between effective and less effective methods of testing throughout psychology's history, including absence-of-bias parameters that show respect for alternative cultures and gender.

18. Application of psychology: Potential for psychology as a change agent
_____ Evaluate intellectual, sociocultural, and other changes stemming from the work of important contributors to the historical development of psychology.
_____ Evaluate (within the context of both contemporary times and the times in which each contributor lived) contributions to societal change resulting from the work of important intellectuals, philosophers, theorists, and researchers throughout psychology's historical evolution.

19. Application of psychology: Applied areas in psychology
_____ Evaluate the contributions of influential historical figures throughout the chronological development of psychology's major and emerging applied subfields.
20. Values in psychology: Curiosity
_____ Apply and sustain curiosity in investigating the claims of key figures in the emergence and development of scientific psychology.
21. Values in psychology: Skepticism
_____ Distinguish between scientific and pseudoscientific explanations of human behavior throughout psychology's history, comparing and contrasting the relative value of these differing explanations.
22. Values in psychology: Tolerance of ambiguity and consideration of human diversity
_____ Evaluate competing psychological explanations of human behavior throughout psychology's history, with an expectation of complexity, tentativeness, and variability across populations and sociohistorical contexts.

Evaluative criterion and grading rubric: In scoring the repertory grid assignments, I examine the underlying logic and connection between students' numerical ratings and accompanying written justifications.

A = Demonstrates thorough understanding of psychological contributor's views and well-conceived arguments in support of all numerical ratings.
B = Evidences an overall understanding of psychological contributor's views but a few inaccuracies in providing rating justifications.
C = Shows moderate difficulty in connecting numerical ratings to logical supporting arguments.
D = Displays limited understanding of psychological contributor's views and recurring inconsistencies in arguing logically in support of numerical ratings.
F = Fails to support numerical ratings with logical justifications in most or all instances.

Note. Adapted from *Teaching, Learning, and Assessing in a Developmentally Coherent Curriculum* (pp. 29–32), by the American Psychological Association, 2008b, Washington, DC: Author. Copyright 2008 by the American Psychological Association.

	Construct ratings											
	1	2	3	4	5	6	7	8	9	10	11	
1. Mind	—	—	—	—	—	—	—	—	—	—	—	Body
2. Nature	—	—	—	—	—	—	—	—	—	—	—	Nurture
3. Subjectivism	—	—	—	—	—	—	—	—	—	—	—	Objectivism
4. Holism	—	—	—	—	—	—	—	—	—	—	—	Elementalism
5. Free will	—	—	—	—	—	—	—	—	—	—	—	Determinism
6. Utility	—	—	—	—	—	—	—	—	—	—	—	Purity
7. Verity	—	—	—	—	—	—	—	—	—	—	—	Falsity
8. Major contribution	—	—	—	—	—	—	—	—	—	—	—	Minor contribution

Figure 6.6. Eight, 11-point construct scales used in the repertory grid assignments. From "A Pilot Investigation of the Repertory Grid as a Heuristic Tool in Teaching Historical Foundations of Psychology," by J. A. Mayo, 2004a, *Constructivism in the Human Sciences, 9,* p. 36. Copyright 2004 by the Society for Constructivism in the Human Sciences. Reprinted with permission.

TABLE 6.1
Contributors Covered in Each Unit of a History
and Systems of Psychology Class

Unit 1	Unit 2	Unit 3
Aristotle	Wilhelm Wundt	Gordon Allport
Saint Thomas Aquinas	William James	Jean Piaget
René Descartes	Mary Whiton Calkins	Francis Cecil Sumner
John Locke	Sigmund Freud	Margaret Floy Washburn
Herbert Spencer	Ivan Pavlov	Kurt Lewin
Immanuel Kant	John B. Watson	William McDougall
Hermann von Helmholtz	B. F. Skinner	Abraham Maslow
Gustav Fechner	Max Wertheimer	Richard Dawkins

Note. From "A Pilot Investigation of the Repertory Grid as a Heuristic Tool in Teaching Historical Foundations of Psychology," by J. A. Mayo, 2004a, *Constructivism in the Human Sciences, 9,* p. 35. Copyright 2004 by the Society for Constructivism in the Human Sciences. Adapted with permission.

EXHIBIT 6.4
Student-Completed Repertory Grid on Aristotle's Writings

					Construct ratings							
	1	2	3	4	5	6	7	8	9	10	11	
1. Mind									X			Body
2. Nature											X	Nurture
3. Subjectivism									X			Objectivism
4. Holism	X											Elementalism
5. Free will								X				Determinism
6. Utility			X									Purity
7. Verity				X								Falsity
8. Major contribution		X										Minor contribution

Justification for each construct rating:

1. Aristotle was both a realist and a naturalist. His later view was monistic, believing that the psyche is not separable from the body. Yet his early writings gave future Christian theologians adequate material to justify their dualism. (*Rating* = 9)
2. Aristotle did not believe that the human psyche is born with knowledge. Instead, he felt that human beings arrive at intellectual understanding through their environmental experiences. (*Rating* = 11)
3. Aristotle possessed an empirical outlook that stressed the value of inductive reasoning where you generalize from observed cases. He viewed psychology as an objective science that depends on experimentation and observation of behavior. But he never fully distanced himself from the metaphysical concerns of Greek Hellenic thinking. (*Rating* = 9)
4. Aristotle believed that form and matter are inseparable. While form accounts for people being human rather than another type of animal, matter makes people the unique individuals that they are. Aristotle also viewed the psyche as a functional process of steps involved in thinking, rather than a physical or mental essence located somewhere in the body. (*Rating* = 1)
5. Aristotle believed that reasoning was limited only to human beings as the top level of the hierarchy of psyches. Since reason's function is to know and reflect, it refines the information we gain from our senses. So, Aristotle probably would have argued that reasoning allows for the human capacity to make informed life choices using input from the senses. Yet Aristotle's view is more directly connected to environmental determinism, seeing psychology as a natural science of behavior in response to environmental manipulations. (*Rating* = 8)
6. It is true that Aristotle sought to explain behavior through natural causes. Regardless, he lived in a time in history where his theories were too far ahead of his contemporaries. So, Aristotle's views could not be fully appreciated or applied in his own lifetime. Yet his far-reaching theories would become very useful in the development of modern naturalistic psychology. (*Rating* = 3)
7. Aristotle's writings include obvious myths and errors and are sometimes as primitive as the nontechnological times in which they were written. Generally, though, his theories have withstood the test of time and are amazingly similar to the views expressed in modern scientific psychology. (*Rating* = 4)
8. In my opinion, Aristotle made a major contribution to the eventual development of psychology as a science, in spite of being wrong in some of his best guesstimates. In many ways the "father of psychology" as we know it today, Aristotle's writings provide us with the first organized account of psychological topics like sensation, perception, learning, memory, and development. (*Rating* = 2)

7

ANALOGICAL REASONING

In linking cognition and language, thinking and speech can be viewed as inherently metaphorical processes such that people define and organize conceptual systems in comparative terms (Lakoff & Johnson, 1980, 2003). As part of everyday practice, people identify, comprehend, and experience most concepts in relation to other concepts. Consequently, people cannot avoid thinking metaphorically or analogically, regardless of their level of awareness of the interdependence between thought and language. For example, imagine the thought processes involved when pioneering computer software designers were searching for a phrase to capture the essence of boxes on a screen as a user interface (Kopp, 1998). After some consideration, they arrived at the self-descriptive term *windows*. To illustrate further how metaphors pervade all language and communication (see Lakoff & Johnson, 1980, pp. 46–51, for similar illustrations), ponder some of the opportunities for embedded figurative language (shown in italics in the list that follows) inherent in the popular phrase, "Life is like a box of chocolates—you never know what you're going to get," from the box-office hit *Forrest Gump* (Zemeckis, 1994).

1. Take a *bite* out of life by seizing every opportunity for success.
2. At times, life can be *bittersweet* for those striving to *taste* its many *flavors*.

3. Life may involve *sticky* situations that are difficult to handle.
4. Some people display an intense *hunger* for life.

THEORETICAL FOUNDATIONS FOR USING
ANALOGICAL REASONING IN THE CLASSROOM

Because thinking and speech are interwoven with analogies and metaphors (Lakoff & Johnson, 1980, 2003), it should not be surprising that teachers across disciplines have long relied on these language tools in their classes (e.g., Hesse, 1966). A considerable body of theory, research, and practice has shown that analogy construction holds favorable pedagogical implications (e.g., Glynn, 1991; Kaufman, Patel, & Magder, 1996; Mayo, 2001b; Pittman, 1999; Wong, 1993a, 1993b). What factors underlie the success of analogical reasoning in the classroom? Refer to the following paragraphs for a descriptive list of 10 theoretical bases for using analogical reasoning as a teaching and learning aid.

1. *Comparing familiar and unfamiliar concepts*. Translated from its Greek derivative, the term *metaphor* means to "carry something across" or "transfer" (Kopp, 1998, ¶ 1). As such, analogies provide an interpretive bridge in comparing, or structurally aligning (*mapping*), the features of familiar (*analog*) and unfamiliar (*target*) concepts (Cyrs, 1994; Gentner & Holyoak, 1997; Genter & Markman, 1997). In a sense, analogies serve a conduit function in facilitating transfer of learning between old and new understandings (Reddy, 1993). In analogical reasoning, learners work to arrive at hybrid conceptualizations that invoke shared similarities between previously established knowledge and newly presented information (Wittrock & Alesandrini, 1990).

2. *Allowing inferences from prior experiences*. Case-based reasoning involves analogical inferences that connect to prior experiences (*cases*) and apply toward understanding and solving authentic problems (Kolodner, 1997). Within this problem-focused framework, case-based reasoning emphasizes the utility of long-term memory retrieval of analogs that characterize personal experiences. For example, introductory psychology students may rely on their personal experiences to speculate about what is wrong with using *confirmation bias*—seeking or interpreting information to validate a preconceived belief while ignoring contradictory evidence (e.g., Sternberg, 2007)—to objectively

analyze a real-world problem. Then, these students may recall different ways that they have successfully sidestepped this problem-solving bias in their own lives.

3. *Stimulating creativity and critical thinking.* Analogy construction encourages a generative process of knowledge creation and integration (Wong, 1993a, 1993b). It also hones comparison–contrast skills as part of an evaluative process of uncovering similarities and differences between analog and target concepts (Glynn, 1991).

4. *Promoting abstract reasoning.* Because all analogies break down somewhere (Glynn, Law, & Doster, 1998), the metacognitive processes involved in analogy construction promote abstract reasoning more as a means than as an end. For instance, in generating a steady stream of refined analogies, students act as problem finders more so than problem solvers (Wong, 1993a). Learners search continuously for ways to improve their abstract conceptualizations but never achieve the ever-elusive perfect analogy. As an indicator of abstract reasoning, it is important for students to comprehend the pitfalls of even well-conceived analogies (Glynn, Law, Gibson, & Hawkins, 1994).

5. *Enlivening and varying content delivery.* With proper use, teacher-generated analogies can energize communication and capture student attention as complementary or alternative modes of content delivery (Kopp, 1998). If teachers adeptly incorporate humorous, interesting, and thought-provoking analogies throughout their classroom presentations, this instructional strategy can go a long way in combating the functional limits of student attention span in lecture-heavy classes (Cyrs, 1994).

6. *Simplifying the complex.* Analogies are a concise means of communication (Kopp, 1998). In a modicum of words, analogies can express complex ideas and help students more readily conceptualize abstract models.

7. *Functioning as advance organizers.* Advance organizers provide students with a theoretical foundation upon which to build solid conceptual understandings (Ausubel, 1977). As similar-acting exploratory devices, analogies can serve an invaluable function for students who must first visualize a concept (particularly an abstract one) before comprehending and internalizing it (Duit, 1991; Mayo, 2006d; Orgill & Bodner, 2004).

8. *Personalizing course concepts.* Consistent with a constructivist educational philosophy, analogy construction permits students to generate new insights on the basis of personalized anecdotes,

discoveries, and life reflections (Mayo, 2006d). Incorporating personal relevance and meaningfulness into the learning process is a robust tool for stimulating conceptual understanding and growth (Clinchy, 1995).

9. *Tailoring teaching to fit the needs of the learning environment.* Analogies and metaphors exist in diverse forms, just as the needs of learning environments differ widely. Finding an appropriate fit between analogy and learning context is vital to the success of analogical reasoning in the classroom (Mayo, 2006d).

Understanding the differences between literal and metaphorical analogies (Holyoak, 1984) is useful in matching analogy to learning environment. *Literal analogies* involve close similarities between features of analog and target concepts (e.g., "An ant colony is like a termite colony"). These tightly mapped analogies require less reflective thinking on the part of students. In contrast, *metaphorical analogies* invoke comparisons between distinctly different ideas (e.g., "An ant colony is like a corporate enterprise"; Thrasher, 2008). These loosely mapped analogies push students to reason more abstractly.

The distinction between frozen and novel metaphors (Littlemore, 2001) is another important consideration in connecting figurative language to the learning situation. *Frozen metaphors* are clichés, such as "sharp as a tack" or "looking like a million bucks," that are used in everyday language. In contrast, *novel metaphors* bring together ideas in new or unusual ways. In the annals of famous musical lyrics from the early 1970s, examples of novel metaphors include Paul Simon's (P. F. Simon & Garfunkel, 1970, Track 1, Side 1) "like a bridge over troubled water" and Jim Croce's (1973, Track 8) "meaner than a junkyard dog." Interestingly, although both of these metaphors were unique at the time of original inception, they have since entered the realm of frozen metaphors.

10. *Serving as diagnostic assessment tools.* As a snapshot measure of conceptual understanding at a given moment in time, students may experience a *breakthrough analogy* as the sudden coming together of the elements of a problem where no insight into a viable solution had existed previously (Herstatt & Kalogerakis, 2005; Mayo, 2006d). Through pre–post analysis, students may also demonstrate changing conceptions over time, beginning with a *baseline analogy* that assesses entry-level comprehension and proceeding through a series of revised analogies that move

progressively closer to conceptual mastery (Mayo, 2006d; Ruhl, 1999).

APPLYING AUTHENTIC ASSESSMENT TO LEARNING THROUGH TEACHER-PROVIDED ANALOGIES

Exhibit 7.1 describes an assignment that uses teacher-generated analogies of contemporary developmental theories as a means to facilitate students' levels of comprehension and application of these views (Mayo, 2001b). This assignment addresses outcomes within three learning goals for the undergraduate psychology major: (a) knowledge base of psychology, (b) critical thinking skills in psychology, and (c) values in psychology.

EXHIBIT 7.1
Applying Authentic Assessment to Learning Through
Teacher-Provided Analogies

Levels of student proficiency: Basic and developing

Course: Life-span developmental psychology

Assignment: Learning through teacher-provided analogies

Instructional context: The introduction of teacher-provided analogies as part of the instructional process in life-span developmental psychology classes can be traced to textbook presentations of analogies that portray the nature of human development. For example, in epitomizing a characteristic element of stage theory, Santrock (1999) invoked a "staircase" analogy (Case, 1992) that highlights the notion of discontinuity in which "developmental peaks" (i.e., significant milestones) alternate with "developmental plateaus" (i.e., relative absences of qualitative change). Empirical evidence (Mayo, 2001b) supports the pedagogical usefulness of teacher-supplied analogies within the framework of a developmental psychology curriculum.

Purpose of the assignment: In traditional classroom practice, teachers have widely recognized the explanatory value of analogies in bridging the gap between new and preexisting knowledge (Thagard, 1992). As a simple demonstration of the pervasive use of analogies in introducing new concepts to students, educators often unwittingly preface their explanations with analogy-laden icebreakers, such as "likewise," "similarly," and "just as" (Glynn, Law, & Doster, 1998).

Teacher-provided analogies have been used to explain concepts across multiple undergraduate disciplines, including the physical and behavioral sciences. For example, in teaching the mechanics of nerve conduction to physics students, the "traveling flame" analogy has been used to compare transmitting an electrical wave in a nerve cell to burning a cigarette (Sircar & Tandon, 1996). As another illustration, students in psychological research-methods classes have been introduced to scientific reasoning by drawing analogies between aspects of a grid-based board game and processes involved in inductive and deductive reasoning (Stadler, 1998). In the present assignment, I rely on my own teacher-supplied analogies to depict major developmental theories as a way to help students better understand and apply these perspectives (Mayo, 2001b).

(continues)

Instructional methodology: At the start of the term, I complete several hours of preliminary instruction on the conceptual foundations of major developmental theories: ethological, contextual, psychodynamic, learning, cognitive, humanistic, and sociocultural. Afterward, I expose students to a series of my own analogies that I design to exemplify features of each theory. Several examples of these teacher-generated analogies, along with the theoretical stance that I intend each to represent, are shown in Exhibit 7.2.

As a written assignment—offered in or out of class, depending on an instructor's preference and the available class time—that each student completes individually, students match each analogy to one or more of the developmental theories. As part of this process, students offer a well-considered justification for each of their choices. In an effort to foster students' reflexivity and creativity, I tell students that no selection is automatically deemed incorrect if accompanied by a suitable supporting argument. This assignment is worth 5% of the final course average.

Once I have scored all completed assignments and returned them to students, I allot class time for whole-class discussion revolving around students' analogical reasoning. As an active and interactive learning experience, I encourage students to openly communicate their responses and constructively critique those of their classmates.

Learning goals and outcomes:

1. Knowledge base of psychology: Contemporary perspectives in psychology
   _____ Examine, compare, and contrast contemporary developmental perspectives on the basis of teacher-provided analogies.
2. Knowledge base of psychology: Overarching themes of psychology
   _____ Use reasoning based on teacher-supplied analogies to apply overarching developmental themes (e.g., nature vs. nurture, free will vs. determinism) in identifying and discussing contemporary developmental theories.
3. Knowledge base of psychology: General content domains of psychology
   _____ Apply contemporary theories of life-span development to various analogical contexts.
4. Critical thinking skills in psychology: Association skills
   _____ Relate contemporary developmental theories to appropriate analogical frameworks.
5. Critical thinking skills in psychology: Argumentation skills
   _____ Use reasoning grounded in teacher-provided analogies to develop defensible arguments that relate to contemporary developmental theories.
6. Values in psychology: Curiosity
   _____ Apply curiosity to examining contemporary developmental theories by means of reasoning that stems from teacher-supplied analogies.

Learning task and grading rubric: Comprehending and applying contemporary developmental theories through reasoning that derives from teacher-provided analogies.

   A = Displays thorough understanding and application of developmental theories based on teacher-provided analogies.
   B = Manifests minimal inaccuracies in comprehending and applying developmental theories based on teacher-provided analogies.
   C = Shows moderate difficulty in understanding and applying developmental theories based on teacher-provided analogies.
   D = Exhibits prominent and recurring difficulties in comprehending and applying developmental theories based on teacher-provided analogies.
   F = Fails, in most or all respects, to understand and apply developmental theories based on teacher-provided analogies.

EXHIBIT 7.2
Examples of Teacher-Provided Analogies for Prominent Developmental Theories

1. "In development as in life, it's too late to close the barnyard gate once the horses have run out." In depicting the ethological concept of development known as *critical periods* (Greenough, Emde, Gunnar, Massinga, & Shonkoff, 2001), this analogy underscores how the presence or absence of formative early life experiences (e.g., social bonding) impacts organisms well beyond the anticipated initial occurrence of these events.
2. "The core of personality development is like a dark and murky cavern full of sinister shadows." The dark and sinister implications of this analogy symbolize Freud's (1940/1970) pessimistic view of human nature, which argues that personality development is controlled largely by the sexual and aggressive instincts of the unconscious mind.
3. "In human development, it's never too late to pick up the pieces from an early fall." This analogy conceptualizes an important tenet of Erikson's (1963) psychosocial stage theory: Trauma experienced during early personality development is potentially reversible through subsequent life-affirming environmental influences.
4. "Optimal human development mirrors the famous Army recruiting slogan, 'Be all that you can be . . . '." This maxim embodies one of the basic principles of humanistic psychology (Maslow, 1968, 1970): People strive for continuing personal growth in relation to increasing levels of inherent self-motivation.
5. "Cognitive competencies develop just like in the old Beatles' lyric, 'I get by with a little help from my friends'." The analogous reference to "a little help from my friends" is consistent with Vygotsky's (1962/1986) sociocultural conception of *guided participation* that captures a child's intellectual progression through social assistance from more experienced peers.

Note. Analogies 1, 2, 4, and 5 (and the narrative descriptions accompanying each) are from "Using Analogies to Teach Conceptual Applications of Developmental Theories," by J. A. Mayo, 2001b, *Journal of Constructivist Psychology, 14,* pp. 191–192. Copyright 2001 by Taylor & Francis. Adapted with permission.

EDUCATIONAL IMPLICATIONS AND APPLICATIONS OF GENERATIVE ANALOGIES

Despite the overall classroom effectiveness of analogical reasoning, analogies can also be misleading if pushed to an unsubstantiated extreme (Duit, 1991). In protecting against such misconceptions, educators should adopt proactive measures in consideration that analogies can act as "double-edged swords" (Glynn et al., 1998, p. 205), holding the potential for both benefit and detriment as heuristic devices. As in the illustrative case of the commonly used analogy, "The human eye is like a camera" (Bell & Staines, 1979), when the instructional process turns to the dissimilarities between analog and target concepts, it should become clear that the human eye and a traditional camera focus in very different ways. Whereas the human eye focuses by using the cornea and the muscles surrounding the lens, a camera is focused by altering the distance between lens and film. Instead of ignoring this analogical inconsistency, teachers should encourage students to uncover the circumstances under which the analogy becomes shaky (Mayo, 2001b, 2006d; Thagard, 1992; Venville & Treagust, 1997).

Another problem inherent in analogical reasoning is that weak analogical transfer may enter into learning situations in which students demonstrate underdeveloped knowledge structures in relation to the target problem domain (Wong, 1993a). Bridging analogies are useful in addressing learners' restricted background knowledge (D. E. Brown, 1994; Clement, 1993, 1998). *Bridging analogies* are intermediate metaphorical conceptions that form when an analogy is divided into smaller parts that can be more easily mastered. In helping learners to clarify confusing conceptualizations, classroom educators can use bridging analogies to elucidate comparisons between problem scenarios that students initially find difficult to conceive in analogous terms (Mayo, 2001b). In conjunction with such analogical bridges, asking students to construct multiple analogies further counters the problems associated with students' insufficient knowledge bases (Spiro, Feltovich, Coulson, & Anderson, 1989). Learners are better able to identify components of increasingly more productive analogies when they originally generate an unproductive analogy followed by critical evaluation of its deficiencies (Mayo, 2001b). From this perspective, analogy-enhanced instruction can be viewed as a generative process in which conceptual advancement unfolds through ongoing synthesis of fragmented knowledge and refinement of analogical conceptions (Mayo, 2001b; Wong, 1993b).

In terms of encouraging analytical thinking about underlying learning principles, I have discovered that both teacher-provided and student-generated analogies are valuable instructional instruments in an undergraduate psychology curriculum (Mayo, 2001b). Similar to the observed effectiveness of bridging and multiple analogies, I have also found that students' learning gains are more striking when they create their own analogies through classroom opportunities for student–student critique and instructor feedback (Mayo, 2001b). On the basis of these research findings, I have developed a three-stage GEM model of analogy co-construction (Mayo, 2006d) that asks students to (a) generate original analogies for course principles, (b) evaluate these analogies in accordance with constructive feedback from classmates and instructor, and (c) modify their initial self-generated analogies in light of others' appraisals. This tripartite model (see Figure 7.1) mirrors a cyclical process of outgrowing earlier analogies in favor of adopting increasingly sophisticated conceptualizations.

Knowing that analogy-enhanced instruction engenders its most favorable learning outcomes in cases where students are actively involved in the process of analogy co-construction, I often draw students into the dynamics of learning through analogy-based classroom activities (Mayo, 2006d, 2009). My creative impetus for designing and implementing these activities derives from

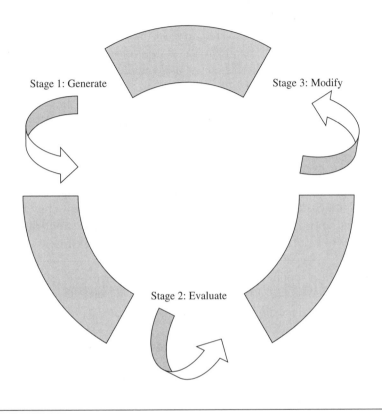

Stage 1: Generate

Stage 3: Modify

Stage 2: Evaluate

Figure 7.1. Three-stage model of analogy co-construction.

numerous teaching suggestions (Bowen, 1998; Carr, 1990; Herreid, 1999; P. James, 2000; Teachers in the English Department, 2001; Wiederman & Nicolai, 2003) that I have synthesized, adapted, and descriptively labeled. In some instances, the activities require the use of simple physical props to highlight psychological principles being taught. In other cases, they delve into reflective reasoning skills and abstract conceptualizations in the absence of tangible cues. The interactive class activities that I describe next—arranged in generally ascending order of task complexity—take into account each of these instructional scenarios.

1. *Fill in the blanks.* Offer a partial analogy to the class (e.g., "The human nervous system is like . . . because . . . "). Afterward, allow students the chance to complete the blanks as part of class discussion.

2. *Object association*. Hold up an object in class and ask students to brainstorm the ways in which the object is similar and dissimilar to the concept being covered. In teaching the notion of *tabula rasa* ("blank slate"), for example, the instructor may digitally manipulate an Etch-a-Sketch screen as symbolic of the way that life experiences compose the story of a person's developmental history. However, unlike the Etch-a-Sketch, which can be shaken clean at will, the positive and negative effects of life experiences are cumulative in determining the course of development.

3. *Personalize an analogy*. Using the name of a well-known person relevant to course content (e.g., B. F. Skinner), ask students to imagine that they actually are that person in the conduct of his or her work. Probe students on how they may feel being that person relative to his or her contributions to the field of psychology (e.g., "If I am B. F. Skinner, I feel like . . . because . . . ").

4. *Free association*. Present the class with a term (e.g., *stream of consciousness*) or a short list of terms (e.g., *unconscious, modeling, free will, connectionism, heredity, mental activities, reward, social interaction*). Next, ask students to generate other words that they associate with the target expression(s). Require students to provide supporting justifications for their responses and encourage them to critique their classmates' comments to clarify any tenuous classifications or associations.

APPLYING AUTHENTIC ASSESSMENT TO THE ANALOGIES LOG

For use in teaching life-span developmental psychology, Exhibit 7.3 introduces a learning assignment that parallels the component stages of the previously described GEM model of analogy co-construction. This assignment, called the *analogies log* (Mayo, 2006d), targets the following three learning goals and designated outcomes for the undergraduate psychology major: (a) knowledge base of psychology, (b) critical thinking skills in psychology, and (c) values in psychology.

EXHIBIT 7.3
Applying Authentic Assessment to the Analogies Log

Levels of student proficiency: Developing and advanced

Course: Life-span developmental psychology

Assignment: Analogies log

Instructional context: The efficacy of analogy-enhanced instruction has been validated in classroom demonstrations (Stadler, 1998) and formal experiments (Mayo, 2001b) involving undergraduate psychology students. Instruction that integrates analogies invites intellectual processes related to thinking creatively (Dagher, 1995), reasoning abstractly (Duit, 1991), understanding cause–effect relationships (Newton, 1996), discovering connections between complex ideas (Thagard, 1997), and representing and organizing thoughts (Knowles, 1994). In short, classroom-supported analogical reasoning can serve as a versatile pedagogical tool in an undergraduate psychology curriculum.

Purpose of the assignment: In the context of teaching life-span developmental psychology, empirical evidence (Mayo, 2001b) points to the heuristic value of student-created analogies in a single assignment pertaining to contemporary developmental theories. As a more expansive project that builds on this prior use of learner-generated analogies within a developmental framework, the *analogies log* extends the learning gains that flow from the active and interactive processes involved in student co-construction of a logical progression of analogies (Mayo, 2006d). In using the analogies log, the instructional focus shifts markedly toward a student-centered approach that invites minimal instructor prompts. When students generate a series of analogies that make increasing sense to them, they engage in *lateral thinking* (DeBono, 1970) as a vehicle for triggering improvements in problem solving and reflective analysis.

Instructional methodology: Students complete the analogies log in accordance with the following sequential steps that are matched to respective stages in the GEM model of analogy co-construction (Mayo, 2006d). The assignment counts as 15% of the final course grade.

Stage 1: Generate

1. Working independently, students generate one or more analogies for each of a series of contemporary developmental theories (e.g., ethological, contextual, psychodynamic, learning, cognitive, humanistic, sociocultural), linking analog and target concepts in each instance. In applying the operations inherent in the teaching-with-analogies model (Glynn, 1991; Glynn, Duit, & Thiele, 1995; Glynn, Law, Gibson, & Hawkins, 1994), students systematically construct each analogy by identifying relevant features of the analog and target and drawing appropriate conclusions based on similarities and differences between these concepts. Students rely on graphic organization to consolidate their thoughts. The use of graphic organizers in this learning context is also consistent with other research-based practices for representing the elements of analogies (see Marzano, Pickering, & Pollock, 2001). The following illustrates the entire process of analogical creation with the commonplace analogy, "The human brain is like a computer":

(continues)

EXHIBIT 7.3
Applying Authentic Assessment to the Analogies Log *(Continued)*

Features of brain (analog)	Features of computer (target)	Similarities	Differences
Neurons, cognition	Circuits, software	Storage, retrieval	Processing

There are a couple of conclusions that can be drawn from this process. To begin, the human brain is capable of memory storage and retrieval in a manner comparable to how a computer relies on its hardware and software to perform similar functions. However, a computer undertakes completely logical operations while processing information, whereas the human brain combines pure logic with creativity, emotionality, and intuition as it processes information and acquires knowledge and skills.

Stages 2 and 3: Evaluate and modify

2. Students exchange their logs with a minimum of three classmates who evaluate and constructively critique each analogy.
3. As deemed necessary, students modify their original analogies or offer new analogies consistent with peer feedback. In doing so, students provide supporting rationale for any reported changes in analogical reasoning.
4. The week before midterm, students bring their revised logs to class to participate in a whole-class discussion. Students share their analogies and critique those of their classmates. Students are also exposed to facilitating instructor comments.
5. Students record feedback from the class discussion that led to any changes in analogical reasoning. Students undertake a final revision of applicable analogies in line with feedback from the class discussion. Once again, students offer supporting rationale for any such changes.
6. At midterm, the students submit the completed logs—reflecting cumulative products of a generative process of conceptual growth and refinement—to the instructor for grading.

Learning goals and outcomes:

1. Knowledge base of psychology: Contemporary perspectives in psychology
   _____ Analyze, compare, and contrast contemporary developmental perspectives by means of learner-generated analogical reasoning.
   _____ Separate and then synthesize basic assumptions and explanatory concepts of contemporary developmental perspectives through the process of learner-generated analogical reasoning.
2. Knowledge base of psychology: Overarching themes of psychology
   _____ Use learner-generated analogical reasoning to apply overarching developmental themes (free will vs. determinism, subjectivism vs. objectivism, variability and continuity of behavior within and across species, and interaction of heredity and environment) in explaining contemporary developmental theories.
3. Knowledge base of psychology: General content domains of psychology
   _____ Apply and analyze contemporary theories of development across the life span on the basis of learner-generated analogical reasoning.
4. Critical thinking skills in psychology: Association skills
   _____ Relate and apply connections between facts and developmental theories over a wide range of analogical contexts.

EXHIBIT 7.3
Applying Authentic Assessment to the Analogies Log   *(Continued)*

5. Critical thinking skills in psychology: Argumentation skills
   _____ Develop increasingly sophisticated and integrated arguments for contemporary developmental theories through the process of learned-generated analogical reasoning.
6. Critical thinking skills in psychology: Questioning skills
   _____ Differentiate between poorly conceived and well-conceived developmental analogies.
   _____ Evaluate the pitfalls inherent in each developmental analogy.
   _____ Modify developmental analogies to reduce ambiguity in explaining contemporary developmental theories.
7. Critical thinking skills in psychology: Creativity
   _____ Generate novel analogies to explain contemporary developmental theories.
8. Values in psychology: Curiosity
   _____ Apply and sustain curiosity in examining contemporary developmental theories through a generative process of analogy refinement.

Evaluative criterion and grading rubric: In scoring the analogies log, I focus on the extent of sophistication and refinement in each student's analogical reasoning from first- to last-draft analogies.

A = Demonstrates mastery of contemporary developmental theories and significant refinement in analogical reasoning from first to last draft.

B = Reveals an overall understanding of contemporary developmental theories and above-average refinement in analogical reasoning from first to last draft.

C = Displays moderate difficulty in comprehending contemporary developmental theories and average refinement in analogical reasoning from first to last draft.

D = Shows prominent and recurring difficulties in both theory comprehension and analogy creation and refinement from first to last draft.

F = Fails, in most or all respects, to show both theory comprehension and growth in analogical reasoning.

8

COOPERATIVE LEARNING: INTERSECTING COGNITIVE AND SOCIAL CONSTRUCTIVISM

Among the best researched of all teaching strategies (R. T. Johnson & Johnson, 1994; Slavin, 1989–1990), *cooperative learning* occurs when groups of students work together to optimize their own and each other's learning (D. W. Johnson, Johnson, & Smith, 1992). Cooperative learning is a specific type of collaborative learning that involves assessing the group as a whole, along with holding students individually accountable for their own work (Palmer, Peters, & Streetman, 2003). Effective communication that includes the ability to work together in groups, one of the skills fostered in cooperative learning experiences, is also shared within the APA *Guidelines for the Undergraduate Psychology Major* (American Psychological Association [APA], 2007) as a skill set applied within liberal-arts-focused higher education that is further developed in psychology.

In instructional settings that incorporate cooperative learning, "the major interaction is student–student, rather than teacher–student, as teaching is normally understood" (Tang, 1998, p. 116). In these settings, the instructor's role is transformed from dispenser-of-knowledge to facilitator-of-learning (Millis, 2002). Compared with competitive and individualistic learning environments, a sizeable body of experimental and correlational research has shown that cooperative learning promotes higher level reasoning, generation of new ideas and solutions, group-to-individual transfer of learning, achievement, social competence, and cognitive and affective perspective taking (see D. W. Johnson & Johnson, 1989). For prospective college graduates, cooperative learning also has potential benefits for future employment preparations. Applying this argument to instructional activities within undergraduate psychology education, Shapiro (2008) wrote,

> To the extent that learning how to work together in teams in a psychology class prepares an individual to be successful as a team member (or leader) on the job, the psychology teacher who does have team projects is better preparing the student for the workforce than the one who does not. (¶ 3)

As a blend of active and interactive processes, cooperative learning is based on the constructivist premise that learning is produced, not reproduced (Millis, 2002). This form of learning "provides opportunities for students to talk and listen, read, write, and reflect as they approach course content through problem-solving exercises, informal small groups, simulations, case studies, role playing, and other [applied learning] activities" (Myers & Jones, 1993, p. xi).

Co-regulated coordination merges the symbiotic aims of cognitive and social constructivism as reflected in cooperative learning environments (Raeff & Mascolo, 1996). According to Mascolo, Craig-Bray, and Neimeyer (1997), *co-regulated coordination* points to "the intersection of personal and social processes . . . in reconstructing social activity, [where] individuals transform jointly produced meanings in terms of their existing skills and meanings" (p. 21). Anchoring co-regulated coordination to constructivist classrooms that highlight each student's learning activities in relation to his or her peers, instructors should "erect a framework for examining the interpersonal construction of meaning and action . . . without losing the individual in the process" (Mascolo et al., 1997, p. 8).

COOPERATIVE LEARNING PARADIGMS AND CLASSROOM ENVIRONMENTS

Cooperative learning is a flexible pedagogical strategy in which classes can be organized into three different cooperative learning paradigms—small groups, large groups, and whole-class groups—with each configuration possessing curricular advantages and disadvantages (Flowers & Ritz, 1994). *Small-group cooperative learning* (3–5 students) affords students greater opportunities to participate in peer tutoring, establish mutual responsibility toward learning, and build cooperative teamwork. Conversely, though, small-group teaming may also intensify some students' unwilling attitudes toward cooperating with certain other students. Different from small-group organization, *large-group cooperative learning* (six or more students) allows students to experience real-world activities that demand quality operations in large functional teams, such as those observed in business, industry, and the military. Because of the increased number of students involved in large-group cooperative learning tasks, however, these circumstances may be conducive to some students hiding in the crowd and thus failing to complete their assigned work. Lastly, the principles underlying *whole-class cooperative learning* can be used effectively to elicit a broad range of ideas when an entire class discusses or debates important topics. Unless the instructor adopts appropriate advance precautions, however, the amount of each student's active participation generally dwindles in proportion to increases in group size.

In addition to small-group, large-group, and whole-class organizational frameworks, there are three other categories of cooperative learning strategies that can be used separately or in tandem with one another: formal cooperative learning groups, informal cooperative learning groups, and cooperative base groups (D. W. Johnson et al., 1992). In *formal cooperative learning groups*, students work together to complete a specific task or assignment. Formal learning groups, which last from one class period to several weeks, can be used to teach specific course content and problem-solving skills. In contrast, *informal cooperative learning groups* are temporary, impromptu groups that are formed for only one class discussion or one class period. Their primary purpose is twofold: (a) to organize in advance the material to be taught and (b) to facilitate the active processing of this material as it is being covered in class. Finally, *cooperative base groups* consist of three or four students who provide each other with the long-term support necessary to progress academically. Base groups work together throughout the entire term, including possible arrangements to meet outside of class.

In cooperative learning, the group's success is contingent on the successful work of each constituent member, with no one group member in unilateral possession of the knowledge, skills, and resources required to attain the group's targeted learning goals (D. W. Johnson & Johnson, 1989). However, this does not suggest that simply placing students in groups to complete assigned projects will guarantee success. Rather, there are five basic components of cooperative learning environments (D. W. Johnson, Johnson, & Holubec, 1998; R. T. Johnson & Johnson, 1994), and instructors can facilitate group effectiveness and the concerted, equitable participation of all group members by systematically integrating these learning components into the structure of teaching and assessment.

1. *Positive interdependence.* At the core of cooperative learning is the perception that an individual cannot succeed unless the entire group succeeds. This "sink-or-swim-together" perspective of interdependence embodies the positive quality of dual responsibility: Each person in the group learns the assigned material

while at the same time ensuring that everyone else in the group learns it. By carefully designing group work and communicating to that group in a manner that emphasizes the potentially unique contribution of each group member to the joint effort, instructors invite positive interdependence and the resultant cooperative learning experience.

2. *Promotive interaction.* Positive interdependence provides the instructional backdrop in which promotive interaction can occur. With promotive interaction, cooperative learning groups serve as academic and personal support systems. Instructors can build promotive interaction into the directions and procedures for cooperative learning activities by encouraging students to share ideas, resources, and constructive performance feedback; work together in complementary and interconnected roles; check one another for comprehension; and explain to each other how to solve problems or relate concepts.

3. *Individual and group accountability.* Group members must hold each other accountable for completing assigned work; otherwise, *social loafing* (Latané, 1981) is more likely to take place. With social loafing, there is a diminished degree of effort extended by people during a group activity. Therefore, in cooperative learning situations, it is imperative that accountability exists on two levels: (a) group accountability for achieving its learning goals and (b) individual accountability for each group member shouldering his or her fair share of the work load. There are several ways in which instructors can foster individual accountability within the overall context of group accountability.

- Instructors can ensure more individual accountability within the group by designing group size to be small and observing the in-class activities of the group.
- Instructors can either assign each member of the group to a specific role (e.g., facilitator, recorder, time monitor) or allow the collective group membership to make these assignments on its own. Once established, though, these roles should remain flexible in allowing for individualized adaptations. By periodically rotating roles within the group, students not only become sensitized to multiple responsibilities involved in successfully completing an assigned task but also arrive at many different ways to become active contributors to group processes. As a means of encouraging all group members to exert optimal effort toward completing assignments, instructors can also leave the role of reporter of the group's work unidentified in advance.

- Instructors can randomly spot-check an individual student's active involvement in the group by asking that student to explain his or her group's work to the teacher, same-group classmates, or entire class. By soliciting the services of a group member in the role of checker—who asks other group members to offer a rationale underlying the group's action—instructors can similarly encourage individual accountability. This spot-checking process, called *simultaneous explaining* (R. T. Johnson & Johnson, 1994), increases the level of understanding among all students involved (Hamm & Adams, 1992).

  Keeping with individual and group accountability, what type of grading format works best with cooperative learning experiences? Compared with a grading system that places students in competition with one another for a predetermined number of As, Bs, and so on, a criterion-referenced grading scheme with clearly stated and realistically high performance benchmarks encourages cooperation and allows students to earn appropriate grades (Millis, 2002). Despite the specifics of the grading system adopted, however, "there must be foreknowledge of what will be evaluated and by whom (professor only, professor and students)" (Hornak, 2008, ¶ 3).

4. *Interpersonal and small-group skills.* Cooperative learning presents a special challenge because it requires students to participate concurrently in task work (learning academic content) and team work (functioning productively as a group). Consequently, instructors should teach academic skills and the accompanying social skills needed for high-quality cooperative work, including effective leadership, sound decision making, accurate and unambiguous communication, and constructive conflict resolution. See D. W. Johnson (1991, 1993) for a discussion of procedures and strategies for teaching students the social skills crucial to success of cooperative learning groups.

5. *Group processing.* With continuous improvement of learning as the targeted outcome, a group needs to reflect on (i.e., process) how well it is functioning. At the conclusion of each cooperative group session, group members should allot adequate time to process how effectively they have worked together. It is important to structure the processing to be as specific as possible. As an example, the group as a whole may be asked to briefly discuss several things that the group did well and at least one thing that it could improve, searching for general agreement

among the feedback offered. Afterward, the instructor may also provide feedback to the group on how well its members are working together, along with recommendations for future performance facilitation.

An important way to link cooperative learning tasks to authentic teaching and assessment is to move in the direction of *multimodality teaching* (Sapon-Shevin, Ayres, & Duncan, 1994). In multimodality teaching, the instructional spotlight repositions from conventional pencil-and-paper tasks to those that support more active student engagement. Throughout the remaining pages of this chapter, I provide three examples of cooperative learning tasks (arranged sequentially from small group to large group to whole class) that capture the essence of multimodality teaching: (a) small-group peer review of a student writing assignment, (b) a large-group poster presentation, and (c) whole-class scored discussion. In each of these cooperative learning assignments, authentic assessment takes into account both content and process of the group experience involved.

APPLYING AUTHENTIC ASSESSMENT TO THE COLLEAGUE SWAP

Exhibit 8.1 casts authentic assessment in the light of a small-group cooperative learning assignment called the *colleague swap* (Camplese & Mayo, 1982; Mayo, 2006a), which is designed to enhance the quality of student writing with the help of systematic peer review and feedback. The writing assignment is a term-length research paper in an educational psychology class. Together, the content of the assigned paper and the group processes entailed in the colleague swap canvas outcomes from all five learning goals for the undergraduate psychology major: (a) knowledge base of psychology, (b) research methods in psychology, (c) critical thinking skills in psychology, (d) application of psychology, and (e) values in psychology.

APPLYING AUTHENTIC ASSESSMENT TO A GROUP POSTER PRESENTATION

Exhibit 8.2 links authentic assessment to the content and group processes involved in a large-group cooperative learning task. Applied psychology students work together to design and implement a group poster presentation that includes a reflective essay portfolio component (Mayo, 2004b). This term-long assignment addresses outcomes from all five learning goals for the undergraduate psychology major: (a) knowledge base of psychology, (b) research methods in psychology, (c) critical thinking skills in psychology, (d) application of psychology, and (e) values in psychology.

APPLYING AUTHENTIC ASSESSMENT TO THE SCORED DISCUSSION

Exhibit 8.3 portrays authentic assessment within the framework of a whole-class cooperative learning assignment aimed at bolstering the quality of class discussions—with only limited instructor involvement. I apply this assignment, referred to as the *scored discussion* (e.g., Frazier, 1997), to teaching history and systems of psychology (Mayo, 2002b). The scored discussion taps into outcomes derived from all five learning goals for the undergraduate psychology major: (a) knowledge base of psychology, (b) research methods in psychology, (c) critical thinking skills in psychology, (d) application of psychology, and (e) values in psychology.

EXHIBIT 8.1
Applying Authentic Assessment to the Colleague Swap

Levels of student proficiency: Developing and advanced

Course: Educational psychology

Assignment: Colleague swap

Instructional context: Poor writing skills among students are neither new to college classrooms nor restricted in scope to the discipline of psychology. Although undergraduate courses in English composition usually pave the way for improvements in student performance, generalization of acquired writing skills from these to other college courses remains problematic. This dilemma is exacerbated by the common student misconception that writing well is the exclusive concern of the English major (Camplese & Mayo, 1982).

Purpose of the assignment: In teaching undergraduate psychology, there are two schools of thought on how to improve the quality of student writing. One approach advocates for the development of a separate course for the sole purpose of teaching effective writing skills tailored to psychology (e.g., Calhoun & Selby, 1979). Consistent with a writing-across-the-curriculum argument, a less sweeping solution to the problem involves reinforcing sound writing skills in the existing framework of established courses. The *colleague swap* (Camplese & Mayo, 1982; Mayo, 2006a) is a systematic means of improving student writing skills in line with writing across the curriculum. The primary goal of the colleague swap is to enhance the quality of student writing through peer exchange and review of writing assignments. On the basis of the peer feedback received, students are given the opportunity to revise their term, theme, research, or position papers.

(continues)

Instructional methodology: In an educational psychology class, students complete a term-length research paper in which they compare, contrast, and evaluate the underlying research findings, theories, and educational practices reflected in these contemporary learning models: behavioral, cognitive–behavioral, constructivist, humanistic, and sociocultural. The minimum required length for the paper is 15 pages (minus illustrative figures and tables), including the title page, 150- to 200-word abstract, and reference section containing at least 10 references.

In applying the colleague swap to the present writing assignment, students earn grade-applicable credit by exchanging or swapping their papers with three classmates. Throughout this process that takes place both inside and outside of class, students evaluate, proofread, and critique one another's work. General guidelines governing peer review of the assigned paper are based on the following questions:

1. Does the introduction appropriately launch a connecting thread of ideas?
2. Does the summary effectively recap the main points?
3. Does the train of thought in each paragraph flow logically from the opening sentence?
4. Are relevant ideas expressed accurately, completely, and coherently?
5. Are all grammatical, spelling, and other mechanical errors eliminated?
6. Is the topic thoroughly and convincingly researched?
7. Are references cited properly in the body of the paper and the reference section?

In addition to asking peer reviewers to incorporate their suggested revisions directly into the body of the writing assignment, I use a preprinted *evaluation ticket* (Camplese & Mayo, 1982; a checklist of standard rhetorical, contextual, and bibliographic considerations) to help reviewers organize and present summative comments to their student colleagues. I arrange the evaluation ticket into comprehensive categories that consist of various subheadings. Preliminarily, I review the categories and subheadings in class with an opportunity for students to ask clarifying questions. I assign points to each constituent element in the checklist, providing blank space to the right of each item for writing applicable constructive criticism. Figure 8.1 contains the evaluation ticket used in this assignment, although its contents can be modified to conform to the idiosyncratic needs of the course and writing assignment involved.

After the colleague swaps are completed, I return the marked papers and attached evaluation tickets to their respective student authors. I then allot class time for each student to meet briefly with corresponding peer evaluators. During the resulting work sessions, students explain their critiques and assist one another in improving the quality of their papers.

I set the due date for the assigned paper, which is worth 20% of the final grade average, at 2 weeks before the final examination period. In submitting their assignments to me for grading, I ask students to attach all earlier drafts (including all completed evaluation tickets) to the final revision of the paper.

As a measure of quality control over the peer-critique process, it is useful for both instructor and student authors to rate peer reviewers' critiques in a manner that ties to overall grade determination for the reviewers. Rating systems may vary in accordance with each instructor's individual preferences. Similar to the rating system used in the evaluation ticket, the quality of each peer reviewer's work may also be rated on a Likert-type scale with anchors at 1 (*unsatisfactory*) and 5 (*exceptional*)—including evaluative comments—that can be easily converted into a letter grade format (see Figure 8.2).

Curricular advantages and disadvantages: There are two curricular advantages afforded through the use of the colleague swap. First, once revised papers are submitted to the instructor for final grading, most technical errors are eliminated and the content is typically stronger. With organizational and grammatical mistakes minimized or eliminated, instructors can concentrate more freely on the task of judging each paper's content in the general absence of distracting mechanical errors. Second, allowing students to critique each other's papers creates a more cooperative learning environment and increases student involvement in the content and flow of the course. It is only natural that students develop a greater vested interest in a class in which they believe their feedback visibly matters.

For instructors, the primary disadvantage associated with the colleague swap is devoting class time to student work sessions that could otherwise be used to lecture or discuss salient course topics. However, this difficulty is offset by student's writing gains and the consequent need for significantly less time in correcting content-independent errors in students' revised papers.

Another potential pitfall in the use of the colleague swap surrounds the assignment of students to peer-critique relationships. Because of the high probability of rating inflation, it is wise to avoid allowing students who know each other well to exchange papers. As a related issue for instructors to consider (regardless of the nature of a peer-critique relationship), students are generally inhibited about criticizing a classmate's paper because of personal insecurity, concern for hurting someone's feelings, fear of reprisal, or other factors. Before undertaking the colleague swap, instructors should counsel students on the need for unbiased feedback in their critiques as an important means of helping one another become more proficient writers.

As a final caveat in using the colleague swap, students must know that the suggestions for change offered by their classmates are purely advisory. Ultimate responsibility for researching the necessity, accuracy, and validity of these recommended revisions rests squarely on the shoulders of student authors themselves.

Learning goals and outcomes:

1. Knowledge base of psychology: Contemporary perspectives in psychology
    _____ Compare and contrast the scientific bases, assumptions, practices, and other elements of contemporary learning models.
    _____ Evaluate the practical utility and effectiveness of contemporary learning models.
    _____ Defend one or more contemporary learning models.
2. Knowledge base of psychology: Overarching themes of psychology
    _____ Evaluate the appropriateness of contemporary learning models from the standpoint of psychology's overarching themes: interaction of heredity and environment, variability and continuity of behavior and mental processes, free will versus determinism, subjectivity versus objectivity, and applicability across societal and cultural groups.
3. Knowledge base of psychology: General content domains of psychology
    _____ Analyze and evaluate contemporary learning models in the general content domains of psychology, including learning and cognition, individual and sociocultural differences, and life-span development.
4. Research methods in psychology: Body of evidence
    _____ Analyze and integrate scientific findings related to contemporary learning models.

(continues)

5. Research methods in psychology: Sociocultural context
   _____ Apply sociocultural framework to scientific findings and conclusions pertaining to contemporary learning models.
6. Research methods in psychology: Database skills
   _____ Develop and implement literature search strategies that encompass an adequate scope of appropriately cited research.
7. Research methods in psychology: Limits of scientific reasoning and evidence
   _____ Discuss reasons why research findings and conclusions related to contemporary learning models may change because of sociohistorical factors and the evolving nature of scientific findings.
8. Critical thinking skills in psychology: Use of evidence in psychology
   _____ Collect and use scientific evidence in drawing appropriate conclusions about contemporary learning models.
9. Critical thinking skills in psychology: Association skills
   _____ Relate and apply connections between diverse scientific findings and contemporary learning models across a variety of educational contexts.
   _____ Assess the quality of connections between diverse scientific findings and contemporary learning models over a range of educational environments.
10. Critical thinking skills in psychology: Argumentation skills
    _____ Develop sound, integrated arguments about human learning based on scientific evidence derived from contemporary learning models.
11. Critical thinking skills in psychology: Detection of errors in psychological reasoning
    _____ Detect, evaluate, and reject claims about human learning that arise from poorly supported assertions inherent in contemporary learning models.
12. Application of psychology: Psychological tests
    _____ Differentiate between effective and less effective methods of psycho-educational testing steeped in contemporary learning models and comment on whether these methods demonstrate respect for alternative cultures and gender.
13. Application of psychology: Potential for psychology as a change agent
    _____ Evaluate the impact of contemporary learning models in promoting positive change in diverse educational environments.
14. Values in psychology: Curiosity
    _____ Apply and sustain curiosity in examining contemporary learning models.
15. Values in psychology: Skepticism
    _____ Maintain rigorous standards related to the quality of scientific evidence in support of claims drawn from contemporary learning models.
16. Values in psychology: Tolerance of ambiguity and consideration of human diversity
    _____ Evaluate contemporary learning models, with anticipation that explanations stemming from these models are complex, tentative, and variable across populations and contexts.

EXHIBIT 8.1
Applying Authentic Assessment to the Colleague Swap   (Continued)

Evaluative criterion and grading rubric: In grading completed research papers that incorporate the colleague swap technique, I direct attention to the extent of refinement (first to last draft) in each student author's work on the basis of reflective revisions that derive from constructive peer feedback.

A = Produces a well-conceived and thoroughly researched paper that reflects an increasing level of refinement in quality from first to last draft.

B = Exhibits overall refinement in the quality of the paper from first to last draft, with minimal errors in content, mechanics, logical order in composition, writing style, and/or reference citations.

C = Demonstrates a moderate degree of inaccuracy in content, mechanics, logical order in composition, writing style, and/or reference citations from first to last draft.

D = Displays an ongoing series of prominent difficulties in content, mechanics, logical order in composition, writing style, and/or reference citations from first to last draft.

F = Fails, in most or all respects, to produce a high-quality paper containing visible evidence of improvement from first to last draft.

Directions: Print your own name and the name of the student author in the designated areas. On the blank line appearing to the left of each of the following 26 elements, assign between 1 and 5 points (1 = *unsatisfactory*, 2 = *fair*, 3 = *average*, 4 = *above average*, 5 = *exceptional*) in rating your classmate's paper. Blank space is provided to the right of each element for you to summarize constructive criticism that you believe will improve the quality of the paper. Once you have finished, staple your critique evaluation to the back of the paper.

Your name: _____

Name of student author: _____

A. Writing style   Constructive criticism

    1. _____ Precision   _____

    2. _____ Economy   _____

    3. _____ Fluency   _____

    4. _____ Jargon   _____

    5. _____ Slang   _____

    6. _____ Ambiguity   _____

    7. _____ Sexist language   _____

B. Logical order in composition

    8. _____ Coherence   _____

Figure 8.1. Evaluation ticket. From "How to Improve the Quality of Student Writing: The Colleague Swap," by D. A. Camplese and J. A. Mayo, 1982, *Teaching of Psychology, 9*, p. 122. Copyright 1982 by Taylor & Francis. Adapted with permission.

(continues)

9. _____ Organization _____

10. _____ Transition _____

11. _____ Sentence structure _____

C. Mechanics

12. _____ Punctuation _____

13. _____ Grammar _____

14. _____ Spelling _____

15. _____ Capitalization _____

D. Content

16. _____ Quality _____

17. _____ Relevance _____

18. _____ Accuracy _____

19. _____ Completeness _____

20. _____ Proportion _____

21. _____ Originality _____

E. Reference citations

22. _____ Placement _____

23. _____ Quality _____

24. _____ Completeness _____

25. _____ Form _____

26. _____ Accuracy _____

Figure 8.1. (*Continued*)

Rating scale:

5 = *Exceptional*   4 = *Above average*   3 = *Average*   2 = *Fair*   1 = *Unsatisfactory*

Evaluative comments: _____

_____

_____

Letter-grade conversions: A = 5, B = 4, C = 3, D = 2, and F = 1

Figure 8.2. Sample peer-reviewer rating scale.

EXHIBIT 8.2
Applying Authentic Assessment to a Group Poster Presentation

Levels of student proficiency: Developing and advanced

Course: Applied psychology

Assignment: Group poster presentation

Instructional context: Psychology holds considerable practical significance as an applied science (G. A. Miller, 1969). Accordingly, an important (albeit sometimes overlooked) objective of undergraduate psychology curricula should be to teach students how to examine real-world scenarios through the lens of applied psychology (Hettich, 1980). As an introduction to diverse applications of psychology to daily life and work—including educational, business, and interpersonal contexts—undergraduate course work in applied psychology offers an excellent venue for engaging students in hands-on learning tasks that place learners in conjointly active and interactive roles. One such learning task is to have cooperative teams of students prepare for an in-class poster session, interacting and collaborating with one another in the creation and evaluation of their work (Mayo, 2004b).

Purpose of the assignment: Classroom research and practice have shown that cooperative learning is an active, student-centered, social process (D. W. Johnson & Johnson, 2003; D. W. Johnson, Johnson, & Holubec, 1998). In the present term-long assignment, applied psychology students work together in relatively large groups to design and implement a group poster presentation (Mayo, 2004b). As a part of the assignment, each student completes a reflective essay that speaks to what and how he or she has learned from participating in the assigned task. This cooperative learning assignment serves three complementary functions: (a) exposing students to varied pragmatic applications of psychology, (b) building teamwork and interpersonal skills, and (c) stimulating self-reflection with respect to the first two functions.

Instructional methodology: At the start of the term, I assign each student to one of five groups of six people—either randomly or with forethought toward establishing equivalency across groups in terms of grade point average and other variables. In this case, the total class size equals 30. Different group configurations are possible, however, based on variations in class size.

Once assigned to their respective groups, students meet briefly in class to select individuals to serve in the flexible and rotating capacities of facilitator, recorder, and other defined roles. After each group's dynamics are set, I apprise students of the procedures involved in completing a group poster presentation, which counts as 25% of each student's final course grade. During this information-sharing process, I tell students that their assigned groups will meet both inside and outside of class to accomplish the required task.

In a different applied specialty of psychology that I negotiate with each group (e.g., clinical, social, educational, school, developmental, industrial/organizational, health, sports, forensic), students find documented evidence (e.g., books, journal articles, newspaper and magazine reports) of that psychological subfield's practical applications to everyday life. In a final written report, students summarize the major themes and findings inherent in the content of the documents uncovered and then coherently tie together their work with that of their same-group colleagues. The documentation assigned to each student is decided as part of the interactive processes occurring within each group.

(continues)

Each group poster contains the following separate sections:

- a title page containing the names of each student contributor;
- a 200- to 250-word introduction;
- a concise textual summary that (a) synthesizes and integrates each student's work with that of other group members, (b) cites reference sources, and (c) incorporates any supporting photographs or illustrations;
- a conclusion that recaps the main points and findings of the report and addresses future implications and directions;
- a reference section that includes a minimum of 12 reference citations (at least two supplied by each person in the group); and
- a two-page summary handout (see Hess & Brooks, 1998)—not including references—made available for review before the poster session but not physically displayed as part of the poster.

In addition, each student is required to write a two-page reflective essay that discusses what and how he or she has learned through completing this project. Students follow current APA Style in formatting and typing all assigned work, with the exception of varying font size as follows: 12-point font for the two-page summary handout and the reflective essay, 24-point font for the poster text, 36-point font for the poster illustration titles, and 72-point font for the poster title.

Although there is no explicit minimum or maximum page limit established for this project, I require that groups mount the content of their respective posters on no more than two standard-sized white poster boards. If groups decide to adapt PowerPoint presentations to their full-size poster presentations, I advise a limit of 10 slides or fewer (see Larsson, as cited in Ferguson, 2006).

I schedule the in-class poster session for the final week of the term. However, a preliminary poster proposal that outlines the intended project is due to me early in the term. I inform each group that it should not complete the assignment until I have reviewed and approved its proposal. Unapproved proposals constitute an automatic grade of zero for the assignment.

The class period before the scheduled poster session, I designate each group a suitably large classroom wall, bulletin board, or chalk/white board space (e.g., 4 × 6 feet) on which to display its poster. Students use easily removable duct or masking tape that will not cause structural damage. At the very start of the poster session, all classroom furnishings and equipment are packed together tightly in the center of the room to permit an unobstructed walking and viewing area for the audience, which consists of all participating students and me.

On the day of the poster session, each participating student and I separately evaluate the appearance and content of the posters, along with the quality of accompanying presentations. In addition, 1 week before the session, each student and I receive a copy of the two-page summary handouts for all groups (outside their own, in the case of students). These handouts sensitize the audience to poster content in advance of the session. To allow the six students in each group ample opportunity to evaluate posters prepared by groups other than their own, I afford rotating pairs of students 15 to 25 minutes (depending on the available length of the class period) to review other posters. At the conclusion of the poster session, all students submit their completed evaluations and individual reflective essays to me. I then integrate the student evaluations and instructor-graded reflective essays as distinct components in a comprehensive grading rubric for the assignment (see the Evaluative criteria and grading rubric section later in this exhibit).

Curricular advantages and disadvantages: A poster session has several advantages over individual or group oral presentations (see Levine, as cited in Ferguson, 2006). To begin, the instructor can collapse all reports into a single poster session, thereby reducing considerably the number of presentation days. The static visual display involved in a poster presentation also allows greater opportunity to review the material. Moreover, the less formal interactive setting associated with a poster presentation is more conducive to cultivating an inquiry-based learning atmosphere.

Compared with traditional term-paper assignments, students generally view a poster session as a more attractive alternative in terms of encouraging creativity, independent and shared thought, and communication skills (Baird, 1991). In the words of Hess and Brooks (1998), the "sheer novelty of creating a poster" (p. 155) can bolster student interest and motivation. In addition, term papers fail to reach the maximum student audience because students are typically unaware of each other's work (Ferguson, 2006).

Although poster sessions possess easily identifiable heuristic benefits, using a group format (especially a large group) adds a degree of logistical challenge to classroom poster sessions. In response to this challenge, instructors may form smaller groups to work collaboratively on the assignment, with the trade-off being an increase in the number of group presentations at the poster session. However, an even greater challenge relates to the evaluation process. Although, in some ways a poster session can ease the grading burden on instructors (Baird, 1991), evaluating all posters in a consistent manner within a relatively short period of time may prove difficult—especially to novice student evaluators. However, there are possible remedies to this problem (see Hess & Brooks, 1998). If the time frame for the poster session cannot be reasonably lengthened, requiring that students distribute a two-page summary of the report prior to the session (which I have undertaken in the present assignment as an advance organizational tool) can partially address this dilemma. As another potential solution, the instructor may collect the posters and complete a more thorough evaluation after the session. In this way, the instructor can dedicate more time at the poster session to probing the depth and breadth of students' knowledge while postponing detailed examination of poster aesthetics and construction to a later date.

Learning goals and outcomes:

1. Knowledge base of psychology: Relationship of psychology to science
   _____ Analyze how research in a psychological subfield reflects scientific principles.
   _____ Evaluate a subfield of psychological science as a means of understanding behavior and mental processes.
2. Knowledge base of psychology: Structure of psychology
   _____ Discuss how a subfield of psychology appropriately addresses research and/or behavioral concerns.
3. Knowledge base of psychology: Relationship of psychology to other disciplines
   _____ Integrate knowledge ascertained from a psychological subfield with that of other disciplines.
4. Knowledge base of psychology: Overarching themes of psychology
   _____ Apply overarching themes of psychology (e.g., interaction of heredity and environment, variability and continuity of behavior and mental processes, interaction of mind and body, applicability of theories across societal and cultural groups) in explaining behavior and mental processes from the perspective of a psychological subfield.

(continues)

5. Knowledge base of psychology: General content domains of psychology
   _____ Apply, analyze, evaluate, and synthesize concepts, theories, and research findings within a psychological subfield, using one or more of the following general content domains of psychology: learning and cognition, individual and sociocultural differences, biological bases of behavior and mental processes, and development.
6. Research methods in psychology: Body of evidence
   _____ Analyze differences across research studies related to a subfield of psychology.
   _____ Integrate findings from several studies in a psychological subfield to produce a coherent set of conclusions.
7. Research methods in psychology: Sociocultural context
   _____ Incorporate sociocultural factors in interpreting research findings derived from a subfield of psychology.
8. Research methods in psychology: Database skills
   _____ Create and implement efficient and effective group literature search strategies that address research areas and/or behavioral concerns in a psychological subfield.
9. Research methods in psychology: Limits of scientific reasoning and evidence
   _____ Discuss reasons why empirical findings and conclusions in a psychological subfield may change or require adjustment.
10. Critical thinking skills in psychology: Use of evidence in psychology
   _____ Collect and use scientific evidence in drawing conclusions regarding research areas and/or behavioral concerns in a subfield of psychology.
   _____ Evaluate the quality, objectivity, and credibility of scientific evidence in drawing conclusions relative to a psychological subfield.
11. Critical thinking skills in psychology: Association skills
   _____ Relate and apply connections between diverse facts and theories in a subfield of psychology.
   _____ Assess the quality of connections between diverse facts and theories in a psychological subfield.
12. Critical thinking skills in psychology: Argumentation skills
   _____ Deduce contradictory and oversimplified arguments based on a growing knowledge of available facts and theories in a subfield of psychology.
   _____ Develop sound, integrated arguments grounded on scientific reasoning and empirical evidence in a psychological subfield.
13. Critical thinking skills in psychology: Detection of errors in psychological reasoning
   _____ Detect, evaluate, and reject claims in a psychological subfield that stem from myths, stereotypes, common fallacies, and poorly supported assertions about behavior and mental processes.
14. Critical thinking skills in psychology: Questioning skills
   _____ Differentiate between poorly defined and well-defined questions in scientifically examining research areas and/or behavioral concerns in a subfield of psychology.
   _____ Evaluate and modify questions to eliminate ambiguity throughout the scientific examination of research areas and/or behavioral concerns in a psychological subfield.
15. Critical thinking skills in psychology: Creativity
   _____ Apply alternative strategies to known protocols in a subfield of psychology.

16. Critical thinking skills in psychology: Problem solving
_____ Appraise the quality of solutions to problems in diverse contexts within a psychological subfield.
_____ Select an optimal problem-solving strategy from multiple alternatives within a subfield of psychology.
17. Application of psychology: Potential for psychology as a change agent
_____ Evaluate the power of psychological strategies to promote positive change (personal, social, and/or organizational) in a psychological subfield.
18. Application of psychology: Major or emerging applied areas in psychology
_____ Determine whether an applied specialty in psychology (major or emerging) can engender a solution for a given psychological problem.
19. Values in psychology: Curiosity
_____ Apply and sustain curiosity in investigating research areas and/or behavioral questions in a psychological subfield.
20. Values in psychology: Skepticism
_____ Differentiate between scientific and pseudoscientific explanations of human behavior in a psychological subfield, comparing the relative value of these explanations.
_____ Maintain rigorous standards related to the quality of scientific evidence in support of behavioral claims in a subfield of psychology.
21. Values in psychology: Tolerance of ambiguity and consideration of human diversity
_____ Analyze behavioral explanations in a psychological subfield with the intent of finding an alternative explanation.
_____ Evaluate explanations in a psychological subfield, with anticipation of complexity, tentativeness, and variability across populations and contexts.
_____ Exhibit sensitivity to issues surrounding human diversity (e.g., power, privilege, discrimination) in relation to the critical examination of a subfield of psychology.

Evaluative criteria and grading rubric: The three evaluative criteria for scoring each group poster presentation are (a) poster content, (b) poster layout, and (c) clarity of presentation. My evaluation is recorded separately from an average class rating obtained from the aggregate total of all students' ratings. Students in each group also rate one another in terms of individual contributions to the group (e.g., individual effort, cooperation, dedication to teamwork), with the group's average used for scoring purposes. My rating of each student's reflective essay also factors into that student's overall grade for the assignment.

All evaluative criteria are weighted equally in calculating the cumulative grade for each student. In arriving at this grade, I collapse all evaluative information (including a concise summary of particularly pertinent or consistently cited narrative feedback) onto a master rubric that I distribute to each respective student in the class. The master grading rubric, including a scheme for converting rubric point totals to grade-level percentages, appears in Figure 8.3.

Evaluative criteria: *4 = Outstanding*   *3 = Proficient*   *2 = Basic*   *1 = Unsatisfactory*

1. Poster content (group)

   Instructor _____   _____   _____ _____

   Average class
   rating _____   _____   _____ _____

2. Poster layout (group)

   Instructor _____   _____   _____ _____

   Average class
   rating _____   _____   _____ _____

3. Clarity of presentation (group)

   Instructor _____   _____   _____ _____

   Average class
   rating _____   _____   _____ _____

4. Contribution to group (group)

   Average
   within-group
   rating _____   _____   _____ _____

5. Reflective essay (individual)

   Instructor _____   _____   _____ _____

Total score = _____ / 32 points = _____ %

Summary of evaluative feedback: _____

_____

_____

Converting rubric point totals to grade-level percentages (A = 90–100%, B = 80–89%, C = 70–79%, D = 60–69%, and F = below 60%):

32 points = 100%	23 points = 72%	14 points = 44%	5 points = 16%
31 points = 97%	22 points = 69%	13 points = 41%	4 points = 13%
30 points = 94%	21 points = 66%	12 points = 38%	3 points = 9%
29 points = 91%	20 points = 63%	11 points = 34%	2 points = 6%
28 points = 88%	19 points = 59%	10 points = 31%	1 point = 3%
27 points = 84%	18 points = 56%	9 points = 28%	0 points = 0%
26 points = 81%	17 points = 53%	8 points = 25%	
25 points = 78%	16 points = 50%	7 points = 22%	
24 points = 75%	15 points = 47%	6 points = 19%	

Figure 8.3. Master grading rubric for group poster presentations.

EXHIBIT 8.3
Applying Authentic Assessment to the Scored Discussion

Levels of student proficiency: Developing and advanced

Course: History and systems of psychology

Assignment: Scored discussion

Instructional context: Inviting student participation in class discussion is typically considered an integral component of successful pedagogy. Class discussion can stimulate cognitive growth as students exercise their abilities to listen actively and think critically (Dixon, 2000; S. M. Miller, 1997). Nevertheless, many college instructors feel varying degrees of concern with balancing quantity and quality of classroom discussions. This concern is readily transferable to spontaneous or planned class discussions that accompany teaching history and systems of psychology, in which diverse content and divergent viewpoints often push students toward the interactive exchange of ideas.

Purpose of the assignment: I score class discussions to improve their quality while at the same time allowing students to engage in productive classroom conversations without overreliance on the instructor. The *scored discussion* is an incentive-based system, blending discussion with authentic assessment, which helps to formatively shape classroom interaction toward favorable student involvement (Frazier, 1997). Relying on basic principles of Skinnerian operant conditioning, the scored discussion involves assigning students "credits" for positive contributions and "debits" for negative contributions to classroom dialogue.

In the scored discussion, students direct their questions and comments to one another rather than to the instructor, who instead acts as a discussion facilitator. Rather than serving in a primary or controlling role, the instructor simply asks students to clarify their remarks or subtly moves the group along when a new topic or question is warranted. As a general rule, limited instructor involvement translates into greater learning gains when students ask and answer each other's questions and test out new ideas in the face of peer feedback (Woolfolk, 1998).

Instructional methodology: In the present assignment, I use the scored discussion in the context of a relatively small course (20 students) in history and systems of psychology (Mayo, 2002b). The course consists of three units, broken down as follows (see Hunt, 1993): (a) philosophical/prescientific psychology, (b) the burgeoning years of scientific psychology, and (c) psychology's contemporary subfields. A total of 12 whole-class discussions (4 per unit) occur throughout the term. Overall, class participation is worth 10% of each student's final course grade, weighed equally across the three units.

At the beginning of the term, I instruct students on the precise nature of positive and negative contributions to class discussion. During the ebb and flow of classroom dialogue, I assign one point for making a relevant comment, presenting factual information, taking a stand on an issue, drawing a classmate into the discussion, and/or asking a clarifying question. I award two points for demonstrating critical thinking (e.g., providing applied illustrations, drawing analogies, relating perspectives). Conversely, I subtract one point for making an irrelevant comment, distracting or interrupting others, engaging in a personal attack, monopolizing conversation, refusing to speak when addressed, and/or not paying attention.

On the basis of Zola's (1992) suggestion, I construct a master scoring checklist (see Figure 8.4) on which to record every student's points. After tallying these points,

(continues)

I distribute a respective summative scoring sheet (see Figure 8.5) to each student during the class period immediately following the last whole-class discussion. The latter scoring instrument represents a modification of McGrath's (1998) use of an individual evaluation form.

Curricular advantages and disadvantages: When gearing the scored discussion toward its maximal utility (Mayo, 2002b, 2005a; Mayo & Schliecker, 2009), classroom discourse is lively and productive as students engage in face-to-face promotive interaction as an important component of a cooperative learning environment (D. W. Johnson, Johnson, & Holubec, 1998). Students demonstrate an understanding that effective communication of well-conceived ideas counts more than simply speaking. Through probing inquiries and perceptive comments, students share their reflective analyses and critique their classmates' expressed perspectives. Students remain open to constructive criticism and tolerant of views that challenge their own. Increasingly, students come to appreciate that cooperation and conflict are inherently related (D. W. Johnson & Johnson, 1995), as they volley between harmonious agreement ("We are like-minded on this issue") and conflict management ("We agree to disagree on this point"). With practice in integrating scored discussions into preselected fibers of a course, classroom discourse holds the potential to progress in a favorable direction that involves a steady ascent in positive point awards to students accompanied by a corresponding decrease in negative point attributions (Mayo, 2002b; Mayo & Schliecker, 2009). Of particular interest is increasing evidence of critical thinking.

In balancing the curricular pros and cons, however, there are also potential costs associated with using the scored discussion (Mayo, 2005a). To begin, as with any classroom approach that veers considerably from conventional practice, there are risks (e.g., fear of failure) concomitant with the scored discussion. In addition, logistics may become a problem when instructors implement the scored discussion in an overly mechanical fashion, focusing more attention on the scoring process than on facilitating meaningful classroom dialogue. One way to possibly sidestep this logistical concern is to use the initial class discussion as a trial run in preparation for subsequent, more formal applications of the technique (Leach, 1992). Although the scored discussion involves an entire class of 20 in the present assignment, instructors also have the option to reduce the number of student participants in the case that whole-class discussion becomes overly difficult to score. When scoring larger groups becomes troublesome, groups of five or six students may constitute a more workable configuration (Frazier, 1997; Mayo & Schliecker, 2009). Instructors may also consider isolating smaller, break-out groups of students in conjunction with follow-up, whole-class discussion (Mayo & Schliecker, 2009).

Learning goals and outcomes:

1. Knowledge base of psychology: Structure of psychology
   _____ Speculate about psychology's continuing evolution and refinement of its subfields.
2. Knowledge base of psychology: Historical perspectives in psychology
   _____ Compare and contrast historical perspectives in psychology.
   _____ Assess the relative importance of psychology's historical perspectives.
   _____ Defend one or more historical perspectives in psychology.

3. Knowledge base of psychology: Contemporary perspectives in psychology
   _____ Compare and contrast the assumptions, methods, and other features of contemporary perspectives in psychology.
   _____ Evaluate the utility of psychology's contemporary perspectives.
   _____ Describe how psychology's contemporary perspectives apply their respective findings to promote human welfare.
4. Knowledge base of psychology: Overarching themes of psychology
   _____ Debate the relative merits of each side of overarching historical themes in psychology, including nature versus nurture, mind versus body, variability versus continuity of behavior within and across species, free will versus determinism, and subjectivity versus objectivity.
   _____ Evaluate the appropriateness of competing explanations of behavior and mental processes from the standpoint of overarching themes throughout psychology's history.
5. Knowledge base of psychology: General content domains of psychology
   _____ Analyze, evaluate, and synthesize concepts, theories, and research in the general content domains of psychology (learning and cognition, individual and sociocultural differences, biological bases of behavior and mental processes, and life-span development) while focusing on socio-historical and contextual variables.
6. Research methods in psychology: Body of evidence
   _____ Analyze similarities and differences across related research studies—especially the classic investigations that pervade the chronological development of psychology's subfields (e.g., social psychology).
7. Research methods in psychology: Sociocultural context
   _____ Apply sociocultural context to research-based conclusions that have helped to shape the historical development of psychology as a scientific field.
8. Research methods in psychology: Limits of scientific reasoning and evidence
   _____ Justify the evolving nature of scientific findings throughout psychology's history.
9. Critical thinking skills in psychology: Use of evidence in psychology
   _____ Evaluate the quality, objectivity, and credibility of the anecdotal and scientific evidence used in formulating intellectual perspectives throughout psychology's history.
10. Critical thinking skills in psychology: Association skills
    _____ Relate connections between diverse facts and theories throughout psychology's history.
    _____ Assess the quality of connections between diverse facts and theories over the historical evolution of psychology while emphasizing sociohistorical and contextual variables.
11. Critical thinking skills in psychology: Argumentation skills
    _____ Deduce contradictory and oversimplified arguments throughout psychology's history based on an ever-expanding knowledge base in the discipline.
12. Critical thinking skills in psychology: Detection of errors in psychological reasoning
    _____ Detect, evaluate, and reject historical perspectives in psychology that arise from myths, stereotypes, common fallacies, and poorly supported assertions.

(continues)

13. Critical thinking skills in psychology: Questioning skills
    _____ Distinguish between poorly defined and well-defined questions serving as centerpieces for competing historical perspectives in psychology.
14. Application of psychology: Psychological tests
    _____ Differentiate between effective and less effective testing methods throughout psychology's history and reflect on whether these methods take into account respect for alternative cultures and gender.
15. Values in psychology: Curiosity
    _____ Apply and sustain curiosity with regard to topical concerns examined throughout psychology's history.
16. Values in psychology: Skepticism
    _____ Distinguish between scientific and pseudoscientific explanations of human behavior throughout psychology's history, comparing and contrasting the relative value of these explanations.
17. Values in psychology: Tolerance of ambiguity and consideration of human diversity
    _____ Evaluate competing explanations of human behavior over psychology's historical evolution, with anticipation that these explanations are complex, tentative, and variable across populations and sociohistorical contexts.

Evaluative criteria and grading schemes: To receive a letter grade of A (90%–100%) for participating in each class discussion, a student must earn 12 or more total points; B (80–89%), 8 to 11 total points; C (70%–79%), 4 to 7 total points; D (60%–69%), 1 to 3 total points; and F (below 60%), 0 or negative total points. I use an adaptation of Leach's (1992) general scoring framework—designed to conduct normative comparisons of student performance—to convert letter grades into numerical scores. I assign a score of 100% to the highest average over 12 points and then use that score as a standard of comparison with respect to other letter-grade A point totals. Similarly, I relate letter-grade B point totals to the high score of 89% in that grade category, letter-grade C point totals to the high score of 79%, letter-grade D point totals to the high score of 69%, and letter-grade F point totals to the high score of 59%.

An alternative grading scheme involves transforming total point tallies into a predetermined number of bonus points for each scored discussion (Mayo & Schliecker, 2009). As an example, a student must earn 12 or more total points to receive 4 bonus points, 8 to 11 total points for 3 bonus points, 4 to 7 total points for 2 bonus points, 1 to 3 total points for 1 bonus point, and 0 or negative total points for 0 bonus points. This approach typically translates into a less threatening application of the scored discussion for those students who are naturally uncomfortable speaking in a group.

Note. The description of the grading system is from "Dialogue as Constructivist Pedagogy: Probing the Minds of Psychology's Greatest Contributors," by J. A. Mayo, 2002b, *Journal of Constructivist Psychology, 15,* p. 296. Copyright by Taylor & Francis. Adapted with permission.

Legend for positive behaviors:

1 = Making a relevant comment (+1)   4 = Drawing a classmate into the
                                          discussion (+1)

2 = Presenting factual information (+1)   5 = Asking a clarifying question (+1)

3 = Taking a stand on an issue (+1)   6 = Demonstrating critical thinking (+2)

Place a mark in the appropriate column each time the corresponding positive behavior is shown.

Student's name	Positive behaviors					
	1	2	3	4	5	6
1. _____	___	___	___	___	___	___
2. _____	___	___	___	___	___	___
3. _____	___	___	___	___	___	___

Legend for negative behaviors:

1 = Making an irrelevant comment (−1)   4 = Monopolizing conversation (−1)

2 = Distracting or interrupting others (−1)   5 = Refusing to speak when
                                                   addressed (−1)

3 = Engaging in a personal attack (−1)   6 = Not paying attention (−1)

Place a mark in the appropriate column each time the corresponding negative behavior is shown.

Student's name	Negative behaviors					
	1	2	3	4	5	6
1. _____	___	___	___	___	___	___
2. _____	___	___	___	___	___	___
3. _____	___	___	___	___	___	___

Figure 8.4. Abbreviated version of a master scoring checklist for the scored discussion. From "Dialogue as Constructivist Pedagogy: Probing the Minds of Psychology's Greatest Contributors," by J. A. Mayo, 2002b, *Journal of Constructivist Psychology, 15,* pp. 302–303. Copyright by Taylor & Francis. Reprinted with permission

Student's name: _____ Discussion number: _____ Date: _____

The number of points earned for each of the following behaviors appears below.

Positive behaviors:

1. Making a relevant comment (+1)   = _____
2. Presenting factual information (+1)   = _____
3. Taking a stand on an issue (+1)   = _____
4. Drawing a classmate into the discussion (+1) = _____
5. Asking a clarifying question (+1)   = _____
6. Demonstrating critical thinking (+2)   = _____

Positive point total = _____

Negative behaviors:

1. Making an irrelevant comment (−1)   = _____
2. Distracting or interrupting others (−1)   = _____
3. Engaging in a personal attack (−1)   = _____
4. Monopolizing conversation (−1)   = _____
5. Refusing to speak when addressed (−1)   = _____
6. Not paying attention (−1)   = _____

Negative point total = _____

Overall point total = _____

Evaluative comments: _____

_____

_____

_____

Figure 8.5. Summative scoring sheet for individual participants in the scored discussion. From "Dialogue as Constructivist Pedagogy: Probing the Minds of Psychology's Greatest Contributors," by J. A. Mayo, 2002b, *Journal of Constructivist Psychology, 15,* p. 304. Copyright by Taylor & Francis. Reprinted with permission.

IV

WHAT'S NEXT?

9

CONSTRUCTIVISM MEETS INSTRUCTIONAL TECHNOLOGY

Technology has always influenced education, from the printing press permitting textbooks to be created, to the television informing large audiences, to hypermedia affording opportunities to browse information in a nonlinear fashion (Matusevich, 1995). The growth of the World Wide Web and browser technology since the 1990s has sparked resurgent interest in the classroom use of technological innovations (Lievrouw, 2001; R. A. Reiser, 2002). As the technological landscape in education continues to grow markedly, the obvious question arises, "How can teachers most effectively incorporate technology into their instructional practices?" A productive place to begin in answering this question is to examine the connection between constructivism and instructional technology. The constructivism–computer relationship exists because technology

> facilitates communication, allowing students to present their beliefs and products to broader audiences, and also exposes them to the opinions of a more diverse group of people in the real world beyond the classroom, school and local community—all conditions optimal for constructivist learning. (Becker, as cited in Carvin, 2004, ¶ 2)

Moreover, constructivist educational theory offers a set of guiding principles to assist teachers in creating "learner-centered, collaborative environments that support reflective and experiential processes" (Jonassen, Davidson, Collins, Campbell, & Haag, 1995).

TECHNOLOGY'S ROLE IN CONSTRUCTIVIST LEARNING

In today's ever-changing, technology-enhanced classroom environments where technologies serve as gateways for delivering instruction, the educational focus should still remain on learning rather than on the technologies themselves (Campoy, 1992). Paramount to the day-to-day dynamics of a constructivist classroom, it is not what equipment is used but how it is used to promote learning that bears greatest significance for academic success (Strommen & Lincoln, 1992). Constructivism supplants the traditional view of instructional technologies as passive conveyors of knowledge, replacing it with the view that learners play an active and interactive role in using computers as cognitive tools in learning, researching, networking, collaborating, and problem solving (Lajoie, 2000; Nanjappa & Grant, 2003; Swain & Pearson, 2001). Consistent with McGovern's analysis of the "'cut-and-paste' approach some [of today's students] take to assembling information [that] undercuts their full understanding of it," constructivism advocates that "'digital natives' . . . deal with information literacy to not just navigate, but evaluate information" (as cited in Munsey, 2008, p. 55).

According to Barr (1990), learning should be independent, individualized, and interactive to assume a meaningful quality. In comparing more traditional didactic classroom environments with those that emphasize learner–computer interaction, several observable shifts are consistent with the elements of such meaningful learning (Collins, 1991; Lynch, 1997; Matusevich, 1995):

- from how information is received, stored, and recalled to how knowledge is constructed by students;
- from passive involvement to active engagement of students;
- from competition to cooperation;
- from whole-class to small-group instruction;
- from verbal thinking alone to the integration of audiovisual and verbal thinking through exploration of sounds, images, and text;
- from lecture and recitation to intelligent tutoring systems and multimedia software that rely on coaching and modeling components as learning tasks increase in difficulty; and
- from all students learning the same material to students learning different information.

On the basis of these classroom transformations, there exists a complementary relationship between proper use of interactive, user-friendly computer technologies and appropriate applications of constructivist learning principles, with implementation of each one benefiting the other (Nanjappa & Grant, 2003). In particular, both educational technologies and constructivism call attention to the creation of diverse knowledge-building learning venues. Like the learning environments produced in technology-mediated classrooms where instructional technologies are used effectively as heuristic aids, constructivist learning expounds on the natural curiosities of students by actively engaging them in cooperative learning and creative problem solving that emphasize multiple perspectives of analysis (Driscoll, 2000; Grabinger, Dunlap, & Heath, 1993). These multiple modes of representation, in turn, allow learners to "revisit the same material, at different times, in rearranged contexts, for different purposes, and from different conceptual perspectives . . . [toward the aim of] attaining the goals of advanced knowledge acquisition" (Spiro, Feltovich, Jacobson, & Coulson, 1991, p. 28).

One of the foundations of constructivist learning is for students to experience a wide array of real-world tasks, such as those encountered in case- or story-based instruction (Jonassen, 1991; Wilson & Cole, 1991). New and emerging instructional technologies allow students to access raw data, primary sources, and interactive materials that push them toward authentic task performance (Brooks & Brooks, 1993). Additionally, in a constructivist educational setting, assessment should be context dependent and outcomes should be based on established performance standards (Jonassen, 1991). With a shared emphasis on authentic learning experiences, constructivism and educational technologies are able to converge in assessing student learning. For example, the digital artifacts that students systematically organize and collect through electronic portfolios can be used to demonstrate and assess learning at the course, program, department, and institutional levels (Lorenzo & Ittelson, 2005). By means of hyperlink, electronic portfolios also allow for ease of comparability between selected portfolio items and learning outcomes (Barrett, 1997a, 1997b), which facilitates learners' metacognitive reflections as a bridge between instruction and assessment (Arter & Spandel, 1992).

In summarizing the results of educational technology research from the late 1980s through 2000, there are various instances in which the instructional advantages of technology and constructivism clearly overlap (see Software and Information Industry Association, 2000). To begin, software that includes embedded cognitive strategies (e.g., constructing cognitive maps, drawing analogical inferences, using advanced organizers in computer simulations) can benefit students academically. Software with embedded conceptual-change features can also help students to sequence their learning from faulty preconceptions to increasingly accurate conceptual understandings. In addition, software that utilizes instructional scaffolding (i.e., gradually decreasing tutorial assistance and/or increasing task complexity) can enhance student achievement. Moreover, online classes not only increase involvement for some students who participate sparsely in face-to-face class discussions but also bolster collaboration across classrooms in different geographical locations.

As an abundant resource of information that grows and responds to human participation, the Internet also serves as a powerful constructivist learning platform (Ryder, 1994). Unlike a more traditional library, the Internet is a virtual library that acts as

> a potent environment for generative learning where participants, through interaction, add value to the resources they exploit . . . [and wherein] the flexibility of collaborative environments provides scaffolding for learners in times of rapid change where standard instructional approaches can be less than adequate. (Ryder, 1994, ¶ 1)

A constructivist, Internet-supported, higher education environment permits learners to solve challenging problems, seek and acquire guidance from experts, and promote knowledge development (Tsai, 2008). By using the Internet in ways that supersede the mere accessing of isolated, noninte-grated bits of information, individuals can participate in active knowledge construction as self-directed learners (Jonassen, Mayes, & McAleese, 1992). Consistent with Wittgenstein's (1921/1981) philosophical argument that knowledge formation as a whole grows out of independent iterations of knowledge, knowledge in cyberspace can be represented by hypertext indexes, home-page directories, and other coherent links to knowledge representations (Ryder, 1994).

Theoretical support for the connection between social and Internet-anchored knowledge construction can be traced to Pask's (1975, 1976) *conversation theory*. According to Pask, knowledge construction occurs as people freely engage in dialogue for learning purposes. New knowledge arises through a dialectical process in which individuals compare and contrast personally held conceptions with those of others until agreement, or public knowledge, is reached. Similar to collaborative knowledge construction that takes place via the Internet, this burgeoning database of learner-initiated public knowledge is subject to growth and modification as people continue to interact with one another in reflective dialogue.

What role should educators play in contemporary constructivist-centered and technology-enhanced classrooms? In these learning environments, teachers should serve as facilitators in breeding the social and intellectual climates necessary for students to actively and interactively construct knowledge (Witfelt, 2000). As captured succinctly in the words of Rakes, Flowers, Casey, and Santana (1999), "Technology can provide the vehicle for accomplishing constructivist teaching practices" (p. 3). Within the executive summary of its research report on the effectiveness of technology in educational settings, the Software and Information Industry Association (2000) endorsed the use of technology in support of constructivist instructional methodologies:

> Introducing technology into the learning environment has been shown to make learning more individualized and student-centered, to encourage cooperative learning and to stimulate increased teacher-student interaction. Technology has been used successfully to support constructivist, inquiry-based and project-based instructional methods. (p. 7)

Of special relevance for using the Internet to foster learning is the issue of developing students' skills in communications and information literacy (November, 2001). With communications literacy, students learn the grammar of the Internet for how to validate the authenticity of authors and information that they locate on the Web. In complementary fashion, information literacy requires that students learn how and where to research on the Web, how to judge the quality of their findings, and how to apply these findings to in- and out-of-class learning assignments (Meadows, 2003). Educators can teach their students to be discriminating users of Web-derived information through the constructivist-oriented teaching practice of guided research and problem solving (Meadows, 2003; November, 2001). In this pedagogical approach, students move progressively toward communications and information literacy with subtle instructor-provided coaching and modeling.

Scott Noon, director of the Connected University at Classroom Connect (an online professional development resource for educators), offered a four-stage developmental model for building teachers' technological efficacy (see Jackson, 1999; McKenzie, 2000). According to McKenzie (2000), teachers can progress rapidly through the first three stages as they increase their skill set for using technology to bolster student achievement. However, attaining the final stage requires considerable teacher reflection and relearning that culminate in the development of technologically savvy constructivist educators who use technology to maximize student learning. The sequential stages in Noon's model are as follows.

1. *Stage 1: Preliterate end-users.* Although educators in this initial stage are aware of available instructional technologies, they possess virtually no experience with computers and little interest in becoming literate in using instructional technologies. Only by convincing these educators of the immediate value of technology in their own classrooms (e.g., more efficient use of time, more rapid teacher–student communication, greater ease of record keeping) will they see the need to advance through the remaining stages in the model.

2. *Stage 2: Software technicians.* Software technicians are sensitized to the utility of integrating technology into curricula predicated on the fact that they presently use common software applications (e.g., word processing, e-mail, Web surfing) to meet their own personal needs.

3. *Stage 3: Electronic traditionalists.* These educators have already successfully incorporated technology into traditional classroom functions (e.g., electronic grading programs, multimedia-supported content delivery, digital instructional resources), but the task remains for them to build on these prior successes by enhancing their proficiency in more advanced uses of technology (e.g., distance learning, virtual simulations and field trips, collaborative online projects).

4. *Stage 4: Techno-constructivists.* Techno-constructivist educators have moved beyond uses of technology to merely complement instruction. Rather, technology serves to redefine curricula in a manner consistent with constructivist learning theory. Within this entirely new instructional framework, students establish connections between learning activities through extrapolating from their own experiences, constructing their own personally meaningful knowledge structures, creating products, and generating solutions to authentic problem-based scenarios across diverse contexts. To enter into the techno-constructivist stage, educators must progress beyond the *expert stage* in Berliner's (1994) paradigm for exemplary teaching performance. Educators accomplish this goal by aligning instruction with a symbiotically blended constructivist- and technology-focused teaching philosophy—either originally founded or subsequently redefined (Meadows, 2003).

CONSTRUCTIONISM: THE HYBRIDIZATION OF CONSTRUCTIVISM

Seymour Papert's groundbreaking work with computers as instruments of learning (Papert, 1980; Papert & Solomon, 1971) has been a precipitating force in the growth of instructional technologies within constructivist classroom environments. One of Piaget's most accomplished protégés, Papert worked with Piaget during the 1960s in Geneva, Switzerland (Johnstone, 2003). In pioneering the concept of artificial intelligence and how technology can afford new ways to learn, Papert built on Piaget's work in constructivist learning theory (Johnstone, 2003; Papert, 1999). *Constructionism*—as

Papert (1987) termed his hybrid learning approach—melds two complementary learning components: (a) a constructivist learning emphasis on actively generating mental representations of the world and (b) a call for experiential learners to construct a meaningful product external to themselves, such as a computer program or its resultant applications (Papert, 1991). Although this "learning-by-making" approach (Papert, 1991, p. 1) has been geared largely to science and mathematics teaching and media studies in the form of inquiry-based science, it holds broader implications that make it applicable to teaching in other disciplines—including psychology.

Constructionism is consistent with the active, student-centered concentration inherent in both cognitive and social constructivism. At the heart of constructionism is the view of teacher-as-mediator who helps and guides students (individually and in groups) in a hands-on discovery process. Through this process, students arrive at their own conclusions by means of constructing concrete or abstract products (Papert, 1987, 1991). With the advent of readily accessible constructing applications on personal computers, constructionism has found a comfortable home in the modern information age. For example, interactive computer applications of the repertory grid (see chap. 6, this volume) are currently available for instructional use in eliciting, interpreting, and comparing students' knowledge structures. One such knowledge management system is WebGrid (Gaines & Shaw, 2009), a free, user-friendly, Web-based application of the repertory grid. As a demonstration of the outcomes of WebGrid grid elicitation and interpretation, I present a sample grid pertaining to key contributors to the early decades of scientific psychology. The data set represents a student's conceptualizations in the context of participating in a history and systems of psychology class that I taught previously. The student completed the conceptual modeling procedures of WebGrid (including online data entry and logical progression through computer-generated grid analyses) as an extra-credit assignment. Figure 9.1 depicts an 8 × 8 × 11 rating-grid display in which the student rates eight bipolar constructs (mind–body, nature–nurture, subjectivism–objectivism, holism–elementalism, free will–determinism, utility–purity, verity–falsity, and major contribution–minor contribution) against eight elements (Wilhelm Wundt, William James, Sigmund Freud, Ivan Pavlov, John B. Watson, B. F. Skinner, Max Wertheimer, and Abraham Maslow) on a series of 11-point Likert-type continua.

Using the data set shown in Figure 9.1, WebGrid offers methods for modeling and visualizing relationships between constructs and elements. As illustrated in Figure 9.2, a cluster analysis technique called FOCUS Clustering affords inferences on whether two constructs are applied similarly to different elements while also depicting how different elements are rated on the same constructs. Additionally, Figure 9.3 reveals the results

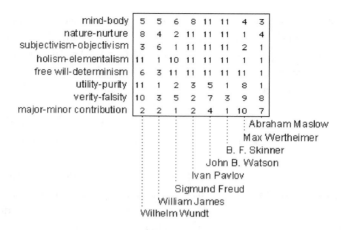

mind-body	5	5	6	8	11	11	4	3
nature-nurture	8	4	2	11	11	11	1	4
subjectivism-objectivism	3	6	1	11	11	11	2	1
holism-elementalism	11	1	10	11	11	11	1	1
free will-determinism	6	3	11	11	11	11	11	1
utility-purity	11	1	2	3	5	1	8	1
verity-falsity	10	3	5	2	7	3	9	8
major-minor contribution	2	2	1	2	4	1	10	7

Abraham Maslow
Max Wertheimer
B. F. Skinner
John B. Watson
Ivan Pavlov
Sigmund Freud
William James
Wilhelm Wundt

Figure 9.1. Sample WebGrid data display. From *Teaching Critical Thinking in Psychology: A Handbook of Best Practices* (p. 132), by D. S. Dunn, J. S. Halonen, and R. A. Smith (Eds.), 2008, London: Blackwell. Copyright 2008 by Blackwell. Reprinted with permission.

of a principal-components analysis known as PrinCom Map, which provides a visual overview of the distribution of constructs and elements in relation to one another.

Internet-based and other interactive technology-mediated constructionist applications hold the potential to move contemporary educators toward

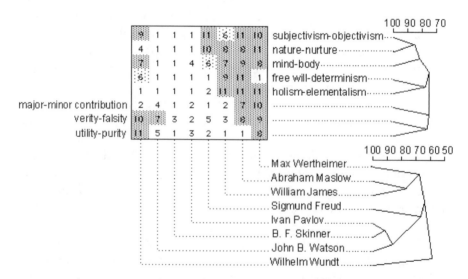

Figure 9.2. Sample WebGrid FOCUS Clustering. From *Teaching Critical Thinking in Psychology: A Handbook of Best Practices* (p. 133), by D. S. Dunn, J. S. Halonen, and R. A. Smith (Eds.), 2008, London: Blackwell. Copyright 2008 by Blackwell. Reprinted with permission.

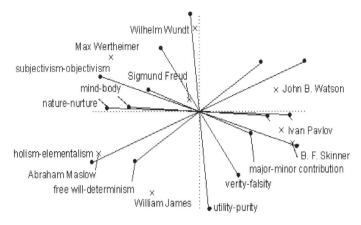

Figure 9.3. Sample WebGrid PrinCom Map. From *Teaching Critical Thinking in Psychology: A Handbook of Best Practices* (p. 133), by D. S. Dunn, J. S. Halonen, and R. A. Smith (Eds.), 2008, London: Blackwell. Copyright 2008 by Blackwell. Reprinted with permission.

a unifying constructivist educational paradigm (Matusevich, 1995). According to Collins (1991), instructional technologies " . . . will eventually foster a shift in society's beliefs toward a more constructivist view of education" (p. 33). However, positive changes in learning environments attributed to an interface of computer technology and constructivism are more evolutionary than revolutionary (Software and Information Industry Association, 2000). Before technology-rich classrooms will more closely approximate the favorable learning outcomes associated with a constructivist approach, students need to further develop their communications and information literacy and teachers must acquire more experience in using instructional technologies to maximize learning benefits.

10

THE FUTURE OF UNDERGRADUATE PSYCHOLOGY EDUCATION

Every year in America since 1995, there have been more than 70,000 new college graduates earning a bachelor's degree in psychology (Snyder & Hoffman, 2003). Along with the number of psychology baccalaureate graduates, enrollment in undergraduate and Advanced Placement (AP) high school psychology courses remains robust in the United States (Belar, 2008; Park & Fineburg, 2008). These contemporary trends in psychology education underlie the view that "designing the best possible psychology curriculum is more important today than ever before" (Munsey, 2008, p. 55). As I turn my attention to the future of undergraduate psychology education, various topics emerge as relevant to effective curriculum programming, including advancing liberal education, psychology's impact on education for other professions, internationalizing curricula, bridging the gap between 2- and 4-year curricula, and new directions for educational reform.

ADVANCING LIBERAL EDUCATION

In providing an overview of the sixth annual Education Leadership Conference (ELC) sponsored by the American Psychological Association

(APA) and convened in 2007, Nelson (2008) discussed the recurring theme of psychology's role in promoting undergraduate liberal education. This theme is predicated on the premise that "education for most, if not all, professions builds on an undergraduate foundation of a liberal education" (Nelson, 2008, p. 6). As defined by the Association of American Colleges and Universities (AAC&U)—the national organization representing colleges and universities—a liberal education is a "philosophy of education that empowers individuals with broad knowledge and transferable skills, and a strong sense of values, ethics, and civic engagement" (AAC&U, 2008b, ¶ 1). According to AAC&U President Carol Geary Schneider (2008), "America's tradition of providing a liberal education to students at the college level . . . is more important than ever in this turbulent global era" (p. 1). Reflected in the learning goals and outcomes of the APA *Guidelines for the Undergraduate Psychology Major* (APA, 2007), the undergraduate psychology major has embraced the value of a liberal education through knowledge, skills, and values taught in psychology curricula that are consonant with liberal arts education. In the words of Robin Hailstorks, associate executive director and director of precollege and undergraduate programs in the APA Education Directorate, "AAC&U and APA share a similar vision for what college graduates need to know in the 21st century in order to be successful" (as cited in Clay, 2008, p. 56).

In her 2007 ELC presentation, "Liberal Education and the Disciplines We Need Now," Schneider outlined the competencies that American college and university graduates must possess to ensure competitiveness in the global economy and information age (as cited in Nelson, 2008). These competencies are embodied in the following learning outcomes that are essential for all undergraduates (AAC&U, 2007, p. 3):

- knowledge of human cultures and the physical and natural world through study in the sciences and mathematics, social sciences, humanities, history, languages, and the arts;
- intellectual and practical skills, including inquiry and analysis, critical and creative thinking, written and oral communication, quantitative literacy, information literacy, and teamwork and problem solving;
- personal and social responsibility, including civic knowledge and engagement (local and global), intercultural knowledge and competence, ethical reasoning and action, and foundations and skills for lifelong learning; and
- integrative learning, including synthesis and advanced accomplishment across general and specialized studies.

As Schneider (as cited in Nelson, 2008) noted, however, the empirical evidence shows a disconnection between what students deem to be the most important goals for their undergraduate education and what employers demand for employment success. Recent employer surveys suggest that baccalaureate degree graduates in America are particularly ill-prepared to face the challenges of the workplace in the areas of global knowledge, self-direction, writing, and critical thinking (AAC&U, 2008a). To address this issue, the AAC&U designed their learning outcomes to be more consistently aligned with employers' expectations of our college graduates. These outcomes are accompanied by principles of excellence that include recommendations to connect knowledge with choices and actions and to assess students' abilities to apply learning in complex real-world problem scenarios (AAC&U, 2007). The AAC&U learning outcomes and principles rise to an even greater level of significance when considering the fact that over 1 million academically underprepared students enter higher education each year in need of remedial education (McCabe, 2000).

To further identify psychology's role in advancing an undergraduate liberal education, discussion groups at the 2007 ELC explored ways to improve learning experiences and assessment of student learning in undergraduate psychology (Nelson, 2008). Discussions veered into two distinct directions: (a) issues related to the introductory psychology course and (b) questions pertaining to the undergraduate psychology major.

Because introductory psychology is a heavily enrolled general education course and the only psychology offering many U.S. undergraduate students will complete, this course affords an excellent opportunity to inform undergraduates about psychology as a scientific discipline with many pragmatic applications (Nelson, 2008). In chronicling the discussions about introductory psychology, Nelson (2008) reported that ELC participants addressed pedagogy and assessment of student learning within this course as it relates to producing AAC&U learning outcomes for a liberal education. Although discussants concluded that the introductory psychology course may not need to be restructured, they cited substantial challenges in satisfying all AAC&U learning outcomes in this or any single course in an undergraduate psychology curriculum. However, discussants agreed that the introductory psychology course can canvas a predetermined subset of these outcomes, depending on the challenges faced. At the top of this list of challenges is the extensive breadth of topics typically covered in a semester-long introductory psychology class. Many times faculty must pick and choose among topics for effective student learning based on the relevance of psychological principles to students' lives and the problems observed in the surrounding world. Another concern involves the sheer number of introductory psychology textbooks available for adoption, each demonstrating differences in topical emphases and content organization. Compounding the multitude of available textbooks is the appreciable diversity of faculty who teach this course, from least to most experienced and from those employed in community colleges, 4-year liberal arts colleges, and undergraduate programs in large research universities. Along with a diverse faculty, there is accompanying diversity in the student population taking introductory psychology. Some students complete only this course, others enroll in additional psychology courses but are not psychology majors, and still others are psychology majors. Finally, the learning objectives that faculty adopt for introductory psychology often vary considerably from the expectations that students have when enrolling in this course. Faculty members ordinarily view psychology as an empirically grounded science- and service-centered discipline, whereas their students may emphasize pop psychology because their prior knowledge (subject to influence by misinformation in the popular press) is a prominent factor affecting their learning in this course (Thompson & Zamboanga, 2003).

In considering the types of pedagogical approaches that may generate AAC&U learning outcomes, ELC discussants recommended greater attention to problem-oriented over topic-oriented pedagogy, generalizable principles over retention of detailed facts, critical thinking over rote memory, and active student engagement over passive involvement in learning (Nelson, 2008). Even though discussants did not go as far as to offer specific instructional techniques, their recommendations bear striking resemblance to the learning goals and outcomes linked to constructivist classroom strategies presented throughout this book. These constructivist approaches include case-based instruction (chap. 4, this volume), autobiographical and biographical narration (chap. 5), concept mapping and the repertory grid (chap. 6), analogical reasoning (chap. 7), and cooperative learning assignments (chap. 8).

With respect to assessing AAC&U learning outcomes, ELC discussants acknowledged special considerations associated with evaluating student learning in any survey course, particularly when it involves large enrollments (Nelson, 2008). Mindful of these considerations, discussants opted in favor of "ways of examining critical thinking skills and obtaining more substantive feedback from students regarding what they have learned and their assessment of the learning process" (Nelson, 2008, p. 9). To satisfy these assessment objectives, faculty may consider the stance adopted in this book that involves embedded authentic assessments cast in the light of constructivist pedagogical applications and a developmentally appropriate curriculum model. Because this approach stresses assessment of knowledge, skills, and values applicable to any course within and across undergraduate psychology curricula, it should prove useful in meeting the challenges of assessing student learning in introductory psychology within a culture of "owning an outcome" as opposed to "owning a course." However, for the present developmental model (see Tables 1A.1–1A.5 of Appendix 1.1 in chap. 1 of this volume) to be used in conjunction with AAC&U learning outcomes, it must be extended to take into account the last five learning goals articulated in the *APA Guidelines* (APA, 2007). As presented next, these goal statements relate to knowledge, skills, and values enveloped within undergraduate psychology curricula that tie to the collective aims of a liberal education.

> *Goal 6: Information and technological literacy*
> Students will demonstrate information competence and the ability to use computers and other technology for many purposes.
> *Goal 7: Communication skills*
> Students will be able to communicate effectively in a variety of formats.
> *Goal 8: Sociocultural and international awareness*
> Students will recognize, understand, and respect the complexity of sociocultural and international diversity.
> *Goal 9: Personal development*
> Students will develop insight into their own and others' behavior and mental processes and apply effective strategies for self-management and self-improvement.
> *Goal 10: Career planning and development*
> Students will emerge from the major with realistic ideas about how to implement their psychological knowledge, skills, and values in occupational pursuits in a variety of settings. (see APA, 2007, pp. 17–21)

Psychology represents one of the most popular undergraduate majors among arts and sciences disciplines (Belar, 2008). For the first time in history, the latest data available show that more than 90,000 U.S. students received a psychology bachelor's degree in 2006–2007 (Snyder, Dillow, & Hoffman, 2009). Turning attention from the introductory psychology course to the growing undergraduate major, ELC discussants recognized that 75% of bachelor's degree graduates in psychology forego graduate training in psychology or other disciplines for direct entry into the workforce (Nelson, 2008). Within this framework, discussants cited strengths of the psychology major as relevant in satisfying the goals of a liberal education while at the same time readying students for the global economy and increasing their level of marketability (Nelson, 2008). The psychology major holds the potential to teach students to think critically, reason quantitatively, and write effectively—all of which are marketable skills that translate into educated citizen consumers and employees in the workforce. Learning to use computer technology to augment critical thinking and analytical competencies in practice (e.g., using technology to conduct a sound literature review) further bolsters the skill set expected of psychology majors in this modern information era. Despite the identifiable strengths of the psychology major, some discussants favored more opportunities for service learning, civic engagement, and applications of psychology to different occupational fields as desirable components of undergraduate psychology education (Nelson, 2008). In offering ways to enhance psychology undergraduates' learning experiences and assessment of student learning, some ELC discussants argued against the compartmentalization of psychology at undergraduate institutions across the country—often resulting from differing departmental concentrations and faculty research interests (Nelson, 2008). To address this concern, discussants recommended establishing integrative learning communities within psychology and across disciplines, along with interdisciplinary courses for psychology majors.

PSYCHOLOGY'S IMPACT ON EDUCATION FOR OTHER PROFESSIONS

The intellectual roots of psychology as a scientific discipline can be traced to philosophy and the natural and physical sciences, including biology, anatomy and physiology, and physics (Robinson, 1995). Twentieth-century pioneers in the field of psychology acknowledged its relevance to other professions and the many facets of economic and social life in America (Fancher, 1996; Hilgard, 1987).

In the early 1900s, William James, John Dewey, and Edward Thorndike applied learning theory to what would be called educational psychology (Lundin, 1996). Around the same time, the experimentally based work of Hugo Munsterberg in industrial–organizational psychology (Moskowitz, 1977) and Walter Dill Scott in advertising psychology (Hunt, 1993) opened the door for applying psychology in the business world. Early contributors to forensic psychology included J. McKeen Cattell and William Marston, who performed groundbreaking investigations into the psychology of testimony (Bartol & Bartol, 2005).

By the mid-1900s, psychology's significance to other professions grew even larger (Nelson, 2008). For example, Alan Turing's landmark treatise on the philosophy of artificial intelligence catapulted psychology to prominence in the burgeoning discipline of computer science (Boeree, 2006). In recognition of psychology's expanding role in applying its principles to other disciplines and in educating people for other professions, one of the first committees formed in 1951 by the newly established APA Education and Training Board pertained to psychology's impact on other professional schools (Nelson & Stricker, 1992).

Over the past half century, more psychology-trained professionals have pursued primary employment in nonacademic settings, and psychologists now constitute an increasing number of faculty members in colleges and academic departments that prepare students for professions other than psychology (Nelson, 2002, 2008). For instance, estimates show a nearly twentyfold increase in the number of psychologists academically employed in medical schools compared with 50 years ago (Mensch, 1953; S. Williams, Wicherski, & Kohout, 1998). However, psychology educators have devoted a paucity of attention to the noteworthy shifts in academic outcomes that should accompany these momentous changes in employment settings for contemporary psychologists (Nelson, 2008).

A central focus of the 2007 ELC was to address psychology's impact on education for other professions. Nelson (2008) reported on the outcomes of ELC panel discussions regarding psychology's present and future roles in preparing professionals for work in fields outside of psychology. Discussants were doctoral-trained psychologists academically employed in colleges for other professions. Common themes springing from the discussions included psychology's contributions to education for other professions through its knowledge of human cognitive and socioemotional processes and its approaches to identifying, analyzing, and solving problems. Among the challenges faced by psychology in contributing to education for other professions, discussants cited the uneven undergraduate exposure to psychology courses, general hesitance of psychology faculty to participate in interdisciplinary teaching and research, and perceived irrelevance (outside the psychological community) of psychological research to other professions in the context of cultures and practices. In summarizing discussants' concerns, Nelson (2008) stated, "to the extent that psychology [education] remains relatively insular . . . from education for other professions . . . it is likely to become increasingly marginalized in its contributions to those areas" (p. 13). As a partial remedy at the undergraduate level, discussants arrived at the conclusion that psychology faculty should better inform students about psychology's role in other professions and more effectively translate psychological knowledge into information of noteworthy significance to other professions.

The demand for psychologists in program evaluation, working with older adults, and government service has expanded in recent decades (DeAngelis, 2008). These trends provide evidence that the breadth and adaptability of psychology's knowledge base in human behavior is recognized and embraced by an increasing number of other professions. Experts predict that there will also be an escalating number of international applications of psychology to reflect shifting patterns of globalization (DeAngelis, 2008). For example, industrial–organizational psychologists continue to focus more attention on cross-cultural issues grounded in communications and organizational culture. According to APA Executive Director for Science Steven Breckler, there is a growing inclination toward multidisciplinary research and applications, with psychology serving as the hub science linked to a broad array of social, behavioral, mathematical, and biological sciences (as cited in DeAngelis, 2008).

Using the complementary premises that psychological principles are applicable to other disciplines and that knowledge acquired in one course may transfer to others, Schaab (2008) argued in favor of establishing learning communities involving psychology courses as a way to help undergraduate learners "'connect the dots' by clarifying the interrelationships between seemingly different fields of study" (p. 3). In learning communities, two or more courses (including course content and student learning outcomes) are clustered around an interdisciplinary theme and enroll a common cohort of students (B. L. Smith, MacGregor, Matthews, & Gabelnick, 2004). Although typically developed for 1st-year students, learning communities can also act as alternative pathways in general education and minor and major studies (Washington Center for Improving the Quality of Undergraduate Education, 2003). Interactive and peer-supported academic tasks within learning communities afford students viable opportunities to accommodate new learning (Cross, 1998). With shared knowledge and responsibility as common elements in learning community programs (Tinto, 2000), improvements in critical thinking, self-understanding, and interpersonal interaction are beneficial byproducts of the cooperative activities and discussion groups taking place within these programs (Lipka, 2007). As a means of actively engaging students and connecting course content across a wide range of disciplines, learning communities continue to expand in number in colleges and universities throughout the United States (Lange, 2007; MacGregor & Smith, 2005; Montecino & Crouch, 1997; Tu, 2004). This expansion includes computer-mediated distance learning communities and living learning programs of college freshmen who share similar academic interests or schedules and live together in the same residence halls. Although the development of learning communities has become a growing national movement for more than 2 decades, on most American college and university campuses—even those where learning communities have been in place for years—learning community programs exist today as fragile entities (B. L. Smith, 2001). Thus, there is considerable room for the learning community concept to reach its full potential in undergraduate curricula, with psychology situated centrally among the participating disciplines.

INTERNATIONALIZING CURRICULA

Psychology has a long history as an international discipline. This fact is reflected in the convening of the First International Congress of Psychology in 1887 (APA, 2005b). Dating back to early pioneers in psychology—including Wilhelm Wundt, Ivan Pavlov, Max Wertheimer, Sigmund Freud, and Jean Piaget—psychology's knowledge base in science and practice derives partly from international origins (APA, 2005b). As evidence of psychology's growing international prominence, contemporary psychology wields a demonstrative presence in 47 countries around the globe (Adair, Coelho, & Luna, 2002).

Throughout the decades since its inception in 1892, the APA has played a pivotal role in promoting the internationalization of psychology. Although internationalization has been generally underrepresented within existing psychology curricula in the United States (Woolf, Hulsizer, & McCarthy, 2002), the increasing importance of internationalization in the teaching of psychology is highlighted within the *APA Guidelines* (APA, 2007). In this document, "Goal 8: Sociocultural and international awareness" is identified as one of 10 undergraduate psychology learning goals with the following suggested outcomes:

8.1 Interact effectively and sensitively with people from diverse abilities, backgrounds, and cultural perspectives.

8.2 Examine the sociocultural and international contexts that influence individual differences.

8.3 Explain how individual differences influence beliefs, values, and interactions with others and vice versa.

8.4 Understand how privilege, power, and oppression may affect prejudice, discrimination, and inequity.

8.5 Recognize prejudicial attitudes and discriminatory behaviors that might exist in themselves and others.

8.6 Predict how interaction among diverse people can challenge conventional understanding of psychological processes and behavior. (APA, 2007, p. 20)

Similarly, the APA Working Group on Internationalizing the Undergraduate Psychology Curriculum (APA, 2005b, pp. 3–4) recommended the following learning goals:

1. *Psychological knowledge in international perspective.* Students should recognize, acknowledge, and describe sociocultural differences and commonalities between people, and consider how the diversity of human behavior around the world contributes to the study and practice of psychology.

2. *Methodological issues in international research.* Students should be aware of research methods and skills necessary for international research competence.

3. *Discipline of psychology in the international perspective.* Students should be aware of how the discipline of psychology is developed, studied, and applied in and across cultures.

4. *Psychology and interpersonal understanding.* Students should be able to use their psychological knowledge and understanding of cultural differences and behavior to demonstrate skills and values that will help them function effectively in a complex multicultural global world.

5. *Psychology and global issues.* Students should be able to recognize, appreciate, and describe the role that psychological knowledge plays in addressing issues related to the human condition from a global perspective.

As part of an action plan to promote curriculum internationalization, the working group also advocated that these goals and their associated learning outcomes move beyond isolated cross-cultural or multicultural psychology courses to cover the entire gamut of psychology curriculum programming.

Early in 2007, the leadership of APA Division 2 (Society for the Teaching of Psychology) appointed the Task Force on Internationalizing the Teaching of Psychology. As its charge, the group was asked to achieve three interrelated goals: (a) seek collaborations to advance a more global perspective in teaching psychology, (b) ascertain approaches to internationalize undergraduate psychology curricula, and (c) recruit involvement of representatives from other nations in meeting the first two objectives (Velayo, 2008). In light of the overlap between the task force's charge and the central goals of the Curriculum and Training Committee established by APA Division 52 (Division of International Psychology), these two groups have collaborated to sponsor panels and symposia aimed at internationalizing psychology curricula. Another area of intersection between shared initiatives of these two groups relates to compiling and regularly updating a resource of materials centered on curriculum internationalization. These resources include a Web site containing annotated bibliographies for books, chapters, articles, and reports, along with two relevant discussion boards (Velayo, 2008).

Comparable collaborative efforts have been undertaken between APA Division 9 (Society for the Psychological Study of Social Issues) and Division 35 (Society for the Psychology of Women) in sponsoring the Report of the Task Force on Resources for the Inclusion of Social Class in Psychology Curricula (APA, 2008a). This report is intended to enhance diversity considerations in psychology curricula by recognizing socioeconomic status as a variable on par with age, ethnicity, gender, religion, disability, and sexual orientation in defining "marginalized groups." As a new teaching tool designed to encourage the incorporation of social class diversity into psychology education at all levels, available online resources consist of course syllabi, classroom exercises, scholarly books and articles, relevant Web sites, and examples gleaned from fiction and popular media.

Beyond officially sanctioned APA initiatives to internationalize psychology curricula, many psychology departments across the country have embarked on diversity transformation projects over the past decade. The primary emphases of these projects are cross-cultural comparisons as well as diversity awareness and multicultural issues within the United States (Bartolini, Gharib, & Phillips, 2009b; Goldstein, 1995, 2005). In contrast to the development of individual courses steeped in international psychology, more recent American-based efforts have focused on infusing internationalism across undergraduate psychology curricula (Stevens & Wedding, 2004). There are a number of important contemporary considerations in favor of integrating an international perspective throughout undergraduate psychology education, including "globalization, increasing ease of international communication, increasing interest in psychology internationally, the growth of international organizations in psychology, and increasing opportunities for students to work and study internationally" (Bartolini et al., 2009b, ¶ 3). Examples of transforming various undergraduate psychology courses through adding international learning outcomes and assessable assignments can be found in Bartolini, Gharib, and Phillips (2009a; Bartolini et al., 2009b). Refer to Gurung and Prieto (2009) for additional classroom techniques and empirically grounded teaching practices for assimilating diversity into existing psychology courses across educational settings.

BRIDGING THE GAP BETWEEN 2- AND 4-YEAR CURRICULA

As discussed in the opening segments of this volume, the APA Education Directorate, through its Board of Educational Affairs, has openly documented the need to bridge the gap between the *National Standards for High School Psychology Curricula* (APA, 2005a) and the *APA Guidelines* (APA, 2007). In its final report, the APA Task Force on Strengthening the Teaching and Learning of Undergraduate Psychological Science proposed a developmentally appropriate set of intermediate knowledge, skills, and values that psychology students should acquire as they progress from the introductory psychology course through attainment of the baccalaureate degree (APA, 2008b). On the basis of expected student competencies, the task force sought to establish common threads and thus a seamless transition within and across undergraduate psychology curricula. This systematic approach to curriculum coherence is especially important to leveling the playing field for students enrolled in psychology courses at 2-year colleges and those completing similar courses at 4-year institutions.

Another vehicle for establishing curriculum coherence across varying sectors of undergraduate psychology education focuses on involving students in research projects. The National Conferences on Undergraduate Research (2008) endorsed undergraduate student–faculty mentor partnerships in conducting research, scholarship, and creative activity as a salient component of higher education. Contrary to the traditional stereotype, this type of scholarly activity is not restricted to 4-year colleges and research universities. In fact, the trend toward faculty involvement in research—either singularly or in tandem with students—is presently accelerating at 2-year colleges (Malachowski, 2006). According to Lopatto (2006), collaborative student–faculty research can be embedded over a wide range of undergraduate educational opportunities, from 1st-year through capstone experiences. Other venues for embedding collaborative student–faculty research into undergraduate curricula include students working independently on projects or studying abroad, each under the guidance of faculty mentors (Coombs, 2006). In turn, these, and other such educational experiences, can lead to curricular and institutional transformations (Elgren & Hensel, 2006).

As a prime example of the increasing prominence of undergraduate research at the 2-year college level, the Maricopa Student Conference constitutes a platform for students from community colleges in the Phoenix, Arizona, metropolitan area to share their original academic research (e.g., supervised fieldwork in the social and behavioral sciences) in an interdisciplinary scholarly setting (O'Connor, 2008). Initiated in 2006, this annual conference mirrors the structure of graduate student conferences with guest speakers, poster sessions, break-out panels, and opportunities for students and faculty to exchange ideas on numerous scholarly topics. This forum sensitizes students to the importance of undergraduate research as a learning tool while readying them for successful transfer to 4-year colleges and universities. By capturing student interest and generating enthusiasm for the discipline, undergraduate research experiences, such as the Maricopa Student Conference, are particularly promising in preparing and retaining first-generation college students (Crowe, 2006).

As another sign of the growing research emphasis at 2-year colleges, the presence of an institutional review board (IRB) is becoming more widespread at community colleges. Some grants even require the establishment of this formal entity (Conner, 2008). According to Jerry Rudmann (2008b), executive director of the National Honor Society in Psychology for Community and Junior Colleges (Psi Beta), becoming familiar with the IRB review process is a valuable learning experience for students. Psi Beta's National Council recently invited its chapters to participate in the Psi Beta National Research Project. In the context of examining community college students' academic and social connections to their campuses, this national investigation (piloted in spring 2008) exposes psychology majors at 2-year colleges to IRB review, informed consent, and other important components of scholarly research (Psi Beta, 2008). Once a Psi Beta chapter completes its participation in the investigation, that chapter can present its portion of the study at local and regional conferences, with subsequent opportunity to expand its work into a local service project that promotes academic success among 1st-year college students. As a subsidiary benefit of the Psi Beta National Research Project, students who attend 2-year colleges that do not offer a lower division research methods course will have a formal vehicle to become involved in research (Rudmann, 2008a).

In experimentally oriented social sciences such as psychology, one of the primary goals of collaborative, process-oriented, student–faculty research is to advance student learning outcomes that engender new knowledge and skills (Malachowski, 2006). Collaborative research with undergraduates should enhance student educational experiences and promote the faculty mentor's research agenda while making a valid contribution to the field (Elgren & Hensel, 2006; Mills, 2005). Collaborative student–faculty research affords students a more personalized education that stimulates intellectual independence and maturation (Elgren & Hensel, 2006). Undergraduate curricula that incorporate critical inquiry through constructivist-oriented heuristic strategies—including problem-centered learning (Balaban, 2007; H. B. White, 2007) and cooperative and project-based learning (Epstein, Bras, Hodges, & Lipson, 2007; Wenzel, 2007)—are best positioned to allow students to develop the autonomy and exploration skills required for successful research experiences. Related to the desired aims of scholarly research, undergraduate curricula infused with these constructivist pedagogical elements "promote greater exposure to the primary literature; create opportunities to articulate and test hypotheses and intellectual models; and encourage students to contextualize and communicate objectives, approaches, analyses, and conclusions" (Elgren & Hensel, 2006, p. 4).

Regardless of the targeted level of student proficiency, the literature on collaborative student–faculty research identifies a number of tangible learning benefits. For example, undergraduate research experiences hold the potential to produce learning that reflects the meticulous student-engagement benchmark categories identified in the National Student Survey of Engagement. The National Student Survey of Engagement benchmarks include high academic challenge, active collaborative learning, concentrated student–faculty interaction, enriching educational experience, and supportive campus environment (Kuh, 2003). Consonant with these benchmarks, student–faculty collaborative research on the undergraduate level "may facilitate empowered learning (including communication, problem solving, and teamwork), informed learning (allowing students to study the natural and cultural world), and responsible learning (permitting the study of social problems and the self)" (Lopatta, 2006, ¶ 2). Studies (e.g., Rauckhorst, Czaja, & Baxter, 2001) also link undergraduate research experiences to accelerated epistemological development that is evidenced in more committed learners who demonstrate greater sophistication in thinking and reflective judgment.

Using a mixture of quantitative and qualitative methods, Seymour, Hunter, Laursen, and Deantoni (2004) conducted a 3-year investigation to pinpoint the benefits of undergraduate research experiences in the natural sciences, social sciences, and humanities at several liberal arts colleges known for exemplary research-supportive curricula. The students in this study experienced various learning and skill set gains as a result of their involvement in undergraduate research—many of which also realize the goals associated with an undergraduate liberal education as discussed earlier in the present chapter. Student improvements were observed in the following areas:

- hypothesis formation and research design;
- data collection, analysis, and interpretation;
- information and computer literacy;
- communication skills;
- professional development (e.g., increased familiarity with professional behavior and career demands; disciplinary socialization on how professionals conduct their work);
- professional advancement (e.g., résumé building, opportunities for publication and presentation of work as part of student–faculty mentor partnerships); and
- personal growth (e.g., development of self-reliance and perseverance in facing challenges).

The increasing emphasis on undergraduate research intersects with an emerging movement toward service learning in higher education, resulting in community-based research (CBR) as scientific and civic pedagogy (Paul, 2006). When working unilaterally on service learning projects, students often experience a "disconnect between personal action and understanding how action can make a difference [in local communities]" (Paul, 2006, p. 12). This problem can be addressed by engaging undergraduates in collaborative partnerships with faculty mentors designed to apply empirical inquiry to real social issues. In serving the research or information needs of community organizations, CBR constitutes a type of scholarship-rigorous service to the public good. As an example of a CBR partnership, Paul (2006) discussed the Trenton Youth Community-Based Research Corps at the College of New Jersey. In merging collaborative student–faculty research with community engagement, this program applies social scientific inquiry as an instrument for change in the lives of poverty-stricken children living in Trenton, New Jersey. Students are involved in data collection, statistical analysis, and presentation of results. On the basis of its research findings, the full partnership participates in developing recommendations for a community agency's needs. In the case where an agency requests a formal research report, students serve as primary authors with appreciable input from all partners.

Beyond active engagement in learning, there are a number of additional learning benefits associated with CBR (Paul, 2006). In the role of equal partners, students are pushed to develop their leadership, communication, problem-solving, and teamwork skills. In doing so, they discover professional writing as a collaborative process that demands persistence, flexibility, and adaptability during the editing and revising stages. Additionally, students learn to experience research as a useful device when they are confronted with the realities of conducting social scientific research and making pragmatic choices. In maximizing and blending their roles as learners, scholars, and citizens in socially significant environments, students who participate in CBR also increase their marketability to prospective graduate schools and employers.

NEW DIRECTIONS FOR EDUCATIONAL REFORM

Many years have transpired since the 1991 APA National Conference on Enhancing the Quality of Undergraduate Education in Psychology was held at St. Mary's College of Maryland. A more recent national conference convened in summer 2008 to address the dramatically changing landscape in higher education over the past 2 decades. Sponsored by the APA Board of Educational Affairs, the National Conference on Undergraduate Education in Psychology (NCUEP) met on the campus of the University of Puget Sound in Tacoma, Washington. The overarching goal of the NCUEP was to create a blueprint for the future of undergraduate psychology education (Halpern, 2008).

Prominent changes have taken place in undergraduate education between the timing of the St. Mary's Conference and the NCUEP. As a motivating force behind the NCUEP, conference organizer Diane Halpern (2008) argued that many of today's college professors are simply "out of touch with the realities of our students' lives" (p. 4). In the technologically savvy world in which they live, contemporary college students spend considerable time multitasking. As a result, a growing number of students check e-mails, instant or text message, micro-blog (Twitter), and interact with Facebook while participating in class or completing outside assignments—all hotly contested issues among faculty across U.S. college campuses.

A sizeable number of our undergraduates now enter college having already completed a high school psychology course (Belar, 2008). Each year, introductory psychology courses are offered to students in over 5,000 U.S. high schools (Park & Fineburg, 2008). AP psychology is one of the fastest growing and most popular AP courses available in high schools (Park & Fineburg, 2008). According to College Board (2009) statistics, roughly 130,000 students took the AP Psychology Examination in 2008. This exam did not even exist at the time of the St. Mary's Conference.

For those who have not been exposed to high school psychology, nearly half of our current undergraduate students experience their initial exposure to psychology in community colleges (American Association of Community Colleges, 2008). This statistic on community college enrollment represents a shift in U.S. higher education, meaning that undergraduate education in psychology and other disciplines is no longer limited to 4-year college or university campuses (Halpern et al., 2009). In addition to community colleges and a considerable array of professional development venues, informal settings, such as the popular media, podcasts, and Web sites, are also prominent players in the contemporary landscape of undergraduate education (Halpern et al., 2009).

Compared with earlier decades, U.S. college students are more diverse in demographic background and preparation for higher education (Halpern, 2007). For example, our student population is becoming increasingly international. Moreover, not only are a substantial number of students underprepared for college-level work, but also many college graduates do not possess the skills that employers demand in the workforce (Belar, 2008).

There has also been an expanded emphasis on assessing student learning outcomes as a result of forces demanding more educational accountability, including consumers, governmental bodies, accreditation agencies, and leaders in higher education (Belar, 2008). Consider Halpern's (2007, p. 1) analysis in examining why the accountability movement has continued to gain strength in the context of higher education:

> Think about our standard assessments of learning. Student learning is evaluated by each faculty member in each course, with grades varying widely in their meaning. Some professors assign grades according to the belief that grade distributions should be normally distributed; others believe that almost everyone or almost no one is deserving of a high letter grade. When questioned about their grading practices, many professors cite academic freedom as a defense of their right to assign grades in any way they deem appropriate. Academic freedom notwithstanding, there are many external pressures on faculty to assign high grades, including the fact that the faculty member's own teaching effective-

ness is evaluated with student ratings, and funding for one's own academic unit depends on the number of students who are retained. The problem of grade inflation is real, and the result is increasing reliance on external measures of academic achievement, which may not match what has been taught.

As yet another reason why traditional undergraduate education is open to reform, Halpern (2007) cited the proliferation of newer modes of course delivery in the form of distance learning and virtual courses that provide "any-time, any-place learning" (p. 2). Because of the potential for both productive and counterproductive uses, these alternative means of teaching and learning have been met with mixed faculty reactions.

In Halpern's (2007) estimation, "the gap between empirically validated theory and practice is wide" (p. 2) in terms of how faculty members teach students in ways that lead to long-term retention and transfer of learning. By largely ignoring an appreciable volume of literature on the scholarship of teaching and learning, psychology classroom educators apply little of the available knowledge base on how people learn and think.

Within this overall backdrop of change that signals the need for educational redesign, working groups of NCUEP participants addressed various broad themes centering on questions that must be answered to create a world-class undergraduate psychology education that (a) readies students for entry into a highly technical workplace, (b) prepares them for advanced study in a multiplicity of fields, and (c) arms them with the knowledge, skills, and values required of concerned and informed citizens in a global society (Halpern et al., 2009). Recommended principles for quality undergraduate education in psychology include:

- reliance on the introductory psychology course as a prerequisite for all other courses and as an entrée to psychology as a scientific discipline;
- how best to apply the science of learning to the science of psychology based on recent developments in the scholarship of teaching and learning;
- a general guide for developmentally appropriate curricula that incorporates an applied experience and course work that draws from the four basic domains (biological bases, learning and cognition, developmental, and sociocultural influences) and writing, speaking, and critical thinking across the curriculum;
- psychology's increased involvement in interdisciplinary course work because of its pivotal role in the core curricula of other departments (e.g., nursing, education, business) and its natural tie to biology, sociology, and other academic disciplines;

- desired learning outcomes in terms of workplace skills and those required for graduate study in psychology and other disciplines;
- promising innovations in technology-mediated teaching formats that can be used to promote learning;
- various teaching methods for different content, contexts, and students;
- improving psychology instruction through professional training opportunities that support an evidence-based scientist–educator model for quality teaching analogous to the scientist–practitioner model for clinical and other practice; and
- a model of inclusive excellence, stemming from the growing diversity of undergraduate students, which challenges the traditional "one-size-fits-all" approach to curriculum design and implementation. (Halpern et al., 2009)[1]

CONCLUDING REMARKS

Teaching from among a wide assortment of available courses challenges psychology educators and their students to integrate diverse course content across an undergraduate curriculum. Interest in discovering the best pedagogical practices to meet these challenges dates back to critical examination of undergraduate psychology curricula during the first national conference convened at Cornell University in 1952, a follow-up conference held at the University of Michigan in 1960, and the subsequent Kulik's (1973) report. Since the 1980s, the APA has taken the lead in sponsoring other seminal initiatives to bolster the quality of undergraduate psychology education, including the national conference held at St. Mary's College of Maryland in 1991 and the one organized at the University of Puget Sound in summer 2008.

Of particular importance to the content of this book is the final report of the APA Task Force on Strengthening the Teaching and Learning of Undergraduate Psychological Science (APA, 2008b). This report provides a curriculum bridge between the *National Standards* (APA, 2005a) and the *APA Guidelines* (APA, 2007) in proposing a set of developmentally appropriate intermediate outcomes that students should achieve on the journey from the introductory psychology course through the end of the baccalaureate degree. Building from the developmental framework offered in this report, the present volume links varied constructivist teaching applications with embedded authentic assessments of student learning.

---

[1] These, and other NCEUP recommendations, are examined in the book *Undergraduate Education in Psychology: A Blueprint for the Future of the Discipline* (Halpern, 2009).

Effective instruction at all academic levels draws heavily from identifiable connections among teaching, learning, and assessment. Regarding course and program evaluation, formative assessment occurs in advance of instructional planning and affords modification throughout the teaching process. The use of authentic assessments permits the establishment of meaningful associations among what is taught, what is learned, and how it is assessed. Casting these assessments in light of constructivist pedagogical strategies places learners in the role of active and interactive "architects of knowledge" in real-world contexts (Mayo, 2006c). Moreover, reliance on a developmental model that encompasses undergraduate psychology curricula allows educators to embed authentic assessments in the context of constructivist learning assignments across a full range of undergraduate psychology courses. Regardless of the future directions of undergraduate education in psychology, psychology educators may be wise to consider this type of systematic approach to course and program evaluation that brings together teaching, learning, and assessment in clearly stated and measurable terms.

REFERENCES

Adair, J. G., Coelho, E. L., & Luna, J. R. (2002). How international is psychology? *International Journal of Psychology, 37*, 160–170.

Adelman, C. (2008). Accountability "light": Our version is going the way of the dollar vs. the euro. *Liberal Education, 94*(4), 6–13.

Allen, M. J. (2004). *The use of scoring rubrics for assessment and teaching.* (Available from Mary J. Allen, Director, Institute for Teaching and Learning, California State University, 401 Golden Shore, 6th Floor, Long Beach, CA 90802-4210)

American Association of Community Colleges. (2008). *Community college fast facts.* Washington, DC: Author. Retrieved August 6, 2009, from http://www2.aacc.nche.edu/research/home.htm

American Psychological Association. (1999). *National standards for the teaching of high school psychology.* Washington, DC: Author.

American Psychological Association. (2002). *Undergraduate psychology major learning goals and outcomes: A report.* Washington, DC: Author. Retrieved August 6, 2009, from http://apa.org/ed/pcue/taskforcereport2.pdf

American Psychological Association. (2005a). *National standards for high school psychology curricula.* Washington, DC: Author. Retrieved August 6, 2009, from http://apa.org/ed/natlstandards.html

American Psychological Association. (2005b). *APA working group on internationalizing the undergraduate psychology curriculum: Report and recommended learning outcomes for internationalizing the undergraduate curriculum.* Washington, DC: Author. Retrieved August 6, 2009, from http://apa.org/ed/pcue/international.pdf

American Psychological Association. (2007). *APA guidelines for the undergraduate psychology major.* Washington, DC: Author. Retrieved August 6, 2009, from http://apa.org/ed/psymajor_guideline.pdf

American Psychological Association. (2008a). *Report of the task force on resources for the inclusion of social class in psychology curricula.* Washington, DC: Author. Retrieved August 6, 2009, from http://www.apa.org/pi/ses/final_report.pdf

American Psychological Association. (2008b). *Teaching, learning, and assessing in a developmentally coherent curriculum.* Washington, DC: Author. Retrieved August 6, 2009, from http://www.apa.org/ed/pcue/bea_coherent.pdf

Anderson-Inman, L., & Ditson, L. (1999). Computer-based concept mapping: A tool for negotiating meaning. *Learning & Leading With Technology, 26*(8), 6–13.

Anderson-Inman, L., & Zeitz, L. (1993). Computer-based concept-mapping: Active studying for active learners. *Computing Teacher, 21*(1), 6–8, 10–11.

Anthis, K. (2005). From Freud to Erikson to Marcia: Concept maps in personality psychology courses. *Teaching of Psychology, 32*, 263–265.

Aristotle. (2007). *On the generation of animals* (A. Platt, Trans.). Adelaide, South Australia: The University of Adelaide Library. Retrieved August 5, 2009, from http://ebooks.adelaide.edu.au/a/aristotle/generation/book3.html

Arnaud, M. J. (1993). Metabolism of caffeine and other components of coffee. In S. Garattini (Ed.), *Caffeine, coffee and health* (pp. 43–95). New York: Raven Press.

Arter, J. A., & Spandel, V. (1992). Using portfolios of student work in instruction and assessment. *Educational Measurement: Issues and Practice, 11*, 36–44.

Association of American Colleges and Universities. (2007). *College learning for the new global century: A report from the National Leadership Council for Liberal Education & America's Promise.* Retrieved August 6, 2009, from http://www.aacu.org/leap/documents/GlobalCentury_final.pdf

Association of American Colleges and Universities. (2008a). *How should colleges assess and improve student learning? Employers' views on the accountability challenge.* Washington, DC: Author.

Association of American Colleges and Universities. (2008b). *What is liberal education?* Retrieved August 6, 2009, from http://www.aacu.org/leap/what_is_liberal_education.cfm

Association of American Colleges and Universities and the Council for Higher Education Accreditation. (2008). *New leadership for student learning and accountability: A statement of principles, commitments to action.* Washington, DC: Authors. Retrieved August 6, 2009, from http://www.chea.org/pdf/2008.01.30_New_Leadership_Statement.pdf

Atkinson, R. C., & Shiffrin, R. (1968). Human memory: A proposed system and its control processes. In K. Spence & J. Spence (Eds.), *The psychology of learning and motivation* (Vol. 2, pp. 89–105). New York: Academic Press.

Au, K. H. (1990). Changes in a teacher's views of interactive comprehension instruction. In L. C. Moll (Ed.), *Vygotsky and education: Instructional implications and applications of sociohistorical psychology* (pp. 271–286). New York: Cambridge University Press.

Austin, A. W. (1993). *Assessment for excellence: The philosophy and practice of assessment and evaluation in higher education.* New York: Macmillan.

Ausubel, D. P. (1960). The use of advance organizers in the learning and retention of meaningful verbal material. *Journal of Educational Psychology, 51*, 267–272.

Ausubel, D. P. (1963). *The psychology of meaningful verbal learning.* New York: Grune & Stratton.

Ausubel, D. P. (1968). *Educational psychology: A cognitive view.* New York: Holt, Rinehart & Winston.

Ausubel, D. P. (1977). The facilitation of meaningful verbal learning in the classroom. *Educational Psychologist, 12*, 162–178.

Ausubel, D. P. (1980). Schemata, cognitive structure, and advance organizers: A reply to Anderson, Spiro, and Anderson. *American Educational Research Journal, 17*, 400–404. (ERIC Document Reproduction Service No. EJ237870)

Baird, B. N. (1991). In-class poster sessions. *Teaching of Psychology, 18,* 27–29.

Balaban, M. T. (2007). Implementing inquiry- or problem-based learning in the undergraduate science curriculum: Ideas, examples, and concerns. In K. K. Karukstis, H. Mudd, & T. E. Elgren (Eds.), *Developing and sustaining a research-supportive curriculum: A compendium of successful practices* (pp. 41–60). Washington, DC: Council on Undergraduate Research.

Ball, C. T., & Pelco, L. E. (2006). Teaching research methods to undergraduate psychology students using an active cooperative learning approach. *International Journal of Teaching and Learning in Higher Education, 17,* 147–154.

Bandura, A. (1976). *Social learning theory.* Englewood Cliffs, NJ: Prentice Hall.

Barr, D. (1990). A solution in search of a problem: The role of technology in educational reform. *Journal for the Education of the Gifted, 14,* 79–95.

Barrett, H. (1997a). *Collaborative planning for electronic portfolios: Asking strategic questions.* Retrieved August 6, 2009, from http://electronicportfolios.com/portfolios/planning.html

Barrett, H. (1997b). *Electronic teaching portfolios.* Retrieved August 6, 2009, from http://electronicportfolios.com/portfolios/SITEArt.html

Bartol, C. R., & Bartol, A. M. (2005). History of forensic psychology. In I. B. Weiner & A. K. Hess (Eds.), *The handbook of forensic psychology* (3rd ed., pp. 1–27). Hoboken, NJ: Wiley.

Bartolini, L., Gharib, A., & Phillips, W. (2009a). International course transformation process in psychology. In R. Gurung & L. Prieto (Eds.), *Getting culture: Incorporating diversity across the curriculum* (pp. 181–189). Sterling, VA: Stylus.

Bartolini, L., Gharib, A., & Phillips, W. (2009b, April). *Internationalizing psychology courses: E-xcellence in Teaching.* Column posted to the Society for Teaching of Psychology discussion list, archived at http://list.kennesaw.edu/archives/psychteacher.html

Baum, C., Benjamin, L. T., Bernstein, D., Crider, A. B., Halonen, J., Hopkins, J. R., et al. (1993). Principles for quality undergraduate psychology programs. In T. V. McGovern (Ed.), *Handbook for enhancing undergraduate education in psychology* (pp. 17–20). Washington, DC: American Psychological Association.

Belar, C. (2008). Rethinking undergraduate education. *Monitor on Psychology, 39*(1), 52.

Belenky, M. F., Clinchy, B. M., Goldberger, N. R., & Tarule, J. M. (1986). *Women's ways of knowing.* New York: Basic Books.

Bell, P. B., & Staines, P. J. (1979). *Reasoning and argument in psychology.* Sydney, Australia: University of New South Wales Press.

Berliner, D. C. (1994). Expertise: The wonder of exemplary performances. In J. N. Mangieri & C. C. Block (Eds.), *Creating powerful thinking in teachers and students: Diverse perspectives* (pp. 161–186). Ft. Worth, TX: Harcourt Brace. Retrieved August 6, 2009, from http://courses.ed.asu.edu/berliner/readings/expertise.htm

Bertaux, D., & Kohli, M. (1984). The life story approach: A continental view. *Annual Review of Sociology, 10*, 215–237.

Bezzi, A. (1996). Use of repertory grids in facilitating knowledge construction and reconstruction in geology. *Journal of Research in Science Teaching, 33*, 179–204.

Biggs, J. (1996). Enhancing teaching through constructive alignment. *Higher Education, 32*, 347–364.

Blackmon, M., Hong, Y., & Choi, I. (2007). Case-based learning. In M. Orey (Ed.), *Emerging perspectives on learning, teaching, and technology*. Retrieved August 6, 2009, from http://projects.coe.uga.edu/epltt/index.php?title=Case-Based_Learning

Bloom, B. S., Hastings, J. T., & Madaus, G. F. (1971). *Handbook on formative and summative evaluation of student learning*. New York: McGraw-Hill.

Boeree, C. G. (2006). *The history of psychology*. Retrieved August 6, 2009, from http://webspace.ship.edu/cgboer/historyofpsych.html

Bosack, T., McCarthy, M., Halonen, J. S., & Clay, S. (2004). Developing scientific inquiry skills in psychology: Using authentic assessment strategies. In D. S. Dunn, C. M. Mehrotra, & J. S. Halonen (Eds.), *Measuring up: Educational assessment challenges and practices in psychology* (pp. 141–169). Washington, DC: American Psychological Association.

Bowen, C. (1998). *Stuck for words? Word retrieval activities for children*. Retrieved August 6, 2009, from http://www.speech-language-therapy.com/wordretrieval.html

Bower, G. H., & Clark, M. C. (1969). Narrative stories as mediators for serial learning. *Psychonomic Science, 14*, 181–182.

Boyatzis, C. J. (1992). Let the caged bird sing: Using literature to teach developmental psychology. *Teaching of Psychology, 19*, 221–222.

Brewer, C. L. (1997). Undergraduate education in psychology: Will the mermaids sing? *American Psychologist, 52*, 434–441.

Brewer, C. L. (2006). Undergraduate education in psychology: United States. *International Journal of Psychology, 41*, 65–71.

Brewer, C. L., & Halonen, J. S. (2003). *A recent history of curriculum and assessment in undergraduate psychology programs*. Retrieved August 6, 2009, from http://www.pkal.org/documents/History.pdf

Brewer, C. L., Hopkins, J. R., Kimble, G. A., Matlin, M. W., McCann, L. I., McNeil, O. V., et al. (1993). Curriculum. In T. V. McGovern (Ed.), *Handbook for enhancing undergraduate education in psychology* (pp. 161–182). Washington, DC: American Psychological Association.

Brewer, W. F. (1995). To assert that essentially all human knowledge and memory is represented in terms of stories is certainly wrong. In R. S. Wyer (Ed.), *Knowledge and memory: The real story* (pp. 109–120). Mahwah, NJ: Erlbaum.

Brooks, J. G., & Brooks, M. G. (1993). *In search of understanding: The case for constructivist classrooms*. Alexandria, VA: Association for Supervision and Curriculum Development.

Brown, D. E. (1994). Facilitating conceptual change using analogies and explanatory models. *International Journal of Science Education, 16,* 201–214.

Brown, J. S., Collins, A., & Duguid, S. (1989). Situated cognition and the culture of learning. *Educational Researcher, 18,* 32–41.

Bruner, J. S. (1960). *The process of education.* Cambridge, MA: Harvard University Press.

Bruner, J. S. (1966). *Toward a theory of instruction.* Cambridge, MA: Harvard University Press.

Bruner, J. S. (1967). *On knowing: Essays for the left hand.* Cambridge, MA: Harvard University Press.

Bruner, J. S. (1973). *Going beyond the information given.* New York: Norton.

Bruner, J. S. (1975). The ontogenesis of speech acts. *Journal of Child Language, 2,* 1–40.

Bruner, J. S. (1986). *Actual minds, possible worlds.* Cambridge, MA: Harvard University Press.

Bruner, J. S. (1990). *Acts of meaning.* Cambridge, MA: Harvard University Press.

Bruner, J. S. (1996). *The culture of education.* Cambridge, MA: Harvard University Press.

Bunge, M. A. (1983). *Treatise on basic philosophy: Epistemology and methodology* (Vol. 5). Hingham, MA: Kluwer Academic.

Cabe, P. A., Walker, M. H., & Williams, M. (1999). Newspaper advice column letters as teaching cases for developmental psychology. *Teaching of Psychology, 26,* 128–130.

Calhoun, L. G., & Selby, J. W. (1979). Writing in psychology: A separate course? *Teaching of Psychology, 6,* 232.

California Portable Assisted Study Sequence. (2006). *Socratic teaching.* Retrieved August 6, 2009, from http://www.capassprogram.org/methodology/socratic.html

Camplese, D. A., & Mayo, J. A. (1982). How to improve the quality of student writing: The colleague swap. *Teaching of Psychology, 9,* 122–123.

Campoy, R. (1992). The role of technology in the school reform movement. *Educational Technology, 32,* 17–22.

Carey, S. (1985). *Conceptual change in children.* Cambridge, MA: MIT Press.

Carr, K. (1990). *How can we teach critical thinking?* Urbana, IL: Eric Clearinghouse on Elementary and Early Childhood Education. (ERIC Document Reproduction Service No. ED326304)

Carvin, A. (2004). *The constructivism–computer connection.* Retrieved August 8, 2009, from http://www.edwebproject.org/constructivism.tlc98.html

Case, R. (Ed.). (1992). *The mind's staircase: Stages in the development of human intelligence.* Mahwah, NJ: Erlbaum.

Cheng, X. (2003, October). Socratic method for engineering education. *CDTL Brief, 6*(10). Retrieved August 6, 2009, from http://www.cdtl.nus.edu.sg/brief/V6n10/default.asp

Clay, R. A. (2008). Are our students learning? *Monitor on Psychology, 39*(5), 54–56.

Clement, J. J. (1993). Using bridging analogies and anchoring intuitions to deal with students' preconceptions in physics. *Journal of Research in Science Teaching, 30,* 1241–1257.

Clement, J. J. (1998). Expert–novice similarities and instruction using analogies. *International Journal of Science Education, 20,* 1271–1286.

Clinchy, B. M. (1995). A connected approach to the teaching of developmental psychology. *Teaching of Psychology, 22,* 100–104.

Cobb, P. (1996). Where is the mind? A coordination of sociocultural and cognitive constructivist perspectives. In C. T. Fosnot (Ed.), *Constructivism: Theory, perspectives, and practice* (pp. 34–52). New York: Teachers College Press.

College Board. (2009). *2008 psychology grade distribution.* Retrieved August 6, 2009, from http://www.collegeboard.com/student/testing/ap/psych/dist.html?psych

Collins, A. (1988). *Cognitive apprenticeship and instructional technology* (Tech. Rep. No. 6899). Cambridge, MA: BBN Labs, Inc.

Collins, A. (1991, September). The role of computer technology in restructuring schools. *Phi Delta Kappan, 73,* 28–36.

Conner, F. (2008, April 21). Society for the Teaching of Psychology Moderated Discussion List. Message posted to PsychTeacher Listserv electronic discussion list, archived at http://list.kennesaw.edu/archives/psychteacher.html

Coombs, V. M. (2006). Research, scholarly, and creative activity at the University of Wisconsin—River Falls. *Peer Review, 8*(1), 8–11.

Cranston-Gingrass, A., Raines, S., Paul, J., Epanchin B., & Roselli, H. (1996). Developing and using cases in partnership environments. *Teacher Education and Special Education, 19,* 158–168.

Croce, J. J. (1973). Bad, bad Leroy Brown. On *Life and times* [Album]. Los Angeles: Vertigo Records.

Cross, K. P. (1998, July–August). Why learning communities? Why now? *About Campus,* 4–11.

Cross, K. P., & Stedman, M. H. (1996). *Classroom research: Implementing the scholarship of teaching.* San Francisco: Jossey-Bass.

Crowe, M. (2006). Creative scholarship through undergraduate research. *Peer Review, 8*(1), 16–18.

Cyrs, T. E. (1994). *Essential skills for college teaching: An instructional systems approach.* Las Cruces: New Mexico State University.

Dagher, Z. R. (1995). Analysis of analogies used by science teachers. *Journal of Research in Science Teaching, 32,* 259–270.

Dagher, Z. R. (2006). Does the use of analogies contribute to conceptual change? *Science Education, 78,* 601–614.

Davis, B. D. (1985). Dependency grids: An illustration of their use in an educational setting. In N. Beail (Ed.), *Repertory grid technique and personal constructs:*

Applications in clinical and educational settings (pp. 319–332). Cambridge, MA: Brookline Books.

DeAngelis, T. (2008). Psychology's growth careers. *Monitor on Psychology, 39*(4), 64–71.

DeBono, E. (1970). *Lateral thinking: Creativity step by step.* New York: Harper Colaphon Books.

DeMarco, R., Hayward, L., & Lynch, M. (2002). Nursing students' experiences with and strategic approaches to case-based instruction: A replication and comparison study between two disciplines. *Journal of Nursing Education, 41,* 165–174.

Descartes, R. (2008). *The passions of the soul* (P. Easton, Ed.; Anonymous, Trans.). Claremont, CA: Claremont Graduate University. (Original work published 1649) Retrieved August 5, 2009, from http://net.cgu.edu/philosophy/descartes/Passions_Part_One.html

Dewey, J. (1896). The reflex arc concept in psychology. *Psychological Review, 3,* 357–370.

Dewey, J. (1916). *Democracy and education: An introduction to the philosophy of education.* New York: MacMillan.

Dickson, S. V., Chard, D. J., & Simmons, D. C. (1993). An integrated reading/writing curriculum: A focus on scaffolding. *LD Forum, 18*(4), 12–16.

Dillon, J. (1997). Questioning. In D.W. Hargie (Ed.), *The handbook of communication skills* (pp. 103–133). New York: Routledge.

Ditson, L., Kessler, R., Anderson-Inman, L., & Mafit, D. (2001). *Concept mapping companion* (2nd ed.). Eugene, OR: International Society for Technology in Education.

Dixon, F. A. (2000). The discussion examination: Making assessment match instructional strategy. *Roeper Review, 23,* 104–108.

Doyle, M. E., & Smith, M. K. (2007). *Jean-Jacques Rousseau on nature, wholeness, and education.* Retrieved August 6, 2009, from http://www.infed.org/thinkers/et-rous.htm

Driscoll, M. P. (2000). *Psychology of learning for instruction* (2nd ed.). Boston: Allyn & Bacon.

Duit, R. (1991). On the role of analogies and metaphors in learning science. *Science Education, 75,* 649–672.

Dunn, D. S., McCarthy, M., Baker, S., Halonen, J., & Hill, G. W. (2007). Quality benchmarks in undergraduate psychology programs. *American Psychologist, 62,* 650–670.

Dunn, D. S., Mehrotra, C. M., & Halonen, J. S. (Eds.). (2004). *Measuring up: Educational assessment challenges and practices for psychology.* Washington, DC: American Psychological Association.

Elgren, T., & Hensel, N. (2006). Undergraduate research experiences: Synergies between scholarship and teaching. *Peer Review, 8*(1), 4–7.

Epstein, A. W., Bras, R., Hodges, K., & Lipson, A. (2007). Team-oriented, project-based learning as a path to undergraduate research. In K. K. Karukstis, H. Mudd, & T. E. Elgren (Eds.), *Developing and sustaining a research-supportive curriculum: A compendium of successful practices* (pp. 69–86). Washington, DC: Council on Undergraduate Research.

Erikson, E. H. (1959). *Identity and the life cycle*. New York: Norton.

Erikson, E. H. (1963). *Childhood and society* (2nd ed.). New York: Norton.

Ernst, R., & Petrossian, P. (1996). Teachings of psychology in secondary schools (TOPSS): Aiming for excellence in high school psychology instruction. *American Psychologist, 51*, 256–258.

Ertmer, P. A., & Russell, J. D. (1995). Using case studies to enhance instructional design education. *Educational Technology, 35*, 23–31.

Executive Office of the President. (1990). *National goals for education*. Washington, DC: Author. (ERIC Document Reproduction Service No. ED319143)

Fancher, R. E. (1996). *Pioneers of psychology* (3rd ed.). New York: W. W. Norton & Company.

Ferguson, D. A. (2006, November). *The use of poster sessions to present student research in the methods classroom*. Paper presented at the annual convention of the National Communication Association, San Antonio, TX. Retrieved August 6, 2009, from http://www.cofc.edu/communication/posters.doc

Fernald, D. (1996). Heads and tales in introductory psychology. *Teaching of Psychology, 23*, 150–158.

Fetherstonhaugh, T., & Treagust, D. F. (1992). Students' understanding of light and its properties: Teaching to engender conceptual change. *Science Education, 76*, 653–672.

Feuerstein, R., & Feuerstein, S. (1991). Mediated learning experience: A theoretical review. In R. Feuerstein, P. S. Klein, & A. J. Tannenbaum (Eds.), *Mediated learning experience (MLE): Theoretical, psychosocial, and learning implications* (pp. 3–52). Tel Aviv, Israel: Freund Publishing House Ltd.

Finke, G. R., & Davis, S. F. (1988, April). *The introductory psychology journal: A technique for increasing course relevance*. Paper presented at the annual meeting of the Southwestern Psychological Association, Tulsa, OK.

Fisher, K. M. (1990). Semantic networking: The new kid on the block. *Journal of Research in Science Teaching, 27*, 1001–1018.

Fisher, K. M., Faletti, J., Patterson, H., Thornton, R., Lipson, J., & Spring, C. (1990). Computer-based concept mapping. *Journal of College Science Teaching, 19*, 347–352.

Flowers, J. C., & Ritz, J. M. (1994). *Cooperative learning in technology education* (Monograph 13 of the Virginia Council on Technology Teacher Education). Retrieved August 6, 2009, from http://teched.vt.edu/vctte/VCTTEMonographs/VCTTEMono13(CoopLearn).html

Flynn, A., & Klein J., (2001). The influence of discussion groups in a case-based learning environment. *Educational Technology Research & Development, 49,* 71–86.

Fosnot, C. W. (1996). Constructivism: A psychological theory of learning. In C. W. Fosnot (Ed.), *Constructivism: Theory, perspectives, and practice* (pp. 8–33). New York: Teachers College Press.

Frazier, C. H. (1997). The development of an authentic assessment instrument: The scored discussion. *English Journal, 86,* 37–40.

Fredholm, B. B., Battig, K., Holmen, J., Nehlig, A., & Zvartau, E. E. (1999). Actions of caffeine in the brain with special reference to factors that contribute to its widespread use. *Pharmacological Reviews, 51,* 83–133.

Freud, S. (1970). *An outline of psychoanalysis* (J. Strachey, Trans.). New York: Norton. (Original work published 1940)

Gagne, R. (1962). Military training and principles of learning. *American Psychologist, 17,* 263–276.

Gagne, R. (1965). *The conditions of learning and the theory of instruction.* New York: Holt, Rinehart & Winston.

Gagne, R. (1977). *The conditions of learning and the theory of instruction* (3rd ed.). New York: Holt, Rinehart & Winston.

Gagne, R. (1985). *The conditions of learning and the theory of instruction* (4th ed.). New York: Holt, Rinehart & Winston.

Gagne, R., Briggs, L., & Wager, W. (1992). *Principles of instructional design* (4th ed.). Fort Worth, TX: HBJ College Publishers.

Gagne, R., & Driscoll, M. (1988). *Essentials of learning for instruction* (2nd ed.). Englewood Cliffs, NJ: Prentice Hall.

Gaines, B. R., & Shaw, M. L. G. (2009). *WebGrid* [Computer program]. Alberta, Canada: Knowledge Science Institute. Available at http://tiger.cpsc.ucalgary.ca/

Garlikov, R. (2000). *The Socratic method: Teaching by asking instead of telling.* Retrieved August 6, 2009, from http://www.garlikov.com/Soc_Meth.html

Garrett, E. (1998). *The Socratic method.* Retrieved October 2, 2008, from http://www.law.uchicago.edu/socrates/soc_article.html

Gentner, D., & Holyoak, K. J. (1997). Reasoning and learning by analogy. *American Psychologist, 52,* 32–34.

Gentner, D., & Markman, A. B. (1997). Structure mapping in analogy and similarity. *American Psychologist, 52,* 45–56.

Gerretson, H., & Golson, E. (2005). Synopsis of the use of course-embedded assessment in a medium sized public university's general education program. *The Journal of General Education 54,* 139–149.

Glynn, S. M. (1991). Explaining science concepts: A teaching-with-analogies model. In S. M. Glynn, R. H. Yeany, & B. K. Britton (Eds.), *The psychology of learning science* (pp. 219–240). Hillsdale, NJ: Erlbaum.

Glynn, S. M., Duit, R., & Thiele, R. (1995). Teaching with analogies: A strategy for constructing knowledge. In S. M. Glynn & R. Duit (Eds.), *Learning science in the schools: Research reforming practice* (pp. 247–273). Mahwah, NJ: Erlbaum.

Glynn, S. M., Law, M., & Doster, E. C. (1998). Making text meaningful: The role of analogies. In C. R. Hynd (Ed.), *Learning from text across conceptual domains* (pp. 193–208). Mahwah, NJ: Erlbaum.

Glynn, S. M., Law, M., Gibson, N. M., & Hawkins, C. H. (1994). *Teaching science with analogies: A resource for teachers and textbook authors.* Washington, DC: Office of Educational Research and Improvement. (ERIC Document Reproduction Service No. ED378554)

Gobbo, C., & Chi, M. T. (1986). How knowledge is structured and used in novice and expert children. *Cognitive Development, 1,* 221–237.

Godshalk, V. M., Harvey, D. M., & Moller, L. (2004). The role of learning tasks on attitude change using cognitive flexibility hypertext systems. *Journal of Learning Sciences, 13,* 507–526.

Goldstein, S. (1995). Cross-cultural psychology as a curriculum transformation resource. *Teaching of Psychology, 22,* 228–232.

Goldstein, S. (2005). Cross-cultural perspectives in the psychology curriculum: Moving beyond "add culture and stir." In B. Perlman, L. McCann, & W. Buskist (Eds.), *Voices of experience: Memorable talks from the National Institute on the Teaching of Psychology* (pp. 45–57). Washington, DC: American Psychological Society.

Gonzalez-DeHass, A., & Willems, P. P. (2005). Case study instruction in educational psychology courses. *Journal of College Teaching & Learning, 2,* 1–4. Retrieved August 6, 2009, from http://cluteinstitute-onlinejournals.com/PDFs/200596.pdf

Grabinger, R. S., Dunlap, J. C., & Heath, S. (1993, January). *Definition of learning environments.* Paper presented at the annual conference of the Association for Educational Communications and Technology, New Orleans, LA.

Graesser, A. C., & Ottati, V. (1995). Why stories? Some evidence, questions, and challenges. In R. S. Wyer (Ed.), *Knowledge and memory: The real story* (pp. 121–132). Mahwah, NJ: Erlbaum.

Grasha, A. F. (1998). "Giving psychology away": Some experiences teaching undergraduates practical psychology. *Teaching of Psychology, 25,* 85–88.

Greenough, W., Emde, R. N., Gunnar, M., Massinga, R., & Shonkoff, J. P. (2001). The impact of the caregiving environment on young children's development. *Zero to Three, 21*(5), 16–23.

Gurung, R. A. R., & Prieto, L. R. (2009). *Getting culture: Incorporating diversity across the curriculum.* Sterling, VA: Stylus.

Gurung, R. A. R., & Schwartz, B. M. (2008). *Optimizing teaching and learning: Practicing pedagogical research.* Malden, MA: Blackwell.

Hake, R. R. (1998). Interactive-engagement vs. traditional methods: A six-thousand-student survey of mechanics test data for introductory physics courses. *American Journal of Physics, 66,* 64–74.

Halonen, J. S., Bosack, T., Clay, S., & McCarthy, M. (2003). A rubric for learning, teaching, and assessing scientific inquiry in psychology. *Teaching of Psychology, 30*, 196–208.

Halpern, D. F. (2007). Redesigning undergraduate education in psychology: Imagine the possibilities. *Psychology Teacher Network, 17*(3), 1–3.

Halpern, D. F. (2008, Winter). The National Conference on Undergraduate Education in Psychology: A blueprint for the future of our discipline. *Educator, 6*, 4–5.

Halpern, D. F. (Ed.). (2009). *Undergraduate education in psychology: A blueprint for the future of the discipline*. Washington, DC: American Psychological Association.

Halpern, D. F., Anton, B., Beins, B., Blair-Broeker, C., Brewer, C., Buskist, W., et al. (2009). 2008 APA National Conference on Undergraduate Education in Psychology: Blueprint for the discipline's future. *Psychology Teacher Network, 19*(1), 1–16.

Hamm, M., & Adams, D. (1992). *The collaborative dimensions of learning*. Norwood, NJ: Ablex Publishing.

Harding, T. S., Vanasupa, L., Savage, R. N., & Stolk, J. D. (2007, October). *Work-in-progress—Self-directed learning and motivation in a project-based learning environment*. Paper presented at the annual ASEE/IEEE Frontiers in Education Conference, Milwaukee, WI.

Hassard, J. (2006). *Advance organizers*. Retrieved September 30, 2008, from http://scied.gsu.edu/Hassard/mos/8.3a.html

Hativa, N. (2001). *Teaching for effective learning in higher education*. Dordrecht, The Netherlands: Kluwer Academic.

Hein, G. E. (1991, October). *Constructivist learning theory*. Paper presented at the annual International Committee of Museum Educators Conference, Jerusalem, Israel. Retrieved August 6, 2009, from http://www.exploratorium.edu/IFI/resources/constructivistlearning.html

Henry, E. R. (1938). A survey of courses in psychology offered by undergraduate colleges of liberal arts. *Psychology Bulletin, 35*, 430–435.

Hepler, G. R., & Lloyd, M. A. (1999, February). *Teaching the psychology of adjustment*. Roundtable discussion at the annual Southeastern Conference on the Teaching of Psychology, Atlanta, GA.

Herreid, C. F. (1997). *What is a case? Bringing to science education the established teaching tool of law and medicine*. Retrieved August 6, 2009, from http://ublib.buffalo.edu/libraries/projects/cases/teaching/whatis.html

Herreid, C. F. (1999). Dialogues as case studies: A discussion on human cloning. *Journal of College Science Teaching, 29*, 245–249.

Herstatt, C., & Kalogerakis, K. (2005). How to use analogies for breakthrough innovations. *International Journal of Innovation and Technology Management, 2*, 331–347.

Hess, G., & Brooks, E. (1998). The class poster conference as a teaching tool. *Journal of Natural Resources and Life Sciences Education, 27*, 155–158.

Hesse, M. B. (1966). *Models and analogies in science*. Notre Dame, IN: University of Notre Dame Press.

Hettich, P. (1976). The journal: An autobiographical approach to learning. *Teaching of Psychology, 3*, 60–63.

Hettich, P. (1980). The journal revisited. *Teaching of Psychology, 7*, 105–106.

Heylighen, F. (1997). Epistemological constructivism. In F. Heylighen, C. Joslyn, & V. Turchin (Eds.), *Principia cybernetica web*. Retrieved September 30, 2008, from http://pespmc1.vub.ac.be/CONSTRUC.html

Hilgard, E. R. (1987). *Psychology in America: A historical survey*. San Diego, CA: Harcourt Brace Jovanovich.

Hintikka, J. (2007). *Socratic epistemology: Explorations of knowledge-seeking by questioning*. Cambridge, England: Cambridge University Press.

Hjelle, L. A., & Ziegler, D. J. (1992). *Personality theories: Basic assumptions, research, and applications* (3rd ed.). New York: McGraw-Hill.

Hogan, K., & Pressley, M. (Eds.). (1997). *Scaffolding student learning: Instructional approaches and issues*. Cambridge, MA: Brookline Books.

Holyoak, K. (1984). Analogical thinking and human intelligence. In R. P. Honeck & R. R. Hoffman (Eds.), *Cognition and figurative language* (pp. 393–423). Hillsdale, NJ: Erlbaum.

Hornack, R. T. (2008, July 18). Society for the Teaching of Psychology Moderated Discussion List. Message posted to PsychTeacher Listserv electronic discussion list, archived at http://list.kennesaw.edu/archives/psychteacher.html

Hunt, M. (1993). *The story of psychology*. New York: Anchor Books.

Hunt, M. (2007). *The story of psychology* (2nd ed.). New York: Anchor Books.

Institute for Human and Machine Cognition. (2009). *CmapTools: Knowledge modeling kit* [Computer program]. Pensacola, FL: Author. Available at http://cmap.ihmc.us/download/

Jackson, R. (1999). Just in time: Web delivered professional development. *Technological Horizons in Education Journal, 26*, 26–27.

Jacobs-Lawson, J. M., & Hershey, D. A. (2002). Concept maps as an assessment tool in psychology courses. *Teaching of Psychology, 29*, 25–29.

James, P. (2000). "I am the dark forest": Personal analogy as a way to understand metaphor. *Art Education, 53*, 6–11.

James, W. (1907). *Pragmatism: A new name for some old ways of thinking—Popular lectures on philosophy*. New York: Longmans, Green, and Co.

James, W. (1958). *Talks to teachers on psychology and to students on some of life's ideals*. New York: Norton. (Original work published 1892)

Jegede, O. J., Alaiyemola, F. F., & Okebukola, P. A. O. (1990). The effect of concept mapping on students' anxiety and achievement in biology. *Journal of Research in Science Teaching, 27*, 951–960.

Jensen, E. (2000). *Brain-based learning* (rev. ed.). San Diego, CA: The Brain Store.

Johnson, D. W. (1991). *Human relations and your career* (3rd ed.). Englewood Cliffs, NJ: Prentice Hall.

Johnson, D. W. (1993). *Reaching out: Interpersonal effectiveness and self-actualization* (6th ed.). Needham Heights, MA: Allyn & Bacon.

Johnson, D. W., & Johnson, F. P. (2003). *Joining together: Group theory and group skills*. Boston: Pearson Education, Inc.

Johnson, D. W., & Johnson, R. T. (1989). *Cooperation and competition: Theory and research*. Edina, MN: Interaction Book Company.

Johnson, D. W., & Johnson, R. T. (1995). *Teaching students to be peacemakers* (3rd ed.). Edina, MN: Interaction Book Company.

Johnson, D. W., Johnson, R. T., & Holubec, E. J. (1998). *Cooperation in the classroom* (7th ed.). Edina, MN: Interaction Book Company.

Johnson, D. W., Johnson, R. T., & Smith, K. A. (1992). *Cooperative learning: Increasing college faculty instructional productivity*. (ERIC Document Reproduction Service No. ED347871) Retrieved August 7, 2009, from http://www.ericdigests.org/1992-2/cooperative.htm

Johnson, R. T., & Johnson, D. W. (1994). An overview of cooperative learning. In J. S. Thousand, R. A. Villa, & A. I. Nevin (Eds.), *Creativity and collaborative learning: A practical guide to empowering students and teachers* (pp. 31–44). Baltimore: Paul H. Brookes Publishing.

Johnstone, B. (2003). *Never mind the laptops: Kids, computers, and the transformation of learning*. Bloomington, IN: iUniverse.

Jonassen, D. (1991). Evaluating constructivist learning. *Educational Technology, 31*(9), 28–33.

Jonassen, D. (1994). Thinking technology: Toward a constructivist design model. *Educational Technology, 34*(3), 34–37.

Jonassen, D. (1996). *Computers in the classroom: Mindtools for critical thinking*. Englewood Cliffs, NJ: Merill/Prentice Hall.

Jonassen, D. (1999). Designing constructivist learning environments. In C. M. Reigeluth (Ed.), *Instructional design theories and models: A new paradigm of instructional theory* (Vol. 2, pp. 215–239). Mahwah, NJ: Erlbaum.

Jonassen, D., Ambruso, D., & Olesen, J. (1992). Designing hypertext on transfusion medicine using cognitive flexibility theory. *Journal of Educational Multimedia and Hypermedia, 1*, 309–322.

Jonassen, D., Davidson, M., Collins, M., Campbell, J., & Haag, B. (1995). Constructivism and computer mediated communication in distance education. *The American Journal of Distance Education, 9*, 7–26.

Jonassen, D., Mayes, T., & McAleese, R. (1992). A manifesto for a constructivist approach to uses of technology in higher education. In T. M. Duffy, J. Lowyck, & D. H. Jonassen (Eds.), *Designing environments for constructivist learning* (pp. 231–247). Heidelberg, Germany: Springer-Verlag.

Joyce, B., Weil, M. & Calhoun, E. (2000). *Models of teaching* (6th ed.). Boston: Allyn & Bacon.

Kant, I. (2003). *The critique of pure reason* (J. M. D. Meiklejohn, Trans.). Salt Lake City, UT: Project Gutenberg Literary Archive Foundation. (Original work published 1781) Retrieved September 30, 2008, from http://www.gutenberg.org/etext/4280

Kaufman, D. R., Patel, V. L., & Magder, S. A. (1996). The explanatory role of spontaneously generated analogies in reasoning about physiological concepts. *International Journal of Science Education, 18,* 369–386.

Kelly, G. A. (1955). *The psychology of personal constructs* (Vols. 1–2). New York: Norton.

Keniston, A. H. (2005, October). *Using Watson's prescriptions to infuse critical thinking into history and systems of psychology.* Poster presented at the Engaging Minds: Best Practices in Teaching Critical Thinking Across the Psychology Curriculum Conference, Atlanta, GA.

Khattri, N., & Sweet, D. (1996). Assessment reform: Promises and challenges. In M. B. Kane & R. Mitchell (Eds.), *Implementing performance assessment: Promises, problems, and challenges* (pp. 1–22). Mahwah, NJ: Erlbaum.

Khuwaileh, A. A. (1999). The role of chunks, phrases and body language in understanding coordinated academic lectures. *System, 27,* 249–260.

Kiewra, K. A. (1987). Notetaking and review: The research and its implications. *Instructional Science, 16,* 233–249.

Kilpatrick, W. H. (1951). *The education of man: Aphorisms by Heinrich Pestalozzi.* New York: Philosophical Library.

Klos, D. S. (1976). Students as case writers. *Teaching of Psychology, 3,* 63–66.

Knowles, J. G. (1994). Metaphors as windows on a personal history: A beginning teacher's experience. *Teacher Education Quarterly, 21,* 37–66.

Kolb, D. A. (1984). *Experiential learning: Experience as the source of learning and development.* Englewood Cliffs, NJ: Prentice Hall.

Kolb, D. A., Winter, S. K., & Berlew, D. E. (1968). Self-directed change: Two studies. *The Journal of Applied Behavioral Science, 4,* 453–471.

Kolodner, J. L. (1997). Educational implications of analogy: A view from case-based reasoning. *American Psychologist, 52,* 57–66.

Kopp, B. M. (1998). *Using metaphors in creative writing.* Retrieved August 6, 2009, from http://owl.english.purdue.edu/handouts/general/gl_metaphor.html

Krathwohl, D. R. (2002). A revision of Bloom's taxonomy: An overview. *Theory Into Practice, 41,* 212–218.

Kubler-Ross, E. (1969). *On death and dying.* New York: Macmillan.

Kuh, G. D. (2003). What we're learning about student engagement from NSSE. *Change, 35*(2), 24–32.

Kulik, J. A. (1973). *Undergraduate education in psychology.* Washington, DC: American Psychological Association.

Lafosse, J. M., & Zinser, M. C. (2002). A case conference exercise to facilitate understanding of paradigms in abnormal psychology. *Teaching of Psychology, 29*, 220–222.

Lajoie, S. (2000). *Computers as cognitive tools (Vol. 2)—No more walls: Theory change, paradigm shifts, and their influence on the use of computers for instructional purposes* (2nd ed.). Mahwah, NJ: Erlbaum.

Lakoff, G., & Johnson, M. (1980). *Metaphors we live by.* Chicago: University of Chicago Press.

Lakoff, G., & Johnson, M. (2003). *Metaphors we live by* (2nd ed.). Chicago: University of Chicago Press.

Lambert, M. E., & Lenthall, G. (1988). Using computerized case simulations in undergraduate psychology courses. *Teaching of Psychology, 15*, 132–135.

Lange, N. Q. (2007). An exploratory investigation of first-year students living in designated living-learning programs at Michigan State University. *Spot Light Series, 8*(1). Retrieved on August 7, 2009, from http://www.reslife.msu.edu/assessment/data/2007-2008/Living_Learning/NSLLP%20SpotLight.pdf

Latané, B. (1981). The psychology of social impact. *American Psychologist, 36*, 343–356.

Lave, J. (1988). *Cognition in practice: Mind, mathematics, and culture in everyday life.* Cambridge, England: Cambridge University Press.

Leach, E. L. (1992). An alternative form of evaluation that complies with NCTM's standards. *Mathematics Teacher, 85*, 628–632.

Lever-Duffy, J., McDonald, J. B., & Mizell, A. P. (2005). *Teaching and learning with technology* (2nd ed.). Boston: Pearson Education, Inc. Retrieved August 7, 2009, from http://wps.ablongman.com/ab_leverduffy_teachtech_2/23/6126/1568334.cw/index.html

Lewontin, R. C., Rose, S., & Kamin, L. (1984). *Not in our genes.* New York: Pantheon.

Lievrouw, L. A. (2001, June). Instructional media and the "no significant difference" phenomenon. *International Communication Association Newsletter, 29*(5). Retrieved August 8, 2009, from http://polaris.gseis.ucla.edu/llievrou/ICAjune01NSDshort.pdf

Likert, R. A. (1932). Technique for the measurement of attitudes. *Archives of Psychology, 140*, 1–55.

Lipka, S. (2007, November 9). Helicopter parents help students, survey finds. *The Chronicle of Higher Education, 54*(11), A1.

Littlemore, J. (2001, March). Metaphoric intelligence and foreign language learning. *Humanising Language Teaching, 3*(2). Retrieved August 7, 2009, from http://www.hltmag.co.uk/mar01/mart1.htm

Liu, C. C., Don, P. H., & Tsai, C. M. (2005). Assessment-based linkage patterns in concept maps. *Journal of Information Science and Engineering, 21*, 873–890.

Liu, C. C., & Lee, J. H. (2005). Prompting conceptual understanding with computer-mediated peer discourse and knowledge acquisition techniques. *British Journal of Educational Technology 36*, 821–837.

Liu, C. C., & Tsai, C. M. (2005). Peer assessment through web-based knowledge acquisition: Tools to support conceptual awareness. *Innovations in Education and Teaching International, 42*, 43–59.

Lloyd, C. V. (1990). The elaboration of concepts in three biology textbooks: Facilitating student learning. *Journal of Research in Science Teaching, 27*, 1019–1032.

Lloyd, M. A., & Brewer, C. L. (1992). National conferences on undergraduate psychology. In A. E. Puente, J. R. Matthews, & C. L. Brewer (Eds.), *Teaching psychology in America: A history* (pp. 263–284). Washington, DC: American Psychological Association.

Lombardi, M. M. (2007, May). Authentic learning for the 21st century: An overview. In D. G. Oblinger (Ed.), *EDUCAUSE Learning Initiative, ELI Paper 1*. Retrieved August 7, 2009, from http://net.educause.edu/ir/library/pdf/ELI3009.pdf

Lopatto, D. (2006). Undergraduate research as a catalyst for liberal learning. *Peer Review, 8*(1). Retrieved August 7, 2009, from http://findarticles.com/p/articles/mi_qa4115/is_200601/ai_n17171062

Lorenzo, G., & Ittelson, J. (2005, October). Demonstrating and assessing student learning with e-portfolios. In D. Oblinger (Ed.), *EDUCAUSE Learning Initiative, ELI Paper 3*. Retrieved August 7, 2009, from http://www.educause.edu/ir/library/pdf/ELI3003.pdf

Lundin, R. W. (1996). *Theories and systems of psychology* (5th ed.). Lexington, MA: D. C. Heath.

Lynch, E. J. (1997). *Constructivism and distance education*. Retrieved August 8, 2009, from http://seamonkey.ed.asu.edu/~mcisaac/emc703old97/spring97/7/lynch7.htm

MacGregor, J., & Smith, B. L. (2005, May–June). Where are learning communities now? National leaders take stock. *About Campus, 10*(2), 2–8.

Mahoney, M. J. (1999). *What is constructivism and why is it growing?* Retrieved August 7, 2009, from http://orgs.unt.edu/constructivism/aboutthejournal.htm

Malachowski, M. (2006). Undergraduate research as the next great faculty divide. *Peer Review, 8*(1), 26–27.

Marzano, R., Pickering, D., & Pollock, J. (2001). *Classroom instruction that works: Research-based strategies for increasing student achievement*. Alexandria, VA: Association for Supervision and Curriculum Development.

Mascolo, M. F., Craig-Bray, L., & Neimeyer, R. A. (1997). The construction of meaning and action in development and psychotherapy: An epigenetic systems perspective. In G. J. Neimeyer & R. A. Neimeyer (Eds.), *Advances in personal construct psychology* (Vol. 4, pp. 3–38). Greenwich, CT: JAI Press.

Maslow, A. H. (1968). *Toward a psychology of being* (2nd ed.). Princeton, NJ: Van Nostrand.

Maslow, A. H. (1970). *Motivation and personality* (2nd ed.). New York: Harper & Row.

Mathie, V. A. (2002). Building academic partnerships in psychology: The psychology partnerships project. *American Psychologist, 57*, 915–926.

Matusevich, M. N. (1995). *School reform: What role can technology play in a constructivist setting?* Retrieved August 7, 2009, from http://delta.cs.vt.edu/edu/fis/techcons.html

Mayer, R. (2003). *Learning and instruction.* Boston: Pearson Education, Inc.

Mayo, J. A. (2001a). Life analysis: Using life-story narratives in teaching lifespan developmental psychology. *Journal of Constructivist Psychology, 14,* 25–41.

Mayo, J. A. (2001b). Using analogies to teach conceptual applications of developmental theories. *Journal of Constructivist Psychology, 14,* 187–213.

Mayo, J. A. (2002a). Case-based instruction: A technique for increasing conceptual application in introductory psychology. *Journal of Constructivist Psychology, 15,* 65–74.

Mayo, J. A. (2002b). Dialogue as constructivist pedagogy: Probing the minds of psychology's greatest contributors. *Journal of Constructivist Psychology, 15,* 291–304.

Mayo, J. A. (2003a). Journal writing revisited: Using life-adjustment narratives as an autobiographical approach to learning in psychology of adjustment. *Journal of Constructivist Psychology, 16,* 37–47.

Mayo, J. A. (2003b). Observational diary: The merits of journal writing as case-based instruction in introductory psychology. *Journal of Constructivist Psychology, 16,* 233–247.

Mayo, J. A. (2004a). A pilot investigation of the repertory grid as a heuristic tool in teaching historical foundations of psychology. *Constructivism in the Human Sciences, 9,* 31–41.

Mayo, J. A. (2004b, August). *Reflective teaching through constructivist pedagogy.* Invited address at the inaugural faculty-development workshop of the Center for Excellence in Teaching and Learning, Georgia College and State University, Milledgeville, GA.

Mayo, J. A. (2004c). Repertory grid as a means to compare and contrast developmental theories. *Teaching of Psychology, 31,* 178–180.

Mayo, J. A. (2004d). Using case-based instruction to bridge the gap between theory and practice in psychology of adjustment. *Journal of Constructivist Psychology, 17,* 137–146.

Mayo, J. A. (2004e). Using mini-autobiographical narration in applied psychology to personalize course content and improve conceptual application. *Journal of Constructivist Psychology, 17,* 237–246.

Mayo, J. A. (2005a). "Shaping" classroom dialogue through the scored discussion. *Psychology Teacher Network, 15*(1), 3–5.

Mayo, J. A. (2005b). A student training guide to concept mapping as a heuristic tool. *Psychology Teacher Network, 15*(4), 21–22.

Mayo, J. A. (2006a). Colleague swap revisited: The use of peer critique to improve student writing skills. *Psychology Teacher Network, 16*(2), 7, 14.

Mayo, J. A. (2006b, March). *Journal writing as a versatile heuristic tool in the under-graduate curriculum*. Paper presented at the annual Teaching Matters Conference, Barnesville, GA.

Mayo, J. A. (2006c). Learning to teach, teaching to learn. In J. G. Irons, B. C. Beins, C. Burke, B. Buskist, V. Hevern, & J. E. Williams (Eds.), *The teaching of psychology in autobiography: Perspectives from exemplary psychology teachers* (Vol. 2, pp. 77–84). Washington, DC: American Psychological Association. Retrieved August 7, 2009, from http://teachpsych.org/resources/e-books/tia2006/tia2006.php

Mayo, J. A. (2006d). Reflective pedagogy through analogy construction. *South-eastern Journal of Psychology, 1*, 1–6. Retrieved August 6, 2009, from http://www.georgiapsychologicalsociety.org/SEJP%20Volume%201%20Number%201%20Mayo.pdf

Mayo, J. A. (2007, February). *Practical uses of constructivist pedagogy in the under-graduate curriculum*. Symposium presented at the annual Georgia Conference on College and University Teaching, Atlanta, GA.

Mayo, J. A. (2008). Repertory grid as a heuristic tool in teaching undergraduate psy-chology. In D. S. Dunn, J. S. Halonen, & R. A. Smith (Eds.), *Teaching critical think-ing in psychology: A handbook of best practices* (pp. 127–135). London: Blackwell.

Mayo, J. A. (2009). Constructivist pedagogical applications: Student-centered learning across the undergraduate curriculum. In S. A. Meyers & J. R. Stowell (Eds.), *Essays from E-xcellence in Teaching* (Vol. 8, pp. 19–24). Washington, DC: American Psychological Association. Retrieved August 6, 2009, from http://www.teach psych.org/resources/e-books/eit2008/eit2008.php

Mayo, J. A., & Salata, M. (2002). [Cross-disciplinary applications of concept mapping in the undergraduate curriculum]. Unpublished raw data.

Mayo, J. A., & Schliecker, E. M. (2009). Engaging students through the scored dis-cussion. In J. Horn (Ed.), *Engaging approaches: A collection of papers presented at the seventh annual Teaching Matters conference* (pp. 89–96). Barnesville, GA: Gordon College Publications.

McCabe, R. (2000). *Underprepared students*. Retrieved August 7, 2009, from http://measuringup.highereducation.org/2000/articles/UnderpreparedStudents.cfm

McClure, J. R., Sonak, B., & Suen, H. K. (1999). Concept map assessment of class-room learning: Reliability, validity, and logical practicality. *Journal of Research in Science Teaching, 36*, 475–492.

McCormick, A. C. (2003). Swirling and double-dipping: New patterns of student attendance and their implications for higher education. *New Directions for Higher Education, 121*, 13–24.

McDade, S. A. (1995). Case study pedagogy to advance critical thinking. *Teaching of Psychology, 22*, 9–10.

McGaghie, W. C., & Menges, R. J. (1975). Assessing self-directed learning. *Teach-ing of Psychology, 2*, 56–59.

McGovern, T. V. (Ed.). (1993). *Handbook for enhancing undergraduate education in psychology*. Washington, DC: American Psychological Association.

McGovern, T. V., & Brewer, C. L. (2003). Undergraduate education. In I. B. Weiner & D. K. Freedheim (Eds.), *Handbook of psychology, Vol 1: History of psychology* (pp. 465–481). New York: Wiley.

McGovern, T. V., & Reich, J. N. (1996). Education and training in psychology: A comment on the quality principles. *American Psychologist, 51*, 252–255.

McGrath, K. L. (1998). What is the score on scored discussions? *Mathematics Teaching in the Middle School, 4*, 50–58.

McKeachie, W. J., & Milholland, J. E. (1961). *Undergraduate curricula in psychology*. Chicago: Scott, Forseman.

McKenzie, W. (2000). *Are you a techno-constructivist?* Retrieved August 7, 2009, from http://www.educationworld.com/a_tech/tech005.shtml

McManus, J. L. (1986). "Live" case study/journal record in adolescent psychology. *Teaching of Psychology, 13*, 70–74.

Meadows, D. (2003). *Becoming a techno-constructivist: Moving out of the way—A reflective paper*. Retrieved August 7, 2009, from http://onlineeducator.info/MAED/EDCA691/EDCA691-Paper.pdf

Mensch, I. N. (1953). Psychology in medical education. *American Psychologist, 8*, 83–85.

Merrill, M. D. (2002). First principles of instruction. *Educational Technology Research and Development, 50*, 43–59.

Merseth, K. (1991). The early history of case-based instruction: Insights for teacher education today. *Journal of Teacher Education, 42*, 243–249.

Miami Museum of Science. (2001). *Constructivism and the Five E's*. Retrieved August 7, 2009, from http://www.miamisci.org/ph/lpintro5e.html

Miller, A. H., Imrie, B. W., & Cox, K. (1998). *Student assessment in higher education: A handbook for assessing performance*. London: Kogan Page Ltd.

Miller, G. A. (1969). Psychology as a means of promoting human welfare. *American Psychologist, 24*, 1063–1075.

Miller, S. M. (1997). Language, democracy, and teachers' conceptions of "discussion": Insights and dilemmas from literacy research. *Theory and Research in Social Education, 25*, 196–206.

Millet, C. M., Payne, D. G., Dwyer, C. A., Stickler, L. M., & Alexiou, J. J. (2008). *A culture of evidence: An evidence-centered approach to accountability for student learning outcomes*. Princeton, NJ: Educational Testing Service.

Millis, B. J. (2002, October). *Enhancing learning—and more!—through cooperative learning* (IDEA Paper No. 38). Manhattan, KS: The IDEA Center.

Mills, N. S. (2005, March). *Undergraduate research in chemistry at Trinity University: The value of enlightened self-interest*. Invited symposium presented at the meeting of American Chemical Society, San Diego, CA.

Miner, R. C. (1998). *Verum-factum* and practical wisdom in the early writings of Giambattista Vico. *Journal of the History of Ideas, 59*, 53–73.

Montecino, V., & Crouch, M. L. (1997, February). *A learning community in cyberspace: Computer-mediated distance learning composition*. Paper presented at the annual Symposium on E-Mail, the WEB, and MOOs: Developing the Writing Skills of University Students in Cyberspace, Washington, DC. Retrieved August 7, 2009, from http://mason.gmu.edu/~montecin/gwconf.htm

Moskowitz, M. J. (1977). Hugo Munsterberg: A study in the history of applied psychology. *American Psychologist, 32*, 824–842.

Mueller, J. (2003). *Authentic assessment toolbox*. Retrieved August 7, 2009, from http://jonathan.mueller.faculty.noctrl.edu/toolbox

Munsey, C. (2008). Charting the future of undergraduate psychology. *Monitor on Psychology, 39*(8), 54–57.

Murphy, E. (1997). *Constructivism: From philosophy to practice*. Retrieved August 7, 2009, from http://www.ucs.mun.ca/~emurphy/stemnet/cle.html

Murray, B. (2002). An historic education conference. *Monitor on Psychology, 33*(1), 58–65. Retrieved August 9, 2009, from http://www.apa.org/monitor/jan02/historic.html

Myers, C., & Jones, T. B. (1993). *Promoting active learning: Strategies for the college classroom*. San Francisco: Jossey-Bass.

Nanjappa, A., & Grant, M. M. (2003). Constructing on constructivism: The role of technology. *Electronic Journal for the Integration of Technology in Education, 2*, 38–56. Retrieved August 7, 2009, from http://ejite.isu.edu/Volume2No1/nanjappa.pdf

National Conferences on Undergraduate Research. (2008). *Undergraduate research*. Retrieved August 7, 2009, from http://www.ncur.org/ugresearch.htm

Nelson, P. D. (2002). *Preparing future faculty in psychology: Final narrative report*. Washington, DC: American Psychological Association. Retrieved August 7, 2009, from http://www.apa.org/ed/graduate/pffpsych_final.pdf

Nelson, P. D. (2008, Winter). Sharing psychology: Its role in education for other professions. *Educator, 6*, 1, 6–15.

Nelson, P. D., & Stricker, G. (1992). Advancing the teaching of psychology: Contributions of the American Psychological Association, 1946–1992. In A. E. Puente, J. R. Mathews, & C. L. Brewer (Eds.), *Teaching psychology in America: A history* (pp. 345–364). Washington, DC: American Psychological Association.

Newton, D. P. (1996). Causal situations in science: A model for supporting understanding. *Learning and Instruction, 6*, 201–217.

Neysmith-Roy, J. M., & Kleisinger, C. L. (1997). Using biographies of adults over 65 years of age to understand life-span developmental psychology. *Teaching of Psychology, 24*, 116–118.

Ng, E., & Bereiter, C. (1991). Three levels of goal orientation in learning. *Journal of the Learning Sciences, 1*, 243–271.

Nichols, J. O., & Nichols, K. W. (2000). *The departmental guide and record book for student outcomes assessment and institutional effectiveness* (3rd ed.). New York: Agathon.

Nicol, D. J., & Macfarlane-Dick, D. (2006). Formative assessment and self-regulated learning: A model and seven principles of good feedback practice. *Studies in Higher Education, 31*, 199–218.

Novak, J. D. (1977). *A theory of education*. Ithaca, NY: Cornell University Press.

Novak, J. D. (1990). Concept maps and Vee diagrams: Two metacognitive tools to facilitate meaningful learning. *Instructional Science, 19*, 29–52.

Novak, J. D. (1998). *Learning, creating, and using knowledge: Concept maps as facilitative tools in schools and corporations*. Mahwah, NJ: Erlbaum.

Novak, J. D., & Canas, A. J. (2006). *The theory underlying concept maps and how to construct them* (Tech. Rep. IHMC Cmap Tools 2006-01). Pensacola, FL: Institute for Human and Machine Cognition. Retrieved August 7, 2009, from http://cmap.ihmc.us/Publications/ResearchPapers/TheoryUnderlying ConceptMaps.pdf

Novak, J. D., & Gowin, D. B. (1984). *Learning how to learn*. New York: Cambridge University Press.

Novak, J. D., & Musonda, D. (1991). A twelve-year longitudinal study of science concept learning. *American Educational Research Journal, 28*, 117–153.

November, A. (2001). *Empowering students with technology*. Arlington Heights, IL: Skylight Professional Development.

Null, J. W. (2004). Is constructivism traditional? Historical and practical perspectives on a popular advocacy. *The Educational Forum, 68*, 180–188.

O'Connor, N. (2008). *Undergraduate research: Not just for research universities*. Retrieved August 7, 2009, from http://www.aacu.org/aacu_news/aacunews08/april08/ feature.cfm

Okebukola, P. A. (1992). Concept mapping with a cooperative learning flavor. *The American Biology Teacher, 54*, 218–221.

Olsson, B. (1997). Is musical knowledge aesthetic or social? A pilot study of knowledge formation in music. *Bulletin of the Council for Research in Music Education, 133*, 110–114.

Orgill, M., & Bodner, G. M. (2004). What research tells us about using analogies to teach chemistry. *Chemistry Education: Research and Practice, 5*, 15–32.

Ozmon, H. A., & Craver, S. M. (1999). *Philosophical foundations of education*. Upper Saddle River, NJ: Merrill/Prentice Hall.

Palmer, G., Peters, R., & Streetman, R. (2003). Cooperative learning. In M. Orey (Ed.), *Emerging perspectives on learning, teaching, and technology*. Retrieved, August 7, 2009, from http://projects.coe.uga.edu/epltt/index.php?title=Cooperative_Learning

Papert, S. (1980). *Mindstorms: Children, computers, and powerful ideas*. New York: Basic Books.

Papert, S. (1987). *Constructionism: A new opportunity for elementary science education* (National Science Foundation Award Abstract No. 8751190). Retrieved August 7, 2009, from http://nsf.gov/awardsearch/showAward.do?AwardNumber=8751190

Papert, S. (1991). Situating constructionism. In I. Harel & S. Papert (Eds.), *Constructionism* (pp. 1–11). Norwood, NJ: Ablex Publishing.

Papert, S. (1999). *Jean Piaget*. Retrieved August 7, 2009, from http://www.time.com/time/time100/scientist/profile/piaget.html

Papert, S., & Solomon, C. (1971). *Twenty things to do with a computer* (Artificial Intelligence Memo 248). Retrieved August 7, 2009, from http://www.stager.org/articles/twentythings.pdf

Park, D., & Fineburg, A. (2008). Teaching high school psychology as a career pathway. *Eye on Psi Chi, 12*(2). Retrieved August 7, 2009, from http://www.psichi.org/pubs/articles/article_664.aspx

Pask, G. (1975). *Conversation, cognition, and learning*. Amsterdam: Elsevier.

Pask, G. (1976). *Conversation theory: Applications in education and epistemology*. Amsterdam: Elsevier.

Pass, S. (2004). *Parallel paths to constructivism: Jean Piaget and Lev Vygotsky*. Charlotte, NC: Information Age Publishing.

Passmore, G. G. (1995). Constructing concept maps facilitates learning in radiologic technologies education. *Radiologic Science and Education, 2,* 50–59.

Paul, E. L. (2006). Community-based research as scientific and civic pedagogy. *Peer Review, 8*(1), 12–15.

Peirce, C. S. (1992). How to make our ideas clear. In N. Houser & C. Kloesel (Eds.), *The essential Peirce: Vol. 1* (pp. 124–141). Bloomington: Indiana University Press. (Original work published in 1878)

Perkins, D. (1999). The many faces of constructivism. *Educational Leadership, 57,* 6–11.

Pestalozzi, J. H. (1894). *How Gertrude teaches her children* (L. E. Holland & F. C. Turner, Trans.). London: Swan Sonnenschein. (Original work published 1801)

Phillips, D. C. (1995). The good, the bad, and the ugly: The many faces of constructivism. *Educational Researcher, 24,* 5–12.

Piaget, J. (1929). *The child's conception of the world*. London: Routledge and Kegan Paul.

Piaget, J. (1959). *The language and thought of the child* (3rd ed.; M. Gabain & R. Gabain, Trans.). London: Routledge and Kegan Paul. (Original work published 1926)

Piaget, J. (1970). *Genetic epistemology*. New York: W. W. Norton & Company.

Piaget, J. (1973). *To understand is to invent*. New York: Grossman.

Piaget, J. (1977). *Equilibration of cognitive structures*. New York: Viking.

Piaget, J. (1987a). *Possibility and necessity* (Vol. 1). Minneapolis: University of Minnesota Press.

Piaget, J. (1987b). *Possibility and necessity* (Vol. 2). Minneapolis: University of Minnesota Press.

Pillemer, D. B., Picariello, M. L., Law, A. B., & Reichman, J. S. (1996). Memories of college: The importance of specific educational episodes. In D. C. Rubin (Ed.), *Remembering our past: Studies in autobiographical memory* (pp. 318–340). New York: Cambridge University Press.

Pines, A. L., Novak, J. D., Posner, G. J., & Vankirk, J. (1978). *The clinical interview: A method for evaluating cognitive structure*. Ithaca, NY: Cornell University, Department of Education.

Pittman, K. M. (1999). Student-generated analogies: Another way of knowing? *Journal of Research in Science Teaching, 36*, 1–22.

Plotnick, E. (1997). *Concept mapping: A graphical system for understanding the relationship between concepts.* (ERIC Document Reproduction Service No. ED407938) Retrieved August 7, 2009, from http://www.ericdigests.org/1998-1/concept.htm

Psi Beta. (2008). *Psi Beta national research project—Overview.* Retrieved August 7, 2009, from http://psibeta.org/site/wp-content/uploads/PsiBeta_NPR_overview.pdf

Quiggin, V. (1977). Children's knowledge of their internal body parts. *Nursing Times, 73*, 1146–1151.

Raeff, C., & Mascolo, M. F. (1996, June). *Co-regulated coordination: Representational activities at the intersection of individual, social and cultural processes.* Paper presented at the annual symposium of the Jean Piaget Society, Philadelphia, PA.

Rakes, G. C., Flowers, B. F., Casey, H. B., & Santana, R. (1999). An analysis of instructional technology use and constructivist behaviors in K–12 teachers. *International Journal of Educational Technology, 1*, 1–18.

Rauckhorst, W. H., Czaja, J. A., & Baxter, M. M. (2001, July). *Measuring the impact of the undergraduate research experience on student intellectual development.* Paper presented at the Project Kaleidoscope Conference, Snowbird, UT.

Reddy, M. J. (1993). The conduit metaphor: A case of frame conflict in our language about language. In A. Ortony (Ed.), *Metaphor and thought* (2nd ed., pp. 164–201). Cambridge, England: Cambridge University Press.

Reigeluth, C. (1987). Lesson blueprints based upon the elaboration theory of instruction. In C. Reigeluth (Ed.), *Instructional theories in action: Lessons illustrating selected theories and models* (pp. 245–288). Hillsdale, NJ: Erlbaum.

Reiser, B. J., Black, J. B., & Abelson, R. P. (1985). Knowledge structures in the organization and retrieval of autobiographical memories. *Cognitive Psychology, 17*, 80–137.

Reiser, R. A. (2002). A history of instructional design and technology. In R. A. Reiser & J. V. Dempsey (Eds.), *Trends and issues in instructional design and technology* (pp. 26–53). Upper Saddle River, NJ: Merrill/Prentice-Hall.

Robertson, J. F., & Rane-Szostak, D. (1996). Using dialogues to develop critical thinking skills: A practical approach. *Journal of Adolescent and Adult Literacy, 39*, 552–556.

Robinson, D. N. (1995). *An intellectual history of psychology* (3rd ed.). Madison: University of Wisconsin Press.

Rogers, C. R. (1969). *Freedom to learn.* Columbus, OH: Merrill.

Rogers, C. R., & Freiberg, H. J. (1994). *Freedom to learn* (3rd ed.). Columbus, OH: Merrill/Macmillan.

Rothenberg, J. J. (1994). Memories of schooling. *Teacher and Teacher Education, 10*, 369–379.

Rousseau, J. J. (1993). *Emile* (B. Foxley, Trans.). London: Everyman Publishing. (Original work published 1762)

Rudmann, J. (2008a). Psi Beta launches a national research project. *Psychology Teacher Network, 18*(2), 9–10.

Rudmann, J. (2008b, April 21). Society for the Teaching of Psychology Moderated Discussion List. Message posted to PsychTeacher Listserv electronic discussion list, archived at http://list.kennesaw.edu/archives/psychteacher.html

Ruhl, T. (1999, April–May). *The heart is like a pump: Medical analogies in patient education.* Paper presented at the Society of Teachers of Family Medicine Conference, Seattle, WA.

Ryder, M. (1994). *Augmentation of the intellect: Network instruments, environments and strategies for learning.* Retrieved August 7, 2009, from http://carbon.cudenver.edu/~mryder/augment.html

Sanford, F. H., & Fleishman, E. A. (1950). A survey of undergraduate psychology courses in American colleges and universities. *American Psychologist, 5*, 33–37.

Santrock, J. W. (1999). *Life-span development* (7th ed.). Boston: McGraw-Hill.

Santrock, J. W. (2004). *Life-span development* (9th ed.). Boston: McGraw-Hill.

Sanzenbacher, R. (1997). New awareness of the power of dialogue: A hopeful pedagogy. *College Teaching, 45*, 104–107.

Sapon-Shevin, M., Ayres, B. J., & Duncan, J. (1994). Cooperative learning and inclusion. In J. S. Thousand, R. A. Villa, & A. I. Nevin (Eds.), *Creativity and collaborative learning: A practical guide to empowering students and teachers* (pp. 45–58). Baltimore: Paul H. Brookes Publishing.

Schaab, N. (2008). Learning communities: Creating coherence and engagement in community college classes. *Psychology Teacher Network, 18*(2), 3, 6–7.

Schank, R. C., & Abelson, R. P. (1995). Knowledge and memory: The real story. In R. S. Wyer (Ed.), *Knowledge and memory: The real story* (pp. 1–86). Mahwah, NJ: Erlbaum.

Schmidt, R., Waligora, T., & Vorobieva, O. (2008). Prototypes for medical case-based applications. *Proceedings of the Industrial Conference on Data Mining, 5077*, 1–15.

Schneider, C. G. (2008). Bologna plus: The liberal education advantage. *Liberal Education, 94*(4), 1–2.

Seiferth. M. S. (1997). *Socratic teaching.* Retrieved August 7, 2009, from http://lonestar.texas.net/~mseifert/crit3.html

Sexton, T. L., & Griffin, B. L. (Eds.). (1997). *Constructivist thinking in counseling practice, research and training.* New York: Teachers College Press.

Seymour, E., Hunter, A.-B., Laursen, S. L., & Deantoni, T. (2004). Establishing the benefits of research experiences for undergraduates in the sciences: First findings from a three-year study. *Science Education, 88*, 493–534.

Shapiro, R. G. (2008, July 16). Society for the Teaching of Psychology Moderated Discussion List. Message posted to PsychTeacher Listserv electronic discussion list, archived at http://list.kennesaw.edu/archives/psychteacher.html

Sheldon, J. P. (2000). A neuroanatomy teaching activity using case studies and collaboration. *Teaching of Psychology, 27*, 126–127.

Shulman, J. (1992). *Case methods in teacher education*. New York: Teachers College Press.

Silverman, R., & Welty, W. M. (1990). Teaching with cases. *Journal on Excellence in College Teaching, 1,* 88–97.

Simon, M. (1993, April). *Restructuring mathematics pedagogy from a constructivist perspective*. Paper presented at the meeting of the American Educational Research Association, Atlanta, GA.

Simon, P. F., & Garfunkel, A. I. (1970). Bridge over troubled water. On *Bridge over troubled water* [Album]. New York: Columbia Records.

Simon, S. D. (2001). *From neo-behaviorism to social constructivism: The paradigmatic non-evolution of Albert Bandura*. Retrieved August 7, 2009, from http://www.des.emory.edu/mfp/simon.doc

Singer, J. A. (1996). The story of your life: A process perspective on narrative and emotion in adult development. In C. Magai & S. H. McFadden (Eds.), *Handbook of emotion, adult development, and aging* (pp. 443–463). San Diego, CA: Academic Press.

Sircar, S. S., & Tandon, O. P. (1996). Teaching nerve conduction to undergraduates: The "traveling flame" analogy revisited. *Advances in Physiology Education, 15,* S78–S85.

Skinner, B. F. (1954). The science of learning and the art of teaching. *Harvard Educational Review, 24,* 86–97.

Slavin, R. E. (1989–1990). Research on cooperative learning: Consensus and controversy. *Educational Leadership, 47,* 52–55.

Smith, B. L. (2001). The challenge of learning communities as a growing national movement. *Peer Review, 3–4*(4–1), 4–8. Retrieved August 7, 2009, from http://www.aacu.org/peerreview/pr-fa01/pr-fa01feature1.cfm

Smith, B. L., MacGregor, J., Matthews, R. S., & Gabelnick, F. (2004). *Learning communities: Reforming undergraduate education*. San Francisco: Jossey-Bass.

Smith, R. A., & Murphy, S. K. (1998). Using case studies to increase learning and interest in biology. *The American Biology Teacher, 60,* 265–268.

Snyder, T. D., Dillow, S. A., & Hoffman, C. M. (2009). *Digest of education statistics, 2008* (NCES Rep. No. 2009-020). Washington, DC: U.S. Department of Education.

Snyder, T. D., & Hoffman, C. M. (2003). *Digest of education statistics, 2002* (NCES Rep. No. 2003-060). Washington, DC: U.S. Department of Education.

Software and Information Industry Association. (2000). *2000 research report on the effectiveness of technology in schools: Executive summary*. Washington, DC: Author.

Spiro, R. J., Feltovich, P. J., Coulson, R. L., & Anderson, D. K. (1989). Multiple analogies for complex concepts: Antidotes for analogy-induced misconceptions in advanced knowledge acquisition. In S. Vosniadou & A. Ortony (Eds.), *Similarity and analogical reasoning* (pp. 498–531). Cambridge, MA: Cambridge University Press.

Spiro, R. J., Feltovich, P. J., Jacobson, M. J., & Coulson, R. L. (1991). Cognitive flexibility, constructivism, and hypertext: Random access instruction for advanced knowledge acquisition in ill-structured domains. *Educational Technology, 31,* 24–33.

Spiro, R. J., & Jehng, J. (1990). Cognitive flexibility and hypertext: Theory and technology for the nonlinear and multidimensional traversal of complex subject matter. In D. Nix & R. Spiro (Eds.), *Cognition, education, and multimedia: Exploring ideas in high technology* (pp. 163–203). Hillsdale, NJ: Erlbaum.

Stadler, M. A. (1998). Demonstrating scientific reasoning. *Teaching of Psychology, 25,* 205–206.

Stein, N. L., & Trabasso, T. (1982). What's in a story: An approach to comprehension and instruction. In R. Glasser (Ed.), *Advances in instructional psychology* (pp. 212–267). Hillsdale, NJ: Erlbaum.

Sternberg, R. J. (2007). Critical thinking in psychology: It really is critical. In R. J. Sternberg, H. L. Roediger, III, & D. F. Halpern (Eds.), *Critical thinking in psychology* (pp. 289–296). New York: Cambridge University Press.

Stevens, M. J., & Wedding, D. (2004). International psychology: An overview. In M. J. Stevens & D. Wedding (Eds.), *Handbook of international psychology* (pp. 1–23). New York: Brunner-Routledge.

Sticht, T. G. (1975). Applications of the audread model to reading evaluation and instruction. In L. Resnick & P. Weaver (Eds.), *Theory and practice of early reading* (Vol. 1, pp. 209–226). Hillsdale, NJ: Erlbaum.

Strommen, E. F., & Lincoln, B. (1992). Constructivism, technology, and the future of classroom learning. *Education and Urban Society, 24,* 466–476.

Swain, C., & Pearson, T. (2001). Bridging the digital divide: A building block for teachers. *Learning and Leading With Technology, 28,* 10–13, 59.

Tang, C. (1998). Effects of collaborative learning on the quality of assignments. In B. Dart & G. Boulton-Lewis (Eds.), *Teaching and learning in higher education* (pp. 102–123). Melbourne, Australia: The Australian Council for Education Research Ltd.

Teachers in the English Department, Ecole Nationale Superieure de Telecommunications de Bretagne, France. (2001, March). Vocabulary revision techniques. *Humanising Language Teaching, 3*(2). Retrieved August 7, 2009, from http://www.hltmag.co.uk/mar01/less.htm

Thagard, P. (1992). Analogy, explanation, and education. *Journal of Research in Science Teaching, 29,* 537–544.

Thagard, P. (1997). Medical analogies: Why and how? In P. Langley & M. Shafto (Eds.), *Proceedings of the nineteenth annual conference of the Cognitive Science Society* (pp. 739–744). Mahwah, NJ: Erlbaum.

Thanasoulas, D. (2001). *Constructivist learning.* Retrieved August 6, 2009, from http://www.eltnewsletter.com/back/April2001/art542001.htm

Thomas, L. F., & Harri-Augstein, S. (1985). Exploring learning with the grid. In N. Beail (Ed.), *Repertory grid technique and personal constructs: Applications in clinical and applied settings* (pp. 295–318). Cambridge, MA: Brookline Books.

Thompson, R. A., & Zamboanga, B. L. (2003). Prior knowledge and its relevance to student achievement in introduction to psychology. *Teaching of Psychology, 30,* 96–101.

Thrasher, D. (2008). *Enterprise anthills.* Retrieved August 7, 2009, from http://www.infovark.com/2008/08/06/enterprise-anthills/

Tinto, V. (2000). Learning better together: The impact of learning communities on student success. *Journal of Institutional Research, 9,* 48–53.

Tobacyk, J. J. (1987). Using personal construct theory in teaching history and systems of psychology. *Teaching of Psychology, 14,* 111–112.

Tritelli, D. (2008). From the editor. *Liberal Education, 94*(4), 3.

Tsai, C. C. (2008). The preferences toward constructivist Internet-based learning environments among university students in Taiwan. *Computers in Human Behavior, 24,* 16–31.

Tu, C. H. (2004). *Online collaborative learning communities: Twenty-one designs to building an online collaborative learning community.* Westport, CT: Libraries Unlimited.

Tversky, A., & Kahneman, D. (1981, January 30). The framing of decisions and the psychology of choice. *Science, 211,* 453–458.

Tynjala, P. (1998). Traditional studying for examination versus constructivist learning tasks: Do learning outcomes differ? *Studies in Higher Education, 23,* 173–189.

University of Victoria Counselling Services. (2003). *Learning skills: Organization practice: Mapping.* Retrieved August 7, 2009, from http://www.coun.uvic.ca/learning/note-taking/class1.html

U.S. Department of Education's National Center for Education Statistics. (1997). *Student outcomes information for policy-making: Final report of the National Postsecondary Education Working Group on Student Outcomes From a Policy Perspective* (NCES Rep. No. 97-991). Washington, DC: Author. Retrieved August 7, 2009, from http://nces.ed.gov/pubs97/97991.pdf

Velayo, R. S. (2008, Spring). Internationalizing the teaching of psychology: Interdivisional collaborating between APA Divisions 2 and 52. *Newsletter of the Society for the Teaching of Psychology,* 9.

Venville, G. J., & Treagust, D. F. (1997). Analogies in biology education: A contentious issue. *The American Biology Teacher, 59,* 282–287.

Vico, G. (1988). *De antiquissima italorum sapientia ex linguae originibus eruenda librir tres* [On the most ancient wisdom of the Italians unearthed from the origins of the Latin language] (L. M. Palmer, Trans.). Ithaca, NY: Cornell University Press. (Original work published 1710)

von Glasersfeld, E. (1989a). *An exposition of constructivism: Why some like it radical.* Amherst: University of Massachusetts, Scientific Reasoning Research Institute. (ERIC Document Reproduction Service No. ED309935) von Glasersfeld, E.(1989b). Constructivism in education. In T. Husen & N. Postlewaite (Eds.), *International encyclopedia of education* (Suppl., Vol. 1, pp.162–163). Oxford, England: Pergamon Press.

von Glasersfeld, E. (1999). *Le Moigne's defense of constructivism.* Retrieved August 7, 2009, from http://univie.ac.at/constructivism/EvG/papers/225.pdf

Vygotsky, L. S. (1978). *Mind in society.* Cambridge, MA: Harvard University Press.

Vygotsky, L. S. (1981). *Thought and language* (E. Hanfmann & G. Vakar, Trans.). Cambridge, MA: Harvard University Press.

Vygotsky, L. S. (1986). *Thought and language.* Cambridge, MA: MIT Press. (Original translated work published 1962)

Wade, C. (1998, November). *Teaching less is teaching more.* Invited presentation at the Southwestern Conference for the Teaching of Psychology, Fort Worth, TX.

Wadsworth, B. J. (1996). *Piaget's theory of cognitive and affective development.* White Plains, NY: Longman.

Wallace, J. D., & Mintzes, J. L. (1990). The concept map as a research tool: Exploring conceptual change in biology. *Journal of Research in Science Teaching, 27,* 1033–1052.

Wallace, J. D., Mintzes, J. J., & Markham, K. M. (1992). Concept mapping in college science teaching—What the research says. *Journal of College Science Teaching, 21,* 84–86.

Walls, R. T., Sperling, R. A., & Weber, K. D. (2001). Autobiographical memory of school. *Journal of Educational Research, 95,* 116–127.

Wandersee, J. H. (1990). Concept mapping and the cartography of cognition. *Journal of Research in Science Teaching, 27,* 923–936.

Wandersee, J. H., Mintzes, J. J., & Novak, J. D. (1994). Research on alternative conceptions in science. In D. Gabel (Ed.), *Research in teaching science* (pp. 177–203). Washington, DC: National Science Teachers Association.

Warrick, W. R. (2001). *Constructivism: Pre-historical to post-modern.* Retrieved October 2, 2008, from http://mason.gmu.edu/~wwarrick/Portfolio/Products/PDF/constructivism.pdf

Washington Center for Improving the Quality of Undergraduate Education. (2003). *How widespread are learning communities and what types of colleges and universities are offering them?* Retrieved August 7, 2009, from http://www.evergreen.edu/washcenter/lcfaq.htm#28

Wasserman, S. (1994). *Introduction to case method teaching: A guide to the galaxy.* New York: Teachers College Press.

Watson, D. L., & Tharp, R. G. (1997). *Self-directed behavior: Self-modification for personal adjustment* (7th ed.). Pacific Grove, CA: Brooks/Cole.

Watson, J. B. (1924). *Behaviorism.* Chicago: University of Chicago Press.

Watson, R. (1967). Psychology: A prescriptive science. *American Psychologist, 22,* 435–443.

Webb, W. (1999). Instructor's manual/test bank accompanying *Pathways to personal growth: Adjustment in today's world* (Goethals, Worchel, & Heatherington, 1999). Boston: Allyn & Bacon.

Weiten, W., & Lloyd, M. A. (2000). *Psychology applied to modern life: Adjustment at the turn of the century* (6th ed., Instructor's ed.). Belmont, CA: Wadsworth/ Thomson Learning.

Wenzel, T. (2007). Cooperative learning and project-based laboratories as a way to broaden learning outcomes. In K. K. Karukstis, H. Mudd, & T. E. Elgren (Eds.), *Developing and sustaining a research-supportive curriculum: A compendium of successful practices* (pp. 21–40). Washington, DC: Council on Undergraduate Research.

Wertheimer, M. (1938). Laws of organization in perceptual forms. In W. Ellis (Ed. & Trans.), *A source book of Gestalt psychology* (pp. 71–88). London: Routledge and Kegan Paul. (Original work published 1923)

Wertheimer, M. (1959). *Productive thinking*. New York: Harper & Row.

West, D. C., Park, J. K., Pomeroy, J. R., & Sandoval, J. (2002). Concept mapping assessment in medical education: A comparison of two scoring systems. *Medical Education, 36*, 820–826.

White, H. B., III. (2007). Stimulating attitudes of inquiry with problem-based learning. In K. K. Karukstis, H. Mudd, & T. E. Elgren (Eds.), *Developing and sustaining a research-supportive curriculum: A compendium of successful practices* (pp. 9–20). Washington, DC: Council on Undergraduate Research.

White, S., & Dillow, S. (2005). *Key concepts and features of the 2003 national assessment of adult literacy* (NCES Rep. No. 2006-471). Washington, DC: U.S. Department of Education.

Wiederman, M., & Nicolai, K. (2003, September). *Using peers creatively in moderate-sized classes*. Paper presented at Taking Off: Best Practices in Teaching Introductory Psychology Conference, Atlanta, GA.

Wiggins, G. (1990). The case for authentic assessment. *Practical assessment, research & evaluation, 2*(2). Retrieved August 7, 2009, from http://pareonline.net/getvn. asp?v=2&n=2

Williams, S., Wicherski, M., & Kohout, J. (1998). *1997 employment characteristics and salaries of medical school psychologists*. Washington, DC: American Psychological Association.

Williams, S. M. (1992). Putting case-based instruction into context: Examples from legal and medical education. *Journal of the Learning Sciences, 2*, 367–427.

Wilson, B. G., & Cole, P. (1991). A review of cognitive teaching models. *Educational Technology Research and Development Journal, 39*, 47–64.

Winer, L. R., & Vazquez-Abad, J. (1997). Repertory grid technique in the diagnosis of learner difficulties and the assessment of conceptual change in physics. *Journal of Constructivist Psychology, 10*, 363–386.

Witfelt, C. (2000). Educational multimedia and teachers' needs for new competencies to use educational multimedia. *Educational Media International, 37*, 235–241.

Wittgenstein, L. (1981). *Tractatus logico-philosophicus* [Logical–philosophical treatise] (D. R. Pears & B. F. McGuinness, Trans.). London: Routledge. (Original work published 1921)

Wittrock, M. C. (1974). Learning as a generative process. *Educational Psychology, 11,* 87–95.

Wittrock, M. C., & Alesandrini, K. L. (1990). Generation of summaries and analogies and analytic and holistic abilities. *American Educational Research Journal, 27,* 489–502.

Wlodkowski, R. J., & Ginsberg, M. B. (1995). *Diversity and motivation: Culturally responsive teaching.* San Francisco: Jossey-Bass.

Wolfle, D. L. (1947). The sensible organization of courses in psychology. *American Psychologist, 2,* 437–445.

Wong, E. D. (1993a). Self-generated analogies as a tool for constructing and evaluating explanations of scientific phenomena. *Journal of Research in Science Teaching, 30,* 367–380.

Wong, E. D. (1993b). Understanding the generative capacity of analogies as a tool for explanation. *Journal of Research in Science Teaching, 30,* 1259–1272.

Woolf, L. M., Hulsizer, M. R., & McCarthy, T. (2002). *International psychology: A compendium of textbooks for selected courses evaluated for international content.* Retrieved August 7, 2009, from http://teachpsych.org/otrp/resources/woolf02intcomp.pdf

Woolfolk, A. (1998). *Educational psychology* (7th ed.). Boston: Allyn & Bacon.

Yadav, A., Lundeberg, M., DeSchryver, M., Dirkin, K., Schiller, N., Maier, K., et al. (2007). Teaching science with case studies: A national survey of faculty perceptions of the benefits and challenges of using cases. *Journal of College Science Teaching, 37,* 34–38.

Yager, R. E., & Tweed, P. (1991). Planning more appropriate biology education for schools. *The American Biology Teacher, 53,* 479–483.

Zablotsky, D. (2001). Why do I have to learn this if I'm not going to graduate school? Teaching research methods in a social psychology of aging course. *Educational Gerontology, 27,* 609–622.

Zemeckis, R. (Director). (1994). *Forrest Gump* [Motion picture]. United States: Paramount Pictures.

Zola, J. (1992). Middle and high school scored discussions. *Social Education, 56,* 121–125.

INDEX

213

Analogical reasoning, 113–125
    about, 113–114
    and analogies log, 122–125
    baseline, 116
    educational implications and
        applications of, 119–124
    teacher-provided analogies,
        117–119
    theoretical foundations of, 114–117
Analogies
    as advance organizers, 46
    breakthrough, 116–117
    bridging, 120
    co-construction of, 120–122
    literal vs. metaphorical, 116
    partial, 121
    personalization of, 122
    teacher-provided vs. student-
        generated, 117–120
Analogies log, 122–125
Analogs, in analogical reasoning, 114
Animism, 82
Anthis, K., 95
APA. See American Psychological
    Association
APA Guidelines. See Guidelines for the
    Undergraduate Psychology Major
Apperception, 36
Application of psychology
    in CBI, 66, 69, 72
    in concept mapping, 101
    in cooperative learning, 136, 143,
        148
    in narrative psychology, 82, 84, 87, 90
    in psychology curricula, 28
    in RGT, 108–109
Applied psychology, 6–7, 79, 85–88,
    132–133, 139–144
Apprenticeship, cognitive, 51
Argumentation skills
    in analogical reasoning, 118, 125
    in CBI, 68, 72, 75
    in cooperative learning, 136, 142,
        147
    in narrative psychology, 90
    in psychology curricula, 27
    in RGT, 108
Aristotle, 73, 111
Assessment, 13. See also Authentic
    assessment
    classroom, 5

in constructivist educational
        practice, 52–56
    course vs. program, 56
    embedded, 54–56
    formative, 56
    goals of, 53–54
    and grading, 178–179
    with instructional technologies, 155
    in introductory psychology courses,
        166–167
    summative, 54
Assimilation
    of knowledge, 37–38, 45
    theory, 53
Association of American Colleges
        and Universities (AAC&U),
        15, 164–167
Association skills
    in analogical reasoning, 118, 124
    in CBI, 63, 66, 72
    in concept mapping, 101
    in cooperative learning, 136, 142, 147
    in narrative psychology, 82, 84, 87, 90
    in psychology curricula, 27
    in RGT, 108
Ausubel, David, 45–46, 53, 94
Authentic assessment, 54–56, 181
    with analogies log, 122–125
    with colleague swap, 132–138
    with concept mapping, 98–102
    with dialogue method, 62, 73–75
    with fictional case studies, 61–64
    with group poster presentations,
        132–133, 139–144
    with life-adjustment narrative, 79,
        83–85
    with life analysis and life-narrative
        journal, 79–83
    with life-change log, 61–62, 67–69
    with "live" research case analysis,
        62, 69–72
    with mini-autobiographical narratives,
        79, 85–88
    with observational diary, 80, 88–91
    with real-life case studies, 61, 65–66
    with RGT, 105–111
    with scored discussion, 133, 145–150
    with teacher-provided analogies,
        117–119
Autobiographical memories, 78
Autobiographical narrative learning,
        51, 78–91

ABOUT THE AUTHOR

Joseph A. Mayo, EdD, earned bachelor's degrees in psychology and political science from Bloomsburg University of Pennsylvania and master's and doctoral degrees in educational psychology from West Virginia University in Morgantown. He is presently a professor of psychology at Gordon College in Barnesville, Georgia, where he has served in both administrative and faculty positions since 1989. Dr. Mayo's classroom research on constructivist pedagogical applications has been published in various book chapters and peer-reviewed journals, including *Teaching of Psychology*, the *Journal of Constructivist Psychology*, and *Constructivism in the Human Sciences*. He also contributes regularly to *Psychology Teacher Network*—the quarterly newsletter of the American Psychological Association (APA) Education Directorate—and presents often at regional, national, and international teaching conferences. Based on his ongoing commitment to the scholarship of teaching and learning, Dr. Mayo was chosen to receive a 2003 Board of Regents' Research in Undergraduate Education Award for the University System of Georgia and the 2005 Wayne Weiten Teaching Excellence Award of the Society for the Teaching of Psychology (APA Division 2). In April 2005, he was selected to serve on the APA Board of Educational Affairs Task Force on Strengthening the Teaching and Learning of Undergraduate Psychological Science.